D1225116

NEW TEEN TITANS

ARCHIVES ▾ VOLUME 4

ARCHIVE EDITIONS

THE NEW TEEN TITANS ARCHIVES
VOLUME 4

ISBN 978-1-4012-1959-8

DC COMICS
1700 BROADWAY
NEW YORK, NY 10019

A WARNER BROS. ENTERTAINMENT COMPANY.

PRINTED IN HONG KONG.
FIRST PRINTING.

THE DC ARCHIVE EDITIONS

COVER ILLUSTRATION BY GEORGE PÉREZ

COLOR RECONSTRUCTION BY DREW MOORE.

SERIES DESIGN BY ALEX JAY/STUDIO J.

PUBLICATION DESIGN BY TERNARD SOLOMON

THE NEW TEEN TITANS CREATED BY MARV
WOLFMAN AND GEORGE PÉREZ

TABLE OF CONTENTS

TABLE OF CONTENTS

INTRODUCTION

GROWING UP WAS EASY TO DO

By Marv Wolfman

When we began The New Teen Titans, co-creator George Pérez and I were certain it wouldn't last more than six issues. This wasn't because we didn't believe in either our new characters or the approach we were taking; quite the opposite. We put everything we could into the book, but we were sure it would fail because, sadly, DC was still trailing far behind Marvel in those days and no new title had lasted more than six issues. We figured we'd work our butts off doing the book exactly the way we always wanted to see a comic done, and when it was cancelled, we'd move sadder but wiser on to other projects. But The New Teen Titans had indeed sold, and sold incredibly well, and George and I couldn't have been happier. The book we did "because we wanted to do a comic our way," worked, not only for us, but also for most of comics fandom.

The first ten or so issues were filled with growing pains. We created dozens of new characters and began to develop our main heroes as well. We then hit our teenage days and did a lot of one-issue stories where we focused on our main characters, brought back a few of our villains, and tried to solidify what we had begun only a year before.

We were now in our 20s and knew if we wanted to survive we couldn't keep doing the same thing yet again, but we had to grow up. We had characters our readers liked, so George and I decided to go for broke and start pushing them in ways we hadn't previously dreamed possible. We dropped the one-issue stories and went to longer and more complex tales. We also introduced a number of new villains whose origins and motivations were very different from the norm of the day.

We had introduced Deathstroke

the Terminator in issue #2, although he had been hinted at in our premiere issue. Trigon was introduced in issue #5, and though we created other villains we hoped could rival them, none came close until we introduced Brother Blood in issue #21.

Whereas our later creation, Joe Wilson - Jericho, was clearly more George's concept than mine, I think I can say Brother Blood was more mine than George's. Of course, once an idea was put out there, it was fully developed by both of us to the point that it's often hard to remember today who suggested exactly what. But when I was at Marvel I wrote a horror book called TOMB OF DRACULA, the same book that introduced Blade, The Vampire Hunter to an unsuspecting world. By its nature, ToD dealt with supreme evil and its control over people, including those in demon and dark religious cults. I wanted to further explore this concept, this time in the guise of the super-hero book, yet I wanted to go just as dark and just as twisted as before.

Brother Blood and his acolytes, overseen by Mother Mayhem, was our look into the darkest side of religious cults and their ability to control not only their believers, but others as well. Besides introducing Blood and Mayhem, we also created Bethany Snow, a TV reporter, who, it turned out, was more than what she appeared to be. Perhaps it was the early televangelists who were popping up everywhere back then, but it was my belief that if you wanted to whitewash evil, how better than to get a TV newscaster to start a crusade against your potential enemies even before they knew you were there. The Brother Blood stories were all dark. Very dark. Judging from the mail, our older readers seemed to appreciate these stories although our younger ones weren't quite sure what we were doing. But I loved Blood and the complexities of his origin that I had already worked up but wouldn't reveal for a few more years. Add to that, George's designs were incredible. His powerful pencils gave Blood not only strength but a sense of raw sexuality that was indeed threatening. At the same time, because of the way George designed him, you could believe others could believe in him. George had created yet another masterpiece of design. Looking back, the stories may appear tame by today's standards, but they were the very definition of pushing the super-hero envelope in 1982.

Following the two-part Brother Blood story, George and I completely switched gears by doing our longest story yet, a multipart space saga starring Starfire. We revealed in our first issue that Koriand'r had been a runaway slave. We learned Kory had been a princess on her home world, Tamaran, and that it was her father, King Myand'r, who had sold her into slavery in order to save their world. Now, at last, we would return to Tamaran and learn what had become of the war Myand'r had tried to stop by sacrificing the blood of his own daughter. At the same time we would introduce yet another brand-new character, Komand'r, Kory's evil sister.

Before I go too far, a brief digression. I love puns and as far as I'm concerned, the worse the better. Hence, our spicy Starfire is named Koriand'r, after the spice, coriander. Her father, who can never make up his mind what to do and keeps going off in the wrong direction, is named Myand'r, or meander (so now you know how to pronounce it). And of course, her ruthless sister the military leader Komand'r, or Commander. Oddly, this final name was not my pun but that of colorist Anthony Tollin. Credit where credit is due.

Being science fiction fans, George and I got involved with some real SF world building. We established a military pecking order not only to our main bad guys, The Citadel, but the Gordanians, our secondary warrior race. We established different worlds, races, and created detailed backgrounds for many of them as well as for their Goddess, X'hal, who, before this story, was merely an exclamation Kory would occasionally spout. We revealed that the star sun Vega had 22 planets and that there used to be 25 before the warrior/Goddess X'Hal went mad and destroyed three worlds. Obviously we made up all these so-called facts, but in reality, several years later, when scientists finally discovered planets around a distant star for the first time – the star Vega, as it turned out, they said they could see between 22 and 25 worlds. You could have knocked me over with that proverbial feather when I read that.

This multi-parter showed what Starfire thought of her family, especially her sister Komand'r. It also had a guest appearance by Superman, the return of the Omega Men, the super-powered freedom fighters from Vega who I had previously introduced in the pages of GREEN LANTERN knowing I would be using them here a year or so later, as well as the introduction of New York District Attorney Adrian Chase who, within a year, would become The Vigilante, a brand-new DC character.

This saga, which concludes in the first Titans Annual, surprises me as I look back on it now. We introduced so many concepts in so few issues that continued to affect the Titans for decades to come. Blackfire even became a semi-regular on the Titans cartoon show, still as evil (though sweet, too) as ever.

In this year we had gone to hell with Brother Blood, and then into space with Komand'r and the

Omega Men. Now it was time to return to Earth in a very real and serious storyline. I don't remember exactly how it came about, or even who suggested it, although I have a hunch it may have been then-DC Publisher Jenette Kahn. Despite worldly adventures, our heroes were still teens. I seem to remember Jenette's asking if we would be interested in working with the National Runaway Association to do a Titans storyline dealing with real runaways. George and I agreed. I went off to research runaway centers and visited several in New York, speaking not only with those in charge, but also with some of the kids themselves. Our story "Runaways", which features one of the most incredible George Pérez covers ever, was our answer. Although this was not a super-hero, super-villain slugfest, this story meant a lot to both of us and we were so incredibly pleased when our readers responded so kindly to it.

Our 20s was definitely our growing-up time. George and I weren't content to just repeat what we had done in our first twenty issues, but we insisted on pushing the boundaries even further. We took everything we learned in these stories and applied them over the next few months with the introduction of a pretty yet particularly quirky young girl named Tara Markov. I wonder how that worked out?

With that storyline we were definitely not looking back.

— Marv Wolfman
May, 2008

FREE! NIGHT FORCE PREVUE PULL-OUT!
THE NEW TEEN TITANS
ALL NEW! 60¢
NO. 21 JULY
APPROVED BY THE COMICS CODE AUTHORITY
EXTRA! INTRODUCING THE NIGHT FORCE BY WOLFMAN AND COLAN IN A SPECIAL FREE 16-PAGE COMIC!
NIGHT FORCE
AN INSTANT COLLECTOR'S ITEM-- FROM THE NEW DC!
DESTROY THE COSTUMED BLASPHEMERS IN OUR MIDST!
OBEY THE HOLY WORD OF-- BROTHER BLOOD!

BEWARE THE WRATH OF... BROTHER BLOOD!

THEY'RE WRONG, YOU KNOW. THE CALL BASEBALL THE GREAT AMERICAN PASTIME.

PERHAPS LONG AGO IN A MORE INNOCENT AGE, IT WAS--BUT NO LONGER.

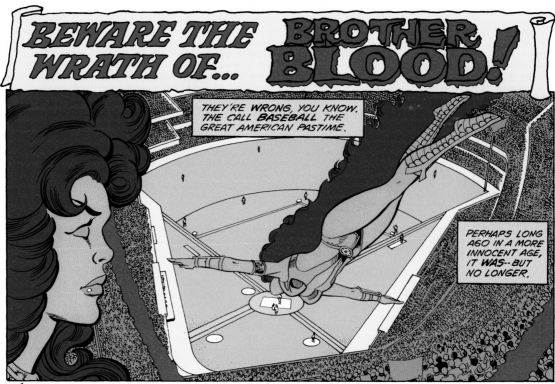

AMERICA'S NEWEST PASTIME, INDEED. THE PASTIME FOR MOST OF THE WORLD TODAY IS A FAR MORE BRUTAL GAME IN WHICH THERE ARE NO WINNERS.

MARV WOLFMAN & GEORGE PÉREZ, WRITER-CO-CREATORS-ARTIST • ROMEO TANGHAL, EMBELLISHER • BEN ODA, LETTERER • ADRIENNE ROY, COLORIST • LEN WEIN, EDITOR

BUT, RAVEN, WE HAVE TO FIND OUT WHERE IT'S HIDDEN.
DO YOU KNOW WHERE IT IS? SPEAK QUICKLY, MAN--THE BOMB... WHERE IS IT?
BOMB? WHAT IN BLAZES ARE YOU TALKING ABOUT, LADY?
I DON'T KNOW ABOUT ANY BOMB. I DON'T EVEN KNOW YOU!

WULL, AH DO, STERN. THIS LI'L LADY'S FROM THEM TITAN KIDS. SPARROW, AH THINK HER NAME IS.
AN' THIS HERE ONE'S STARFLAME, AH THINK.
PLEASE, YOU DON'T COMPREHEND THE URGENCY.
ROS
COACH
MACK
STERN
8

WE HAD REPORTS OF A BOMB PLANTED HERE.
THERE ARE THOUSANDS WHO MIGHT BE KILLED.

NOT REALLY, LADY. WE WERE JUST WAITIN' FOR YOU TO SHOW.
NOW TO GIVE THE GUY PAYIN' THE BILLS A SHOW FOR HIS MONEY.
HE WANTS YOU TWO RUN THROUGH YOUR PACES.
AND THAT'S WHAT HE'S GOING TO GET!

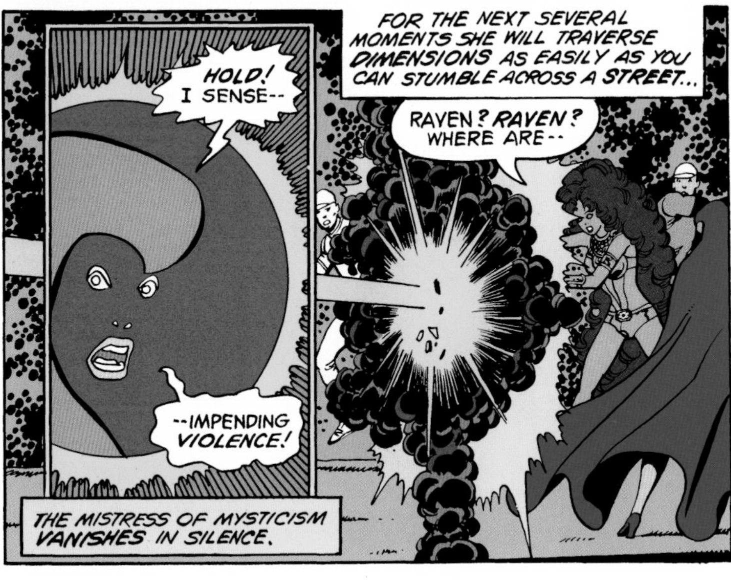
HOLD! I SENSE--
--IMPENDING VIOLENCE!
THE MISTRESS OF MYSTICISM VANISHES IN SILENCE.
FOR THE NEXT SEVERAL MOMENTS SHE WILL TRAVERSE DIMENSIONS AS EASILY AS YOU CAN STUMBLE ACROSS A STREET...
RAVEN? RAVEN? WHERE ARE--

OH.
OKAY.
2

I DON'T NEED ROBIN TO TELL ME THOSE ARE OUR BOMB-PLANTERS AND THAT THEY'RE LOOKING FOR A FIGHT.
I THINK I WOULD VERY MUCH LIKE TO ACCOMMODATE THEM!
BAM
BAM
BAM

BUT...
NO! STARFIRE, PLEASE, NO VIOLENCE.
ALREADY TOO MANY INNOCENTS ARE BEING TRAMPLED IN THEIR MAD EFFORTS TO ESCAPE.

THAT IS SOMETHING PEOPLE LIKE YOU NEVER CONSIDER, DO YOU?

YOU THRIVE AND WALLOW IN DESTRUCTION FOR ITS OWN SAKE.
YOU SICKEN ME!
THIS IS RAVEN'S SOUL-SELF. ITS PROPERTIES ARE UNKNOWN.

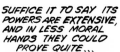

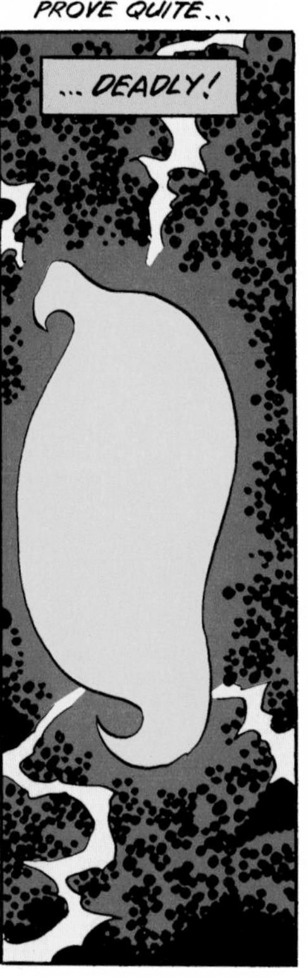
SUFFICE IT TO SAY ITS POWERS ARE EXTENSIVE, AND IN LESS MORAL HANDS THEY COULD PROVE QUITE...
...DEADLY!

THE GAME IS OVER! NOW TALK!
UNLIKE RAVEN, I DO NOT PACIFY MY ENEMIES!
BUT EVEN AS STARFIRE'S DESTRUCTIVE STARBOLTS LASH OUT...

...RAVEN'S MORE CORPOREAL SELF GETS TO THE HEART OF THE MATTER AT HAND...
YOU! THE ONE BEHIND THIS INSANITY --TURN NOW, MAN!
HUH? HOW'D YOU SNEAK UP BEHIND ME?
3

I AM NOT HERE TO ANSWER *YOUR* QUESTIONS. I HAVE QUERIES OF MY OWN.

I DEMAND *INFORMATION*...

WH-WHAT'RE YOU *DOIN'* TO ME?

EXTRACTING KNOWLEDGE... TELL ME WHERE YOU PLACED THE *BOMB.*

TELL ME *NOW!*

NOW!

STARFIRE! IT IS BURIED BENEATH SOMETHING CALLED *THIRD BASE.*

WHAT'S *THAT?*

OVER *THERE,* LADY-- THAT LITTLE *BAG* ON THE FIELD.

THIS IS *IT?* THEN STAND BACK.

THERE IS NO TIME REMAINING!

RAVEN, I THINK I SEE IT, BURIED ABOUT FIVE FEET DOWN!
IT'S QUITE SMALL ACTUALLY.
ALTHOUGH I LEARNED LONG BEFORE I EVER FOUND MYSELF ON YOUR WORLD--

--THAT SIZE IS NO INDICATION OF POWER!
LIKE A GRIM COMET, PRINCESS KORIAND'R OF TAMARAN BURNS THROUGH THE BLUE SKIES OF EARTH...
4

WHY DOESN'T SHE THROW IT?
SHE IS STILL MUCH TOO LOW!

BEFORE WE RUSHED OFF HERE, DICK WARNED ME TO MAKE CERTAIN THE BOMB WAS FAR AWAY FROM MANHATTAN...
...OR ELSE ITS SHOCK-WAVE COULD STILL WREAK HAVOC.
DICK'S ALWAYS PROVEN RIGHT ABOUT THESE THINGS BEFORE...
IT'S JUST MATTERS OF A MORE PERSONAL NATURE THAT HE'S USUALLY WRONG ABOUT.
WHY WON'T HE ADMIT THAT HE LOVES ME? I KNOW HE DOES.
THOUGH I WONDER IF I CAN EVER CARE FOR HIM AGAIN THE WAY I DID BEFORE I MET FRANKLIN.

WILL I BE ABLE TO CARE FOR ANYTHING EVER--

X'HAL! TOO CLOSE!
THE BOMB EXPLODED SOONER THAN I HAD EXPECTED.

C-CAN'T CONCENTRATE ... CAN'T FLY...

GREAT AZAR! KORIAND'R...
SHE'S BARELY CONSCIOUS... SHE NEEDS ME.

WE'RE SO DIFFERENT, THE TWO OF US... YET SHE HAS ALWAYS CALLED ME HER FRIEND...

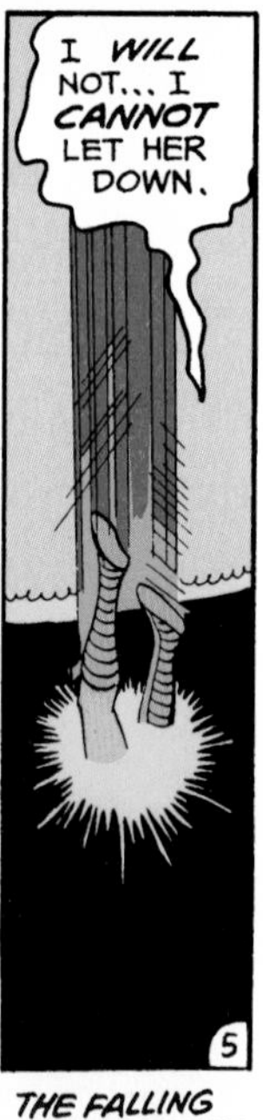

I WILL NOT... I CANNOT LET HER DOWN.
5

THE FALLING ALIEN VANISHES WITHIN RAVEN'S MYSTICAL SOUL-SELF...

...ONLY TO REAPPEAR MOMENTS LATER...
ARE YOU SAFE?
SHE DOESN'T MOVE.

CURSE ME FOR A FOOL! SHE USES THE WARM SOLAR RAYS TO GIVE HER POWER...
THE SUDDENNESS OF BEING ENVELOPED BY MY FRIGID SOUL-SELF THREW HER INTO DEEP SHOCK.
HER FRIEND MAY HAVE ENDANGERED HER, BUT THE EMPATH THAT I AM CAN SAVE HER...

LET HER PAIN BECOME MY OWN ... LET HER AGONIES BECOME MINE.
I MUST SAVE KORIAND'R ...I MUST SAVE...
...MY FRIEND.

SPACE: THERE ARE SEVERAL HUNDRED SATELLITES IN CLUTTERED ORBIT AROUND THE EARTH THESE DAYS...
...THIS IS BUT ONE OF THEM:
FASCINATING! THE EXTENT OF THEIR POWER IS GREATER THAN I HAD IMAGINED!

SUCH INFORMATION WILL PROVE VALUABLE TO MY CLIENTS.
WHO IS THIS MYSTERY MAN? THAT IS A STORY FOR ANOTHER DAY...

FOR NOW, HOWEVER, WE RETURN TO EARTH...
...TO A WOODED ACREAGE NEAR BUZZARD'S BAY, MASSACHUSETTS...
...WHERE A POSSIBLY FAMILIAR FIGURE RACES FOR HER VERY LIFE.
HER NAME IS MARCY (NO LAST NAMES ARE PERMITTED IN THE RETREAT)...
ONCE, MANY YEARS AGO, SHE WAS THE GIRL FRIEND OF VICTOR STONE, WHO HAS SINCE BECOME CYBORG, ONE OF THE NEW TITANS...
SHE DEARLY WISHES HE WAS WITH HER NOW.
OH, MY GOD... MY GOD! THEY'LL KILL ME!
ZWIPPP!
6

ZWIPPP PPP!
ALL THESE MONTHS I'VE BEEN SO *WRONG!* I JUST WANT TO *LEAVE*... THAT'S ALL... THAT'S *ALL*.
I WON'T *SAY* ANYTHING. I WON'T *TELL* ANYBODY!

CHUGCHUGCHUGCHUGCHUGCHUGCHUG
BELIEVE ME, HIS SECRET IS *SAFE*... REALLY IT IS.
JUST LET ME GO HOME TO MY PARENTS. *PLEASE*...

THE *ANSWER* COMES COLDLY AND RELENTLESSLY...
CHUGCHUGCHUGCHUGCHUG
ZWIPPPPPPPP

WHY... WHY? *WHY?*
WHY?
CHUGCHUGCHUGCH

BECAUSE YOU HAVE *SINNED,* SISTER MARCY.
CHUGCHUGCHUG
SINNED AGAINST THE CHURCH OF *BROTHER BLOOD!*

FOR SINNING YOU MUST PAY *PENANCE*.
CHUGCHUGC
YOUR PENANCE IS *EXCOMMUNICATION*.

WHAT?
CHUGCHU

SEVERAL HOURS LATER IN MANHATTAN...
...I'M TELLIN' YA, SARAH, IT'S JUST HARD TO EXPLAIN.
I FEEL GUILTY BECAUSE KNOWIN' ME GOT YOU KIDNAPPED!

BUT I DON'T BLAME YOU, VICTOR. I NEVER DID.
I BLAME MYSELF. THAT'S ENOUGH.
SOMETIMES I EVEN BLAME MY-SELF FOR MY PARENTS DYIN'.

MEBBE IF I HAD HELPED THEM LIKE THEY WANTED ME TO, WHAT HAPPENED TO THEM WOULDN'T HAVE HAPPENED. I DON'T KNOW...
MAYBE I JUST DON'T WANT TO GET TOO CLOSE TO ANYONE.

HELL, SARAH, I DON'T HAVE MYSELF FIGURED OUT...
NOBODY EVER KNOWS THEMSELVES, VICTOR. I'M NOT ASKING FOR US TO BE ANYTHING OTHER THAN GOOD FRIENDS...

...BUT I WAS SO WORRIED WHEN YOU DIDN'T CALL. I--
RRING RRING

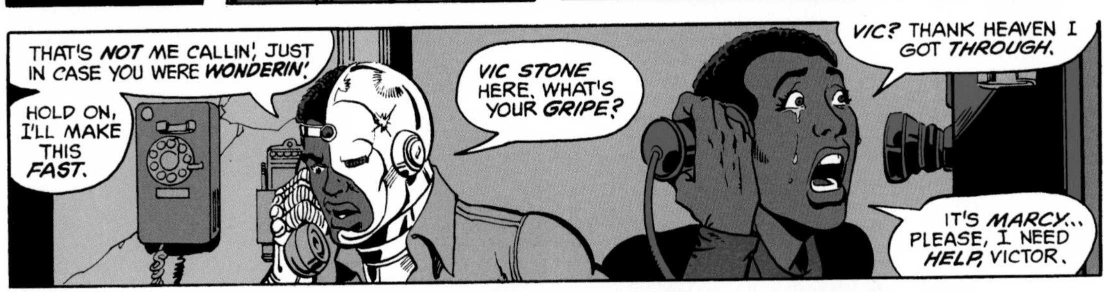
THAT'S NOT ME CALLIN', JUST IN CASE YOU WERE WONDERIN'.
HOLD ON, I'LL MAKE THIS FAST.
VIC STONE HERE. WHAT'S YOUR GRIPE?
VIC? THANK HEAVEN I GOT THROUGH.
IT'S MARCY... PLEASE, I NEED HELP, VICTOR.

THEY'RE AFTER ME, VICTOR.
P-PLEASE HELP ME.
THEY? WHO'S THEY, MARCY? AN' WHERE ARE YOU?

B-BROTHER BLOOD, VIC-- HE'S TRYING TO KILL ME.
I-I'M AT RON'S OLD PLACE... PLEASE COME HERE ...PLEASE...
I'M ALREADY HURT...

SKRA-BLAM
AGGHHH!

MARCY!?! FOR GOD'S SAKE, MARCY!
8

PLEASE, I'LL COME BACK QUIETLY. I WON'T EVER RUN AWAY AGAIN.
JUST DON'T HURT ME.
PLEASE DON'T HURT ME.

OUR SISTER WAS SLAIN TRYING TO GIVE YOU PENANCE, SISTER MARCY.
WE CAN DELAY THE LAST RITES NO LONGER.
YOU MAY SAY YOUR FINAL PRAYERS BEFORE WE CARRY OUT BROTHER BLOOD'S ORDER OF EXCOMMUNICATION.

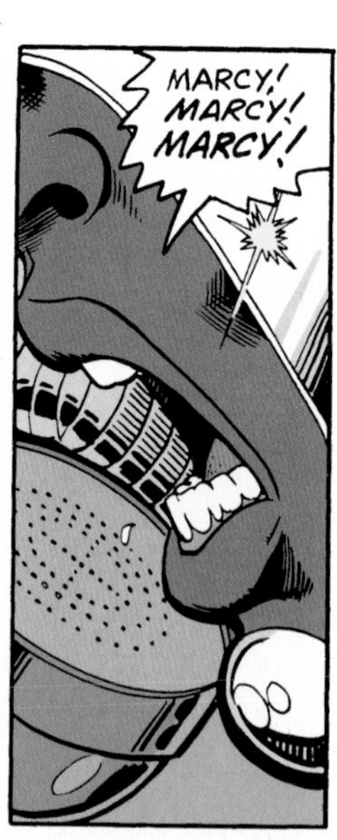

MARCY! MARCY! MARCY!

NARROWIN' IN...

RON'S PLACE ISN'T FAR. JUST A COUPLE MORE BLOCKS.

HUH? WHAT'S THAT CRACKLIN' SOUND I'M PICKIN' UP ON MY EAR AMPLIFIERS?

WON'T WORRY 'BOUT THAT NOW. MARCY'LL EXPLAIN EVERYTHIN'!

WHY?

WHY?
WHY?
WHY?
WHY?
10
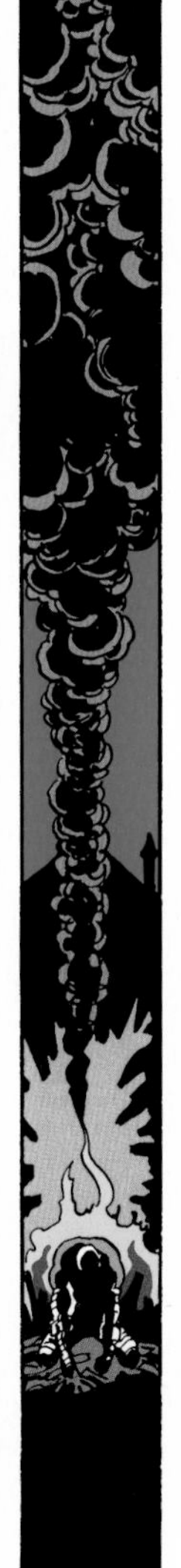
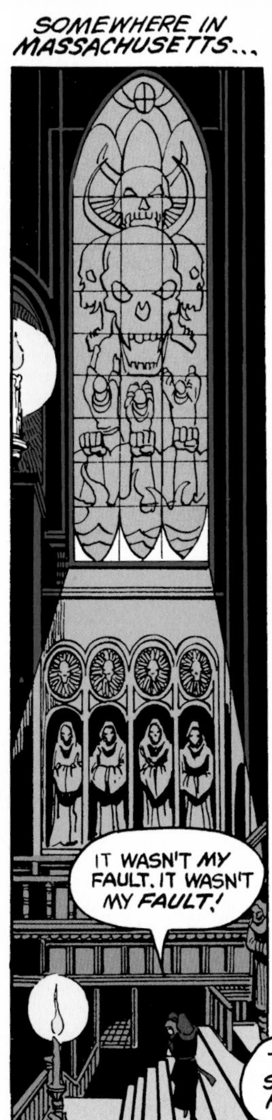
SOMEWHERE IN MASSACHUSETTS...
IT WASN'T MY FAULT. IT WASN'T MY FAULT!

THIS IS SISTER KARYN.
SHE WAS THE ONE.

BUT IT WASN'T MY FAULT.
I'VE BEEN LOYAL TO YOU FOR THREE YEARS NOW.
I WORSHIP YOU. I'VE GIVEN YOU EVERYTHING!
I WOULD NEVER BETRAY YOU.

I AGREE, SISTER KARYN. YOU HAVE GIVEN ME EVERYTHING YOU HAD TO GIVE.

BUT YOU WERE THE ONE WHO VOUCHED FOR OUR LATE SISTER MARCY.
YOU WERE ASSIGNED TO EXPLORE HER HISTORY.
AND YOU FAILED TO LEARN THAT SHE HAD ONCE BEEN THE LOVER OF ONE OF OUR POSSIBLE ENEMIES.
BUT THEY WERE KIDS. IT WAS OVER YEARS AGO.

FIRST LOVES DO NOT DIE, SISTER KARYN. YOU SHOULD HAVE KNOWN BETTER.
I TOLERATE MISTAKES, SISTER KARYN. BUT IN CONFESSION YOU CLAIMED IGNORANCE OF THE TRUE FACTS.

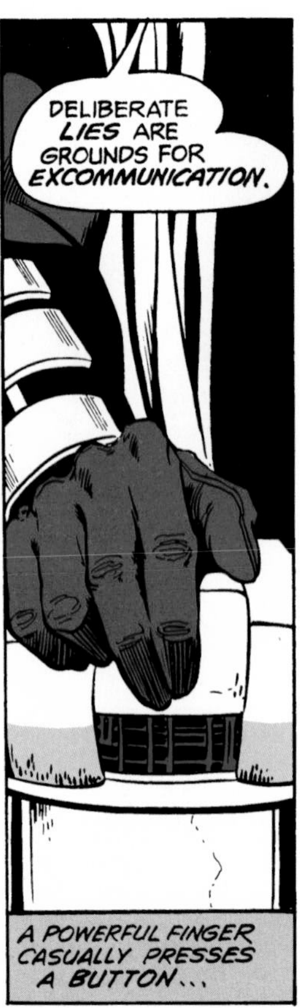
DELIBERATE LIES ARE GROUNDS FOR EXCOMMUNICATION.
A POWERFUL FINGER CASUALLY PRESSES A BUTTON...

...AND INSTANTS LATER A SECTION OF STONE FLOORING SLIDES OPEN...
WH-WHAT?

WH-WHAT ARE YOU GOING TO DO TO ME?
WHAT ARE YOU GOING TO DO TO ME?!?
YAGGHHH!
11

ENOUGH.
PERHAPS THIS SHALL SERVE AS A LESSON TO THE OTHERS IN OUR MIDST WHO DO NOT TRULY BELIEVE IN--
--THE MERCY OF BROTHER BLOOD!
BUT NOW, BECAUSE OF SISTER KARYN'S BLUNDERING, WE HAVE POSSIBLY SPAWNED A NEW ENEMY.
ALERT OUR BELIEVERS IN THE SENATE AND CONGRESS OF THIS COUNTRY TO QUICKLY DEAL WITH THESE TEEN TITANS FOR ME.
I HAVE FAR MORE IMPORTANT DUTIES THAT MUST BE ATTENDED TO THAN THE UNFORTUNATE FATE SOON TO BEFALL THOSE SEVEN YOUNG CHILDREN.
12

TITANS' TOWER:
HEADQUARTERS FOR THE NEW TEEN TITANS SITUATED ON A SMALL ISLAND IN NEW YORK'S EAST RIVER...
...LAST THING SHE SAID WAS SOMETHING ABOUT A BROTHER BLOOD BEING AFTER HER.

I CAN'T TELL YOU HOW SORRY WE ARE, VICTOR.
BUT I PROMISE WE'LL START A COMPUTER CHECK ON THIS BROTHER BLOOD IMMEDIATELY.
HOW ARE YOU HOLDING ON? YOU OKAY?

I'LL BE FINE... JUST FINE. LOOK, I GOT SOME THINGS TO DO.
JUST GET ME THAT INFO, OKAY?

IT'S AS GOOD AS GOTTEN, VIC.
ROBIN, LET ME SPEAK TO VICTOR, PLEASE.

VICTOR, IT'S ME, KORIAND'R. IS THERE ANYTHING I CAN DO FOR YOU?
ANYTHING AT ALL? I'D LIKE TO HELP.

DON'T NEED NO HELP, GOLDIE. BUT THANKS FOR ASKIN'.
JUST MAKE SURE ROBBIE GETS ME THAT STUFF, OKAY?

THEY'LL FIND OUT WHERE THIS BROTHER BLOOD IS.
THEN HE'S MINE!
MINE!
13

HE'S TAKING IT VERY HARD.
LISSEN, I KNOW THAT LUNKHEAD BETTER'N ANYONE. HE'S KEEPIN' MOST OF HIS ANGER INSIDE.
I'M REALLY SCARED OF WHAT'LL HAPPEN WHEN IT BURSTS FREE.
YOU THINK MARCY WAS KILLED BECAUSE SHE KNEW VICTOR?

IS THIS THE WAY THINGS ARE ON YOUR WORLD?
YOU FALL IN LOVE AND YOUR LOVER HAS TO DIE?

BELIEVE ME, KORY, IT'S NOT ALWAYS THAT WAY.
SURE, THERE ARE SOME SICK PEOPLE OUT THERE. BUT MOST OF THE WORLD BELIEVES IN LIFE AND BASIC HONESTY.
WE'RE IN THE MAJORITY, THE VAST MAJORITY. BUT ALL YOU NEED IS A FEW CRUMBS LIKE THIS BROTHER BLOOD...

LISTEN, FOR VICTOR--
--LET'S NAIL THAT CREEP-- FAST!

A DAY PASSES AS WE MOVE TO A CEMETERY ON THE SOUTH SHORE OF QUEENS, NEW YORK.

HOW DO YOU SIMPLY SUM UP THE LIFE OF A GIRL FAR TOO YOUNG TO DIE?

HOW DO YOU MAKE SENSE OF SOMETHING DEVOID OF SENSE?

SADLY, THERE IS NO WAY. INSTEAD, YOU JOIN TOGETHER IN GRIEF AND TRY TO THINK OF THE GOOD TIMES...

...THE TIMES OF SMILES AND LAUGHTER AND LOVE...
14

BUT, ALL TOO OFTEN, THERE ARE TOO MANY SAD REMINDERS...
YOU?!?

I HAD TO COME, MR. REYNOLDS.
MARCY MEANT A LOT TO ME.

YOU...YOU FILTH! YOU KILLED HER!
DAD, PLEASE... REMEMBER YOUR HEART.
DONALD, STOP... STOP IT!

I DIDN'T KILL HER, MR. REYNOLDS. SHE CALLED ME FOR HELP...
...AND I REALLY TRIED TO HELP...
BECAUSE OF YOU SHE DIED. WHY DIDN'T YOU DIE SO SHE WOULDN'T HAVE HAD TO?

PLEASE, DONALD, VICTOR HAD NOTHING TO DO WITH IT. YOU KNOW THAT.
HE CARED FOR HER AND SHE LOVED HIM.

YOUR WIFE IS RIGHT, MR. REYNOLDS.
WHAT ARE YOU DOIN' HERE?

WE'RE YOUR FRIENDS, VICTOR.
MR. REYNOLDS, VICTOR LOVED YOUR DAUGHTER. HE COULDN'T DO ANYTHING TO HURT HER.
HE DROVE HER TO THAT MANIAC, THAT'S WHAT HE DID.
HE'S RESPONSIBLE FOR ALL OF THIS.
MR. AND MRS. REYNOLDS, I FEEL YOUR GRIEF AND SORROW...
...I CAN SENSE YOUR PAIN AND LOSS AND NOTHING I CAN SAY CAN OR EVEN SHOULD REMOVE IT.

CERTAINLY NOTHING COULD EVER BRING MARCY BACK...
...BUT WE WANT TO HELP FIND HER KILLER. WILL YOU HELP US DO THAT... FOR MARCY?
AS WE HAVE STATED, RAVEN IS AN EMPATH, AND HER CALM, WARMING WORDS SOOTHE THE ANGER IN DONALD REYNOLDS' HEART...
15

WE HAVE REASON TO BELIEVE SOMEONE NAMED BROTHER BLOOD WAS RESPONSIBLE.
BLOOD...? LOOK, VICTOR, I'M SORRY I SNAPPED AT YOU. PLEASE UNDERSTAND.
"I DO," VICTOR RESPONDS.

PLEASE, CAN YOU TELL US ANYTHING ABOUT BROTHER BLOOD?

I DON'T KNOW MUCH. MAYBE I SHOULD HAVE CHECKED HIM OUT WHEN THIS ALL BEGAN.

MR. REYNOLDS, DO NOT DWELL ON THE PAST. THAT ACCOMPLISHES NO POSSIBLE GOOD.

W-WHEN I BROKE UP THE ROMANCE BE-TWEEN MARCY AND VICTOR, SHE BECAME SO SILENT, SO SULLEN.

ONE OF HER FRIENDS TOLD HER ABOUT THIS RELIGIOUS GROUP -- THE CHURCH OF BROTHER BLOOD.

OH, I ARGUED WITH HER, BUT SHE STILL BECAME A BELIEVER...

...FINALLY SHE LEFT OUR HOUSE AND MOVED TO BLOOD'S RETREAT. SHE CALLED US A FEW DAYS AGO...

...SAID SHE WANTED TO COME HOME. BUT THAT'S THE LAST WE HEARD FROM HER UNTIL THE POLICE CAME.

DO YOU KNOW WHERE BLOOD'S RETREAT IS, MR. REYNOLDS?

YEAH, I KNOW... I KNOW WHERE THAT DAMNED HOUSE OF DEATH IS.

EVENING...

RICHARD, VICTOR WAS ANGRY.
NOTHING I COULD DO ABOUT IT, RAVEN.
HE COULDN'T JOIN US.
HOLD!

OH, IT'S YOU, BELCHER. ANOTHER DELIVERY?
YEAH. GOT ME SOME PEACH FUZZ RIPE FER PICKIN'.

PEACH FUZZ? WAS THAT AN INSULT?
I THINK THEY MEAN WE'RE YOUNG.
AT LEAST I HOPE THAT'S WHAT THEY MEANT.

ANYWAY, WE MADE IT.
BROTHER BLOOD'S RETREAT, FOR WORSE OR WORSER STILL.

WELCOME, WELCOME TO THE CHURCH OF BROTHER BLOOD.
PLEASE, STEP DOWN AND FOLLOW US FOR PROCESSING.
GREAT! WE'RE NOT PEOPLE, WE'RE CHEESE!
16

UPON FIRST VIEW, BLOOD'S RETREAT IS AWESOME. BUT THEN ITS DECADENT SPLENDOR BECOMES APPARENT...
GROTESQUE GARGOYLES LEER DOWN ON EVERY HALLWAY, THEIR STONY EYES SEEM TO FOLLOW YOUR EVERY STEP...
THE SMELL OF INCENSE IS ALMOST OVER-WHELMING AS IS THE CONSTANT DRONING OF EBON-CLAD WORSHIPPERS...
THESE ARE SOME OF OUR OTHER BELIEVERS ON THEIR WAY TO DARK MASS.
YOU'LL JOIN THEM SOON ENOUGH.
I SENSE VIRTUALLY NO EMOTIONS FROM THOSE PEOPLE. IT IS AS IF THEIR SENSES HAVE BEEN DEADENED.
KEEP SCANNING, RAVEN. TRY TO HOME IN ON BLOOD HIMSELF.
WE'VE HEARD SO MUCH ABOUT BROTHER BLOOD. IS HE REALLY A GOD LIKE THEY SAY?
HE'S BEEN ALIVE FOR MORE THAN 700 YEARS...
...AND HIS CHURCH HAS PROSPERED FOR AT LEAST THAT LONG ON THE BALTIC ISLAND OF ZANDIA.
WHEN DO WE GET A CHANCE TO SEE HIM?
SOON. VERY SOON.
17

MAYBE TOO SOON, WALLY WEST, FOR DEEP BELOW THE GIANT CATHEDRAL...
I'VE GOT THE NEW RECRUITS UNDER BI-SECTORS.
BUT THERE SEEMS TO BE AN ANOMALY HERE.
GET A COMPUTER READOUT OVER TO MOTHER MAYHEM--FAST.

WHAT HAVE WE FOUND, ACOLYTE?
A DEFINITE BIOLOGICAL ANOMALY IN THREE OF THE FOUR NEW RECRUITS...

WELL, WE'VE BEEN EXPECTING SOMETHING LIKE THIS.
BROTHER BLOOD MUST BE NOTIFIED AT ONCE.

MAN, THIS PLACE IS CREEPIER THAN A JOHN CARPENTER MOVIE.

THAT IT IS, WALLY, BUT WHAT BOTHERS ME IS HOW HE MANAGED TO GET SO MANY KIDS HERE--
--WITHOUT SOMEONE FINDING OUT ABOUT IT?
AND DID YOU SEE THOSE SUPPOSED NUNS? NOT ONE OF THEM WEARS A CRUCIFIX.
WHATEVER THIS IS, IT'S NOT A REAL RELIGION.

Y'KNOW WHAT HURTS? SOMETHING TWISTED LIKE THIS THRIVES WHILE MANY REAL RELIGIONS ARE IN TROUBLE.

ARE YOU RELIGIOUS, WALLY?
I GUESS SO. I DON'T GO ALL THE TIME, BUT I BELIEVE. YOU?
I HAVEN'T THOUGHT ABOUT IT MUCH.
18

SOMETHING WRONG?
THIS IS THE FIRST TIME I'VE WORN PANTS.
I DON'T FEEL AT ALL COMFORTABLE.

AND I FEEL EVEN LESS AT EASE WHENEVER I LOOK AT THAT PICTURE.
THERE IS SOMETHING EVIL ABOUT IT, DONNA.
BROTHER BLOOD

JUST THEN...
YOU ARE DRESSED. GOOD. IT IS TIME FOR THE CEREMONY.
COME WITH ME.
EACH NIGHT THERE ARE PRAYERS. EVERYONE JOINS IN.
YOU ARE ON PROBATION HERE FOR SIX MONTHS. IF YOU PASS, YOU BECOME A FULL MEMBER OF THE CHURCH.

NOW, TAKE THESE SEATS AND REMAIN SILENT UNLESS SPOKEN TO BY BROTHER BLOOD.
DO YOU UNDERSTAND?
STRANGE. SHE'S NOT TRYING TO MAKE THIS PLEASANT. HOW DOES SHE EXPECT TO GET RECRUITS?
19

LOOK AT THEM-- EVERYONE'S ACTING LIKE PUPPETS.
SHHH. LOOK AT THE ALTAR.

EVERYONE NOW RISE AND PRAY WITH BROTHER BLOOD.
NO, SISTER. NOT YET.
THERE ARE SOME AMONG US WHO HAVE NO RIGHT TO PRAY IN OUR MIDST.

WE HAVE SINNERS HERE.
LOOK INTO YOUR DAMNED SOULS AND YOU WILL KNOW WHO YOU ARE.
YOU WILL SEE THE HELL YOUR SOUL HAS BEEN CONDEMNED TO.

YOUR ONLY SALVATION IS COMPLETE OBSEQUIOUSNESS TO THE DEMANDS OF YOUR GOD, BROTHER BLOOD.
WILLIAM LORING-- RISE AND CONFESS YOUR SINS.

BR- BROTHER BLOOD, I- I WAS WRONG. I WANTED TO GO HOME TO MY PARENTS.
WILL YOU PAY PENANCE?
I WILL... I WILL. I'LL DO ANYTHING.

GOOD, WILLIAM. FOR THE NEXT SIX MONTHS YOUR LABORS HERE SHALL BE IN-CREASED TWOFOLD. NOW SIT.

WENDY FLETCHER-- RISE AND CONFESS YOUR SINS.
I HAVEN'T SINNED.
I FINALLY SAW THE TRUTH.
YOU'RE NOT A GOD. YOU'RE NOT EVEN A RELIGION. YOU'RE A DEVIL-- A DEVIL!
AND YOU ARE A BLASPHEMER!
20

ONE WHOSE SINS DEMAND IMMEDIATE EXCOMMUNICATION!
ZWIP

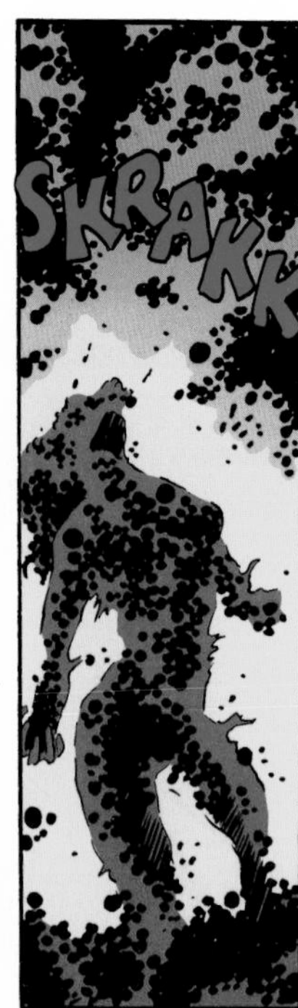
SKRAKK

ARGHH! THE PAIN... THE TERRIBLE, PIERCING PAIN!
THERE, MY TRUE BELIEVERS-- THAT ONE, SHE AND HER FRIENDS...

...THEY HAVE COME HERE TO DESTROY THE CHURCH OF BROTHER BLOOD.
BUT WE SHALL SHOW THEM WHAT HAPPENS TO WOULD-BE DEFILERS! TEAR THEM APART!

DICK, THEY'RE ATTACKING US!
OUR COVER'S OBVIOUSLY BLOWN!

TRY TO GET TO BLOOD.
AND REMEMBER, THESE KIDS ARE JUST BEING DUPED!

I KNOW IT, DICK--

--BUT I CAN'T DO ANYTHING ABOUT IT!

DUPED OR NOT, I'VE GOT TO FIGHT BACK TO GET FREE.

BUT ONCE FREE, MY NEXT STOP IS BROTHER BLOOD HIMSELF!
I'LL TRUSS 'IM UP LIKE A TURKEY BEFORE HE CAN EVEN TURN!
21

AH, THE YOUNG FLASH. ASIDE FROM YOUR AMAZING SPEED YOU ARE STILL QUITE HUMAN.
YOU'LL PROVE NO PROBLEM.
I DON'T LIKE THE WAY HE'S JUST STANDING THERE WAITING.
BETTER BE CAREFUL. HE'S UP TO SOMETHING.

A VALIANT ATTEMPT, THOUGH A FRUITLESS ONE. THE ELECTRICAL FIELD THAT SURROUNDS ME WILL ASSURE YOUR DEFEAT...
...AND MY ULTIMATE VICTORY!
AMAZING. HIS REFLEXES ARE ASTOUNDING.
ARGHH!
HE PULLED AWAY QUICKLY ENOUGH TO AVOID ELECTROCUTION!

STILL, HE IS NO THREAT.
YOU'VE WON!
OF COURSE.
BROTHER BLOOD--

--THE FEMALE IS VANISHING!

SHE'S BRINGING THE OTHER TITANS HERE, BLOOD.
WHICH MEANS YOU AND THIS PSEUDO-RELIGIOUS MADHOUSE ARE DONE FOR.
WHAP!
SPAK!

ROBIN--DUCK!
I'M THE ONE WHO PLAYS "BULLETS AND BRACELETS"--NOT YOU!
DON'T WORRY, WONDER GIRL, I'M NOT HOGGING YOUR ACT.
RAVEN?
I COULD NOT LEAVE YOU THREE IMPERILED LIKE THIS.
THERE IS STILL MUCH HERE I CAN DO!
22

THOUGH I HAD NOT INTENDED TO REVEAL MY PRESENCE IN YOUR COUNTRY, SO BE IT! THE DEED IS DONE!
MY FOLLOWERS ALREADY INFEST YOUR GOVERNMENT!
I HAVE BELIEVERS IN YOUR UNIVERSITIES AND IN YOUR BUSINESS BOARDROOMS.
MY POWER EXTENDS THROUGH THE VERY FABRIC OF YOUR LIVES. INDEED, VERY SOON I SHALL CONTROL YOUR LIVES.
CONVERT NOW AND BE SPARED AN IGNOBLE DEFEAT.

STUFF IT, BLOOD!
YOU'RE FINISHED!

NO, MY YOUNG FOOL, YOU ARE GREATLY MISTAKEN...
YOU DO NOT KNOW WHAT YOU ARE UP AGAINST.

BUDDY, I'VE HEARD THAT FROM EVERY TWO-BIT CREEP WHO EVER CRAWLED OUT OF THE MUD-HOLE THAT SPAWNS YOU TWISTED MADMEN!
AND YOU KNOW SOMETHING, BLOOD? YOU'RE ALL LOSERS!

HISTRIONICS ILL BECOME YOU, CHILD.
I SAID BEFORE YOU DO NOT KNOW THE POWER OF BROTHER BLOOD.
KRAK!

BELIEVE ME, THAT IS NO IDLE BOAST!
ZWAMM
ROBIN!

YOU HAVE SEEN THE POWER OF OUR GOD. NOW SING HIS PRAISES.
MISTER, I'M NOT GIVEN TO MAKING RASH PROMISES, BUT I DO PROMISE THIS--
--IF ROBIN'S DEAD, SO ARE YOU!

AND I ASSUME YOU HAVE THE POWER TO ASSURE THAT?
ZWAM
DO NOT MAKE ME LAUGH, GIRL!
23

I WASN'T JOKING, BLOOD. I MEANT IT!
THOK

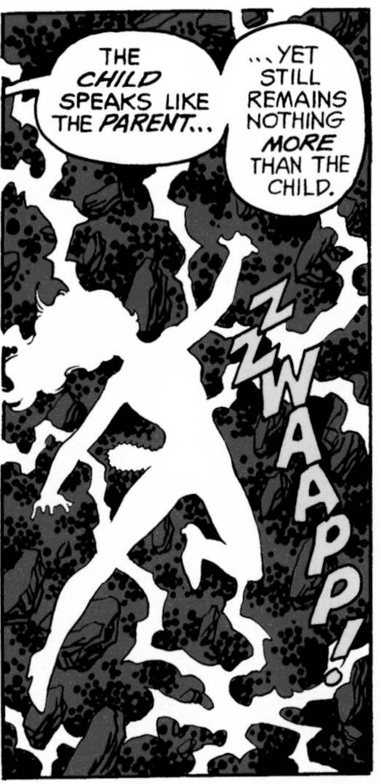
THE CHILD SPEAKS LIKE THE PARENT...
...YET STILL REMAINS NOTHING MORE THAN THE CHILD.
ZZWAAPP!

WONDER GIRL-- ROBIN IS STILL ALIVE! HE WAS MERELY STUNNED.
A TEMPORARY MEASURE, GIRL. BELIEVE THAT.
BRING THE CLOAKED ONE TO ME-- NOW!

BUT NO MAN CAN TOUCH THE GIRL NAMED RAVEN IF SHE DOESN'T WISH TO BE TOUCHED...
SH-SHE'S GONE!

I WILL WORRY ABOUT THAT ONE ANOTHER TIME.
BUT YOU-- YOUR STAMINA IS REMARKABLE!

STILL, IN THE LONG RUN--
--IT WILL HELP YOU VERY LITTLE!
THUNK!

WHY ARE YOU DOING THIS, BLOOD?
I DO NOT OWE YOU EXPLANATIONS.
YET THIS I WILL TELL YOU, GIRL!
THE DESTINY OF BROTHER BLOOD IS TO CONTROL.
THIS DAY I STAND READY AT THE THRESHOLD OF DESTINY'S DOORWAY.
AND NO MAN, WOMAN OR WITCH SHALL DARE BAR MY WAY.
IT IS JUST HIM AND ME... I COULD FIGHT--
24

"BUT WHY...
"...DO I SENSE--

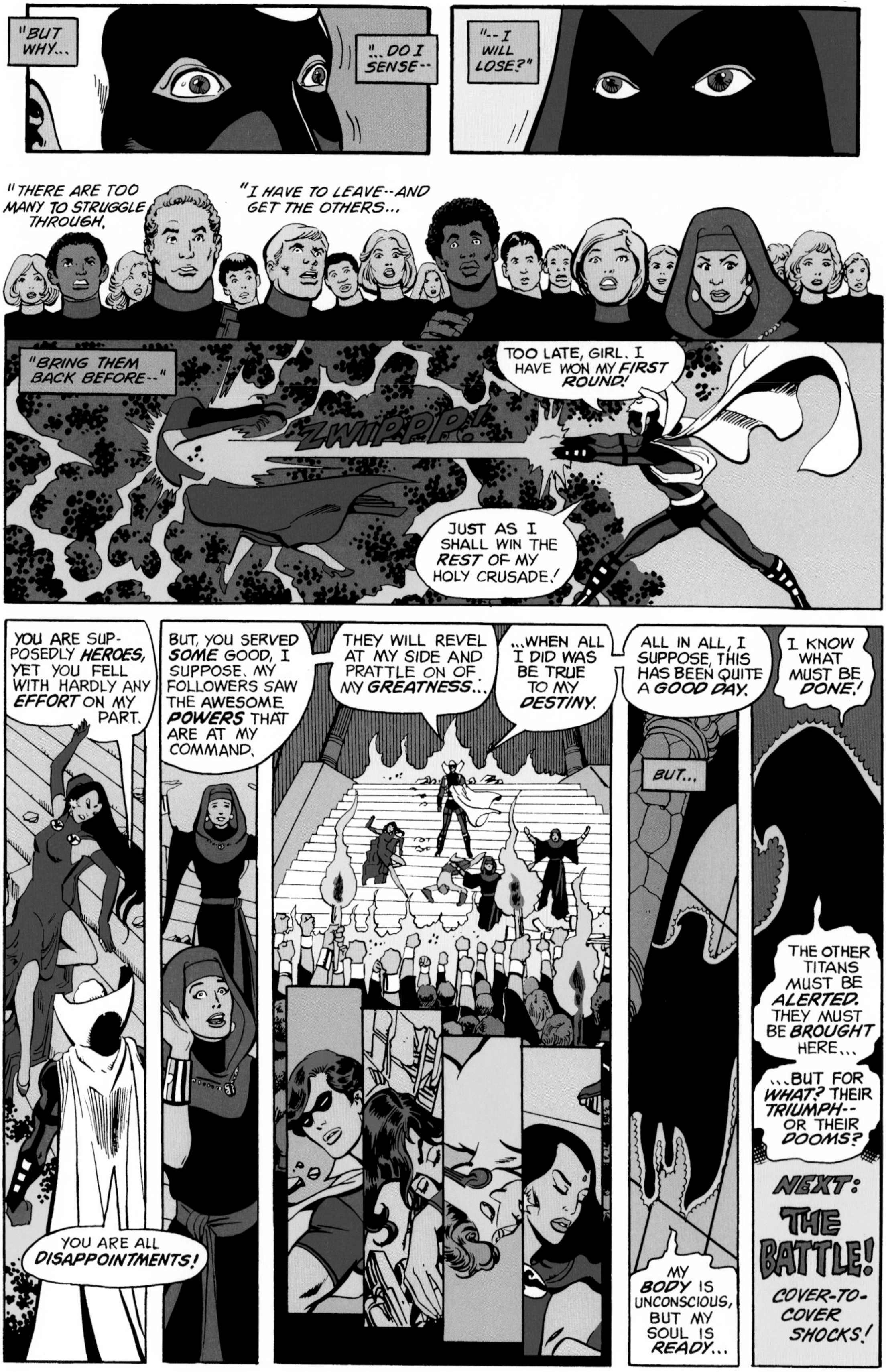

"--I WILL LOSE?"

"THERE ARE TOO MANY TO STRUGGLE THROUGH.
"I HAVE TO LEAVE--AND GET THE OTHERS...
"BRING THEM BACK BEFORE--"
TOO LATE, GIRL. I HAVE WON MY FIRST ROUND!
ZWIPPP!
JUST AS I SHALL WIN THE REST OF MY HOLY CRUSADE!

YOU ARE SUPPOSEDLY HEROES, YET YOU FELL WITH HARDLY ANY EFFORT ON MY PART.

YOU ARE ALL DISAPPOINTMENTS!

BUT, YOU SERVED SOME GOOD, I SUPPOSE. MY FOLLOWERS SAW THE AWESOME POWERS THAT ARE AT MY COMMAND.

THEY WILL REVEL AT MY SIDE AND PRATTLE ON OF MY GREATNESS...

...WHEN ALL I DID WAS BE TRUE TO MY DESTINY.

ALL IN ALL, I SUPPOSE, THIS HAS BEEN QUITE A GOOD DAY.

BUT...

MY BODY IS UNCONSCIOUS, BUT MY SOUL IS READY...

I KNOW WHAT MUST BE DONE!

THE OTHER TITANS MUST BE ALERTED. THEY MUST BE BROUGHT HERE...

...BUT FOR WHAT? THEIR TRIUMPH--OR THEIR DOOMS?

NEXT: THE BATTLE! COVER-TO-COVER SHOCKS!

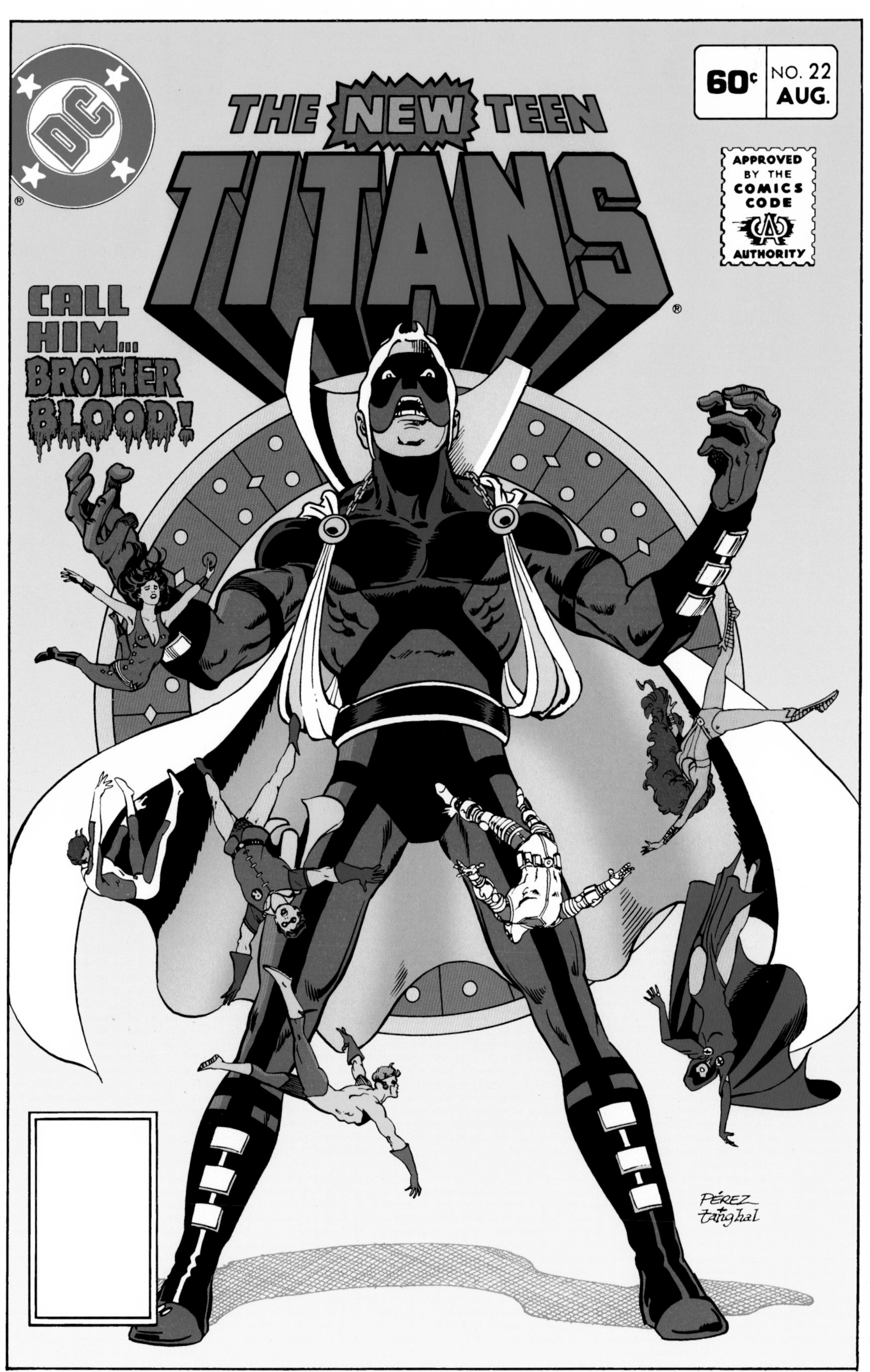
60¢
NO. 22
AUG.
THE NEW TEEN
TITANS
APPROVED BY THE COMICS CODE AUTHORITY
CALL HIM... BROTHER BLOOD!
PÉREZ
Tanghal

THE NEW TEEN TITANS
ASHES TO ASHES!
I HAVE MET THE ENEMY AND THEY ARE MINE!
THEY LIE HUMBLED AND DEFEATED AT MY FEET, SUBJECT TO MY EVERY WHIM!
MOTHER MAYHEM-- SEAL THEM IN THE PITS AND LET THEM DIE!
MARV WOLFMAN & GEORGE PÉREZ
WRITER--CO-CREATORS--ARTIST
ROMEO TANGHAL
EMBELLISHER
BEN ODA — LETTERER
ADRIENNE ROY — COLORIST
LEN WEIN — EDITOR
PLEASE NOTE, GENTLE READER, THAT THIS MAN IS NAMED BROTHER BLOOD!
HE IS NOT VERY NICE!

WAIT! DO NOT TAKE ALL OF THEM...

...LEAVE ME THE NON-POWERED ONE -- THE BOY CALLED ROBIN!

I WANT THE CONFESSOR TO SPEAK WITH HIM!

HE POSSESSES INFORMATION THAT MIGHT BE OF IMPORTANCE TO ME.
ONCE YOU ARE DONE, HURRY BACK HERE.

THAT GIRL -- RAVEN -- HER SHADOW-FORM FLED OUR CATHEDRAL TO ALERT HER BRETHREN.

WE CAN EXPECT THEM TO FOLLOW HER BACK HERE AT ANY TIME.
NOW, YOUNG CHILD --IT IS TIME TO DEAL WITH YOU.
BROTHER BLOOD--?

SENATOR HARDY SAYS THERE IS AN EMERGENCY. HE HAS TO SPEAK WITH YOU.
HARDY? OH YES, MY ACOLYTE IN WASHINGTON.
I WILL TAKE HIS MESSAGE.

MY BELIEVERS, WE ARE ON THE ROAD TO VICTORY!
THE CHURCH OF BROTHER BLOOD WILL PROSPER!
AND THE WORLD WILL BE OURS!

THE OTHERS RAISE THEIR VOICES IN PRAISE OF THEIR GOD AND MASTER, BUT BROTHER BLOOD BARELY HEARS THEM...

LONG AGO HE LEARNED TO IGNORE THE MEWLINGS OF HIS MINDLESS MINIONS...

I AM NOT PLEASED THAT MY PRESENCE IN THIS COUNTRY HAS BEEN DETECTED...
...YET, I FEEL I SHALL TURN THIS TRAGEDY INTO TRIUMPH.
IT WILL BE SO, BROTHER BLOOD. THERE IS NO WAY YOU CAN FAIL.
2

WHAT DO YOU HAVE TO REPORT, HARDY?
BROTHER BLOOD, THE MOTION TO RECOGNIZE ZANDIA AND YOUR CHURCH AS A TRUE ORGANIZED RELIGION IS COMING TO A VOTE TOMORROW.
OUR FOLLOWERS IN BOTH THE HOUSE AND SENATE ARE HAVING A DIFFICULT TIME CONVINCING THE OTHERS.
WE NEED HELP.
I HAVE SUPPLIED YOU WITH MILLIONS. HAVE YOU SQUANDERED THEM AWAY?
N-NO... IT'S JUST THAT SINCE ABSCAM THINGS HAVE BEEN TOUCHY. IT ISN'T AS EASY TO OFFER BRIBES.
HMMM.
LISTEN TO ME, HARDY. TELL YOUR FELLOW SENATORS THAT SINCE THE ZANDIAN PRESIDENT WAS ASSASSINATED SEVERAL WEEKS BACK--*
--OUR NEW PRESIDENT PROMISES TO INSURE DEMOCRACY IN ZANDIA.
AND BE CERTAIN YOU DO NOT WASTE MY TIME.
MY CHURCH HAS ALREADY GROWN THROUGHOUT EUROPE. YET I NEED AMERICA IF MY PLANS ARE TO SUCCEED.
SISTER LUCILLE, CALL OUR REPRESENTATIVE IN THE MEDIA. ARRANGE FOR AN INTERVIEW WITH ME--TONIGHT.
HARDY, PERHAPS I CAN ALLAY THE FEARS OF YOUR COMPATRIOTS.
TELL THEM ANY LIE THEY WILL BELIEVE.
*TITANS #14. --Len
3

BROTHER BLOOD LEAVES AND ARROGANTLY STRIDES THROUGH HIS GREAT CATHEDRAL.

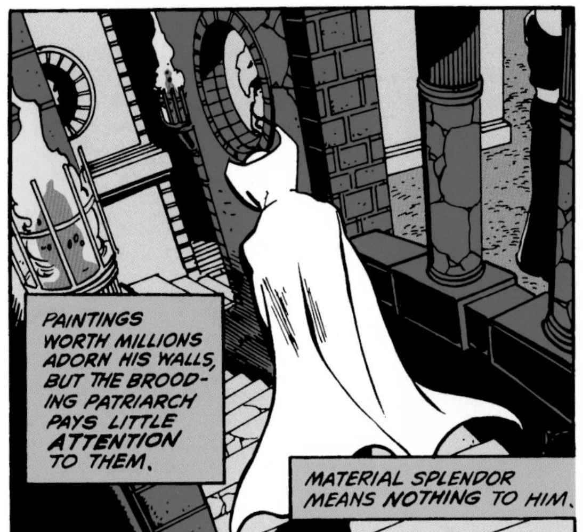
PAINTINGS WORTH MILLIONS ADORN HIS WALLS, BUT THE BROODING PATRIARCH PAYS LITTLE ATTENTION TO THEM.
MATERIAL SPLENDOR MEANS NOTHING TO HIM.

BROTHER BLOOD MERELY CRAVES POWER.
BROTHER RAYMOND, HOW IS THE YOUNG TITAN TAKING HIS CONFESSIONAL?
HE HAS NOT YET SCREAMED OUT IN PAIN, BROTHER BLOOD.
HMM. THAT WILL HAVE TO CHANGE.

CONFESSOR, WHY HASN'T OUR GUEST ADMITTED TO HIS SINS?
HE WILL. HIS BRAVADO WILL FADE LONG BEFORE HIS FLESH IS SEARED FROM HIS BONES!
HE WILL CONFESS TO EVERYTHING!
I GUARANTEE IT!
4

PERHAPS A WORD OF ADVICE MIGHT HELP, BOY. I SUGGEST YOU TELL THE CONFESSOR WHAT HE WANTS TO KNOW.
HIS METHODS ARE MOST... INDELICATE.
AND THE DAMAGE HE CREATES... PERMANENT.

BLOOD, YOU'RE NOT THE HEAD OF SOME RELIGION LIKE YOU CLAIM--YOU'RE JUST A BLASTED KILLER.
AND NO MATTER WHAT YOU DO TO ME, I'LL SEE YOU PAY FOR YOUR CRIMES.

AN AMUSING SPEECH, BOY. I SEE I MUST FIRST BREAK YOUR SPIRIT BEFORE I LOOSEN YOUR TONGUE!

ROBIN BREATHES DEEPLY AS THE ELECTRONIC LASH WHIPS ACROSS HIS NAKED CHEST...

WHILE, ON AN ISLAND IN NEW YORK'S EAST RIVER...
I'VE HAD IT!

YOU HEAR ME? I'M FED UP WAITING!
BROTHER BLOOD KILLED MARCY-- THE FIRST GIRL I EVER LOVED...
...KILLED HER JUST BECAUSE SHE KNEW ME.
SO WHY ARE THE OTHERS GOIN' AFTER BLOOD? WHY AM I STAYIN' BACK HERE PRESSIN' THESE BLASTED TWO-TON WEIGHTS?

VIC, CALM DOWN, FOR PETE'S SAKE.
YOU KNOW WE COULDN'T GO TO BLOOD'S RETREAT... ONLY THE OTHERS COULD INFILTRATE.
FACE IT, PAL-- WE'D BE PRETTY CONSPICUOUS!
I DON'T CARE, LOGAN!
I'M SICK OF COOLING MY HEELS!
SKRAK
I'M SICK OF EVERYTHING!
5

YOU OKAY?
MARCY WAS MY GIRL AND I SHOULD BE DOING SOMETHING ABOUT HER DEATH...
SOMETHIN' MORE'N WAITIN' BACK HERE AND GETTIN' MADDER EVERY SECOND.

NOW YOU KNOW HOW I FELT WHEN FRANKLIN WAS KILLED.
I TELL YOU, VICTOR, ALL WE DO IS SIT HERE TALKING--
--WHILE MORE GOOD PEOPLE DIE!
FOR ONCE, KORIAND'R--YOU AN' I AGREE.

C'MON, VIC, JUST THINK ABOUT IT FOR A MINUTE.
WE AGREED WITH DICK TO WAIT HERE WHILE THE OTHERS DID THEIR WORK.

DICK ALWAYS DOES THINGS THAT WAY...ALWAYS SO SLOWLY.
THAT ISN'T MY WAY, GARFIELD.
I DON'T THINK IT'S VICTOR'S EITHER.

BELIEVE IT, GOLDIE. LET'S YOU AN' ME GO!
NO!
I WON'T LET YOU!

VIC, PLEASE LISTEN TO ME. YOU'RE NOT THINKING...
I WON'T LET YOU MAKE A MISTAKE.
YOU'RE GONNA STOP ME, GREENIE?
FRANKLY, PAL, I DON'T THINK YOU'RE MAN ENOUGH!
MEBBE YOU CAN HOLD BACK SOME LITTLE KID, BUT YOU AIN'T STOPPIN' ME!

WHAT IS GOING ON HERE?
RAVEN? WHAT IN BLAZES ARE YOU DOIN' HERE?
I CAME BACK--WE NEED HELP!
BLOOD CAPTURED THE OTHERS, EVEN BLASTED MY HUMAN BODY.
I BARELY HAD TIME TO FREE MY SOUL-SELF.
THEY NEED US.
VIC--LET ME GO...FOR PITY'S SAKE, LET ME GO.
THEY ALWAYS NEED US.
6

THE PAIN IS... EXCRUCIATING. FAR WORSE THAN ANY HE HAS SUFFERED THROUGH BEFORE...
YET...
TALK, BOY! SPEAK BEFORE YOUR MUCH-VAUNTED MIND IS REDUCED TO LITTLE MORE THAN MUSH!
NO!
THE HUMAN BODY CAN ONLY WITHSTAND SO MUCH AGONY, BOY.
ONCE YOU HAVE PASSED THE THRESHOLD, YOUR NERVOUS SYSTEM WILL COLLAPSE.
ASSUMING YOU EVEN LIVE, YOU WILL BE LITTLE MORE THAN A VEGETABLE!
SAVE YOURSELF, BOY--CONFESS ALL YOU KNOW!
N...
N...
CONFESS! CONFESS!
NOOOOOO!!!
HE WILL NOT TALK, CONFESSOR.
HIS STAMINA FAR EXCEEDS HIS REASON.
I AM SORRY, BROTHER BLOOD. I FAILED YOU.
7

YOU DID YOUR BEST, CONFESSOR.
BROTHER MORRIS AND SIMON, FOLLOW ME WITH THE SINNER.

HIS INFORMATION WOULD HAVE PROVED HELPFUL, BUT IT WAS NOT VITAL TO MY OPERATION HERE.
I DO NOT NEED HIM ANY LONGER.

LET HIM DIE!

UNHHHH...

FALLING... INTO SOME AWFUL PIT.
I'LL BREAK MY BACK IF I LAND LIKE THIS.

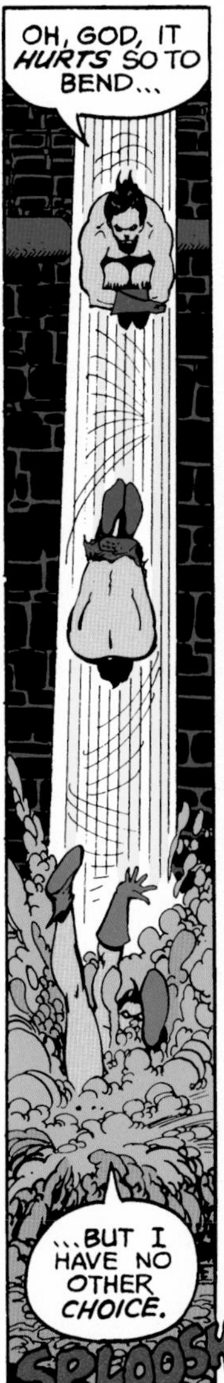
OH, GOD, IT HURTS SO TO BEND...
...BUT I HAVE NO OTHER CHOICE.
SPLOOSH!

FAREWELL, BOY. ENJOY YOUR FINAL MOMENTS.
BROTHER SIMON, SEAL THE PIT.

THERE'S STILL LIGHT IN HERE. HE WANTS ME TO SEE--
OH, NO-- KID FLASH, WONDER GIRL-- EVEN RAVEN. HE'S GOT THEM ALL HERE.
ALL UNCONSCIOUS.

THEN HE HEARS ANOTHER PASSAGEWAY GRIND OPEN, AND...
NO! IT'S IMPOSSIBLE!!
8

THAT'S WHY THE LIGHTS ARE STILL ON DOWN HERE--BLOOD WANTS ME TO SEE THAT HIDEOUS MONSTROSITY!
CURSE HIM. HE'S SICK, EVEN MORE TWISTED THAN THE JOKER!
HE EXPECTS ME TO PANIC, BUT THAT ISN'T HOW I WAS TAUGHT.

THERE'S ALWAYS A WAY OUT OF EVERY TRAP!
JUST HAVE TO LOOK FOR THE LOOPHOLE.

OF COURSE, FIRST I HAVE TO LIVE LONG ENOUGH TO DO THE LOOKING.
TROUBLE IS, ARE THE OTHERS STILL ALIVE? I DON'T KNOW.
BLASTED STINGERS! ALMOST GOT ME!
AGHHH! ITS LEG MOVED FASTER THAN I THOUGHT!

SHOULDER'S KILLING ME--BUT I DON'T THINK I'VE BROKEN ANY BONES.
DONNA'S BREATHING... THAT MUCH I CAN TELL, THANK GOD.

BUT NOW THAT UGLY'S HEADING RIGHT FOR HER.
WELL, THE OTHERS WILL JUST HAVE TO WAIT.

ONE THING AT A TIME. LORD, I HOPE THEY'RE STILL ALIVE.
THESE PAST MONTHS HAVE BROUGHT US SO CLOSE...
NO! CAN'T WEAKEN MY CONCENTRATION. THEY'RE ALIVE. THEY HAVE TO BE.

SO--FOCUS EVERYTHING INTO THE PLAN!
THUK!
DISTRACT THE BEAST FROM DONNA... LURE HIM TOWARDS ME...

RAGGGHHHH!!
WELL, I SURE SUCCEEDED!
NOW I'M HIS TARGET!
WALLY WAS SO STILL... DIDN'T SEE HIS CHEST MOVING.

NO! HAVE TO CLEAR MY THOUGHTS... CONCENTRATE, BLAST IT-- JUST CONCENTRATE!
STAY ALIVE... THINK! THERE'S A WAY OUT.
CAN I SCALE THE WALLS?

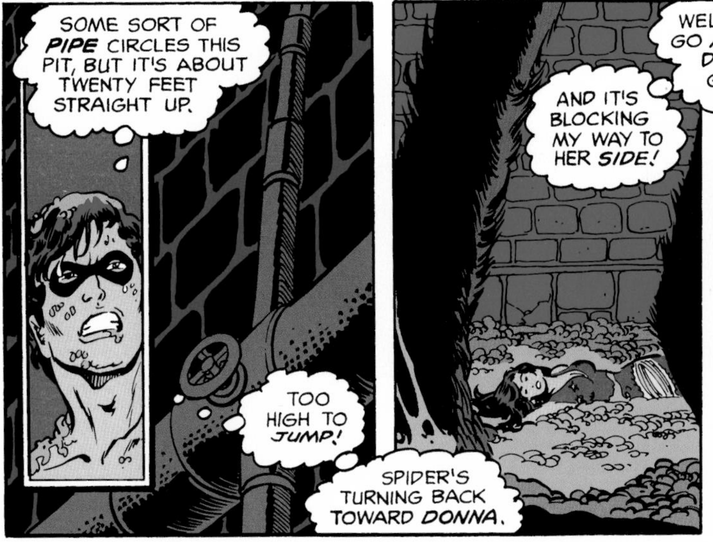
SOME SORT OF PIPE CIRCLES THIS PIT, BUT IT'S ABOUT TWENTY FEET STRAIGHT UP.
TOO HIGH TO JUMP!
AND IT'S BLOCKING MY WAY TO HER SIDE!
SPIDER'S TURNING BACK TOWARD DONNA.

WELL, IF I CAN'T GO AROUND TALL, DARK AND GRUESOME--
--PERHAPS I CAN GO OVER HIM INSTEAD!
FLIP OFF HIS ABDOMEN AND SOMERSAULT RIGHT OVER TO DONNA.

YEAH, I WAS RIGHT... SHE IS STILL BREATHING.
THAT MEANS THE OTHER TWO ARE PROBABLY ALIVE AS WELL.

THOUGH IF I DON'T MOVE QUICKLY ENOUGH, THEY MAY NOT BE FOR MUCH LONGER.
THANK HEAVEN FOR DONNA'S GOLDEN LASSO.

IT JUST MAY SAVE ALL OUR SKINS!
10

MEANWHILE...
LOOK, PAL, I DON'T WANT WHAT *HAPPENED* BACK THERE TO GET *BETWEEN* US, UNDERSTAND?
I'M *SORRY* ABOUT WHAT I SAID.
BUT IT WAS *TRUE*, ANYWAY.

I TURN INTO *ANIMALS*. GREAT! *BIG DEAL*!
I KNOW I *FOUL UP*--
DON'T *GIVE* ME THAT GARBAGE, GAR. *YOU* DON'T FOUL UP ANY MORE'N THE *REST* OF US.

ANYONE HERE FOULS UP, IT'S *ME* AN' MY BIG MOUTH!
I WAS *ANGRY*. I JUST WANTED TO *CRUSH* SOMETHING. YOU GOT IN MY WAY, THAT'S ALL.

I WOULD'A SAID THE SAME THING ABOUT *DICK* OR *DONNA*. I DIDN'T *MEAN* ANY OF IT.
GUYS, WE'RE ALMOST *THERE*. I SEE BLOOD'S *RETREAT*.

BELOW...
THIS IS BETHANY SNOW FOR *WUBC* NEWS. WE HAVE ALL HEARD ABOUT *RELIGIONS* WHICH SUDDENLY SEEM TO SPRING UP OUT OF NOWHERE...
...RELIGIONS THAT HAVE GRABBED THE ATTENTION OF OUR *YOUTH*.
BUT *ONE* SUCH "NEW" RELIGION THAT HAS JUST *RECENTLY* COME TO AMERICA IS ACTUALLY A VERY *OLD* RELIGION.

I AM HERE IN THE *CHURCH OF BROTHER BLOOD*. A CHURCH THAT DATES BACK ALMOST *700 YEARS*.

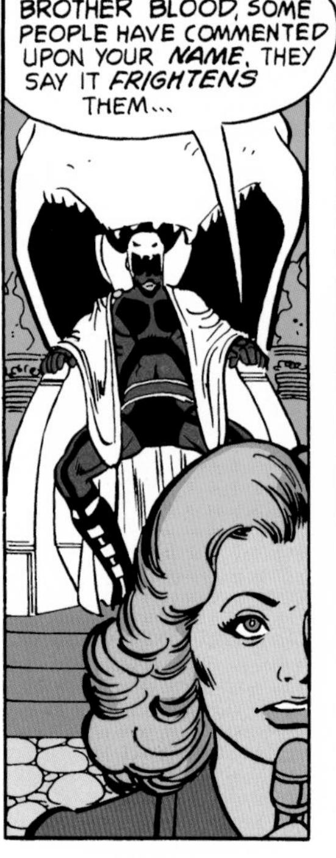

BROTHER BLOOD, SOME PEOPLE HAVE COMMENTED UPON YOUR *NAME*. THEY SAY IT *FRIGHTENS* THEM...

BETHANY, *BLOOD* IS THE LIFE-FLUID THAT FLOWS WITHIN ALL MANKIND.

BLOOD *GIVES* LIFE, AND I *STAND* FOR LIFE. MY NAME SHOULD NO MORE *FRIGHTEN* PEOPLE THAN MY TRADITIONAL *CEREMONIAL GARB*.
11

WHAT ABOUT THE ACCUSATION THAT YOUR COUNTRY IS A NATION WHICH HARBORS TERRORISTS?

THOSE DAYS ARE OVER, BETHANY. OUR FORMER PRESIDENT, WHOM I ALWAYS RESISTED, IS DEAD.
OUR NEW PRESIDENT WANTS STRONG LINKS WITH WESTERN DEMOCRACY.
WE BELIEVE ONLY IN PEACE, AND I WISH ZANDIA TO TAKE ITS PLACE AMONG THE FREE NATIONS OF THIS WORLD.

HMMM. THEY'VE COME. FINALLY.
I HAVE COME HERE SEEKING RECOGNITION FOR OUR COUNTRY AND OUR CHURCH.

YOU GETTING A STRONG SOUND LEVEL ON THIS, HANK?
I HAD TO ADJUST, MORRIE. THAT BLOOD GUY'S VOICE IS BARELY ABOVE A COARSE WHISPER.
BUT HE'S COMING THROUGH LOUD AN' CLEAR.

YOU SEE, WE HAVE BEEN PERSECUTED BECAUSE OUR BELIEFS ARE DIFFERENT.
SOME OF YOUR PEOPLE FEAR US FOR NO REASON.

INDEED, WE HAVE REPORTS THAT A VIGILANTE GROUP OF SUPPOSED SUPER-HEROES HAS BEEN SENT TO EXTERMINATE US.

SURELY, BROTHER BLOOD, THAT SOUNDS LIKE PARANOIA. OUR PEOPLE ARE TOLERANT.
I WOULD HOPE SO, BETHANY, BUT I FEAR MY REPORTS ARE TRUE.

AND SHOULD THEY COME, WE WILL, OF COURSE, HAVE TO SHOW THEM THE STRENGTH OF OUR CONVICTIONS.
THEY SHOULD BE HERE AT ANY MOMENT. THREE... TWO...
12

WE'VE BROKEN THROUGH, VICTOR.
NOW IT'S ONLY A MATTER OF FINDING ROBIN AND THE OTHERS.
BTRAM!
YOU FIND 'EM, GOLDIE--
--I WANT BLOOD!
SKREEEEEE
YOU CAN HAVE HIM.

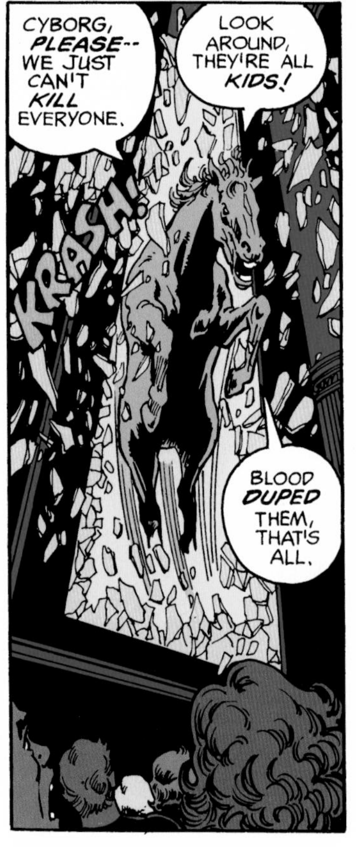

DO YOU SEE, BETHANY? I TOLD YOU THEY WOULD ATTACK MY FOLLOWERS.
WE'RE BEING PERSECUTED FOR OUR BELIEFS!
THIS IS AMAZING. THESE TEEN TITANS, THESE SELF-PROCLAIMED HEROES--

--HAVE INVADED THIS CHURCH, ARE WRECKING MILLIONS IN PRIVATE PROPERTY...
...AND SEEM NOT TO CARE IF ANY OF THESE INNOCENT CHILDREN ARE HURT.
BTAM
BAM!
UNLESS THE TITANS KILL US AS WELL, WE WILL CONTINUE TO BRING YOU THIS STORY AS IT HAPPENS.

WE'RE BEING SET UP. SHE'S DELIBERATELY LYING!
SPAK!
THOOM!
DON'T YOU GUYS SEE THAT?
BLOOD'S MAKING US LOOK LIKE THE VILLAINS!

THAT'S RIDICULOUS, GAR. WE'RE ONLY TRYING TO RESCUE OUR FRIENDS.
BESIDES, EVERYONE CAN SEE THAT BLOOD SENT THOSE KILLERS TO STOP US.
BLAM! BAM!
SKREEEEEEEE!

THE VIOLENCE CONTINUES AS BROTHER BLOOD DESPERATELY TRIES TO DEFEND HIS CHURCH AND BELIEVERS FROM ATTACK.
IS THIS WHAT AMERICA IS COMING TO? ARE WE A COUNTRY OF HOOLIGANS AND TERRORISTS?
SPAMM!
KLUNK!
14

I'VE BEEN LOOKIN' FOR YOU, BLOOD.
SO, YOU HAVE FOUND ME. NOW WHAT DO YOU WANT?

WANNA PAY YOU BACK FOR WHAT YOU DID TO MARCY!
WANNA PAY YOU BACK-- IN KIND!
SKRAK!

YOU ATTACK ME IN MY OWN HOME? THEN I CAN DEFEND MYSELF!
THE AMERICAN PEOPLE WILL LEARN WHO ARE THE VILLAINS HERE!

SPTANG!
UNNNHH! LOGAN WAS RIGHT! BLOOD IS USIN' US! AN' BECAUSE 'A ME, WE FELL RIGHT INTO HIS TRAP!

MEANWHILE...
GOT DONNA SECURED AND THERE'S ENOUGH LASSO TO REACH TO RAVEN.
MAN, I HOPE HER SOUL-SELF GOT FREE...
...BECAUSE I'M BEGINNING TO THINK GETTING OUT OF HERE ISN'T GOING TO BE QUITE SO EASY.
SHE'S NOT BREATHING ...BUT THEN I DON'T KNOW IF SHE DOES BREATHE WHEN HER SOUL-SELF IS OUT OF HER BODY.
THERE'S SO MUCH ABOUT HER WE DON'T KNOW.

IF WE GET OUT OF THIS ALIVE, WE'RE GOING TO HAVE TO TAKE SOME TIME OFF AND TALK!
15

"IF"? I THINK MY ALTERNATIVES ARE RAPIDLY RUNNING OUT.
NO WAY TO CLAMBER BACK UP THAT ROPE IN TIME.
I'M SORRY, RAVEN... I TRIED MY BEST.
BRUCE ... I'M SORRY I LET YOU DOWN!
RICHARD!
WHAT?
RAVEN?
THE OTHERS ARE HERE AS WELL.

BUT FIRST I SEE I MUST SUBDUE THIS CREATURE AS BEST I CAN.
WHAT THIS EMPATH FEELS IS TERRIBLE, ALMOST IMPOSSIBLE PAIN CUTTING THROUGH THE VERY FABRIC OF HER BEING. BUT...

THE CREATURE WAS IN AGONY... BROTHER BLOOD NURTURED ITS APPETITE AND ANGER THROUGH TORTURE.
YEAH, THAT SEEMS TO BE HIS WAY. NICE GUY...

...PROBABLY A CHARTER MEMBER OF THE "MARQUIS DE SADE" FAN CLUB.
YOU OKAY?
JUST WEAK.

BUT WE CANNOT GIVE IN TO WEAKNESS.
OUR FRIENDS NEED OUR HELP. WITHOUT THINKING, THEY ARE JEOPARDIZING EVERYTHING WE BELIEVE IN.
TRY TO AROUSE WALLACE WHILE I OPEN THE PIT DOOR.
16

YOU ARE BROTHER BLOOD... THE ONE BEHIND THIS MADNESS.
YOU'RE THE PURVEYOR OF PAIN, THE ONE WHO REVELS IN THE AGONIES OF OTHERS!
A TITAN, AND YOU STILL LIVE?
BUT I AM COMMITTED TO STOPPING YOU...
...TO REVEALING YOUR TRUE MADNESS TO ALL WHO CAN SEE US.

WE KNOW THE TRUTH--
ARRGHH!
PAIN! TERRIBLE PAIN!
NO, GIRL. ONLY I KNOW THE FULL TRUTH.
THE TRUTH WHICH PERMITS ME TO STEP THROUGH YOUR ALL-ENVELOPING SOUL.

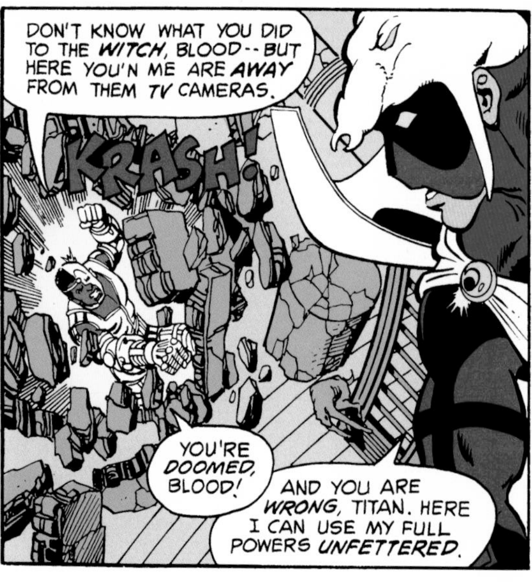

DON'T KNOW WHAT YOU DID TO THE WITCH, BLOOD--BUT HERE YOU'N ME ARE AWAY FROM THEM TV CAMERAS.
KRASH!
YOU'RE DOOMED, BLOOD!
AND YOU ARE WRONG, TITAN. HERE I CAN USE MY FULL POWERS UNFETTERED.

ZIZZZLEEE!
HERE I CAN BEGIN TO DEMONSTRATE WHY BROTHER BLOOD WILL PROVE SUPREME.
17

I... HAVE NEVER FELT ANYTHING LIKE THAT BEFORE.
IT WAS AS IF MY SOUL HAD BEEN TORN ASUNDER.

BLOOD HAS DOWNED VICTOR... I--I SHOULD DO SOME-THING...
...BUT I HAVEN'T HALF THE NECESSARY STRENGTH TO STOP HIM.

THERE IS... TERRIBLE PAIN IN EVERY STEP I TAKE ...PAIN I AM HELPLESS TO CURE.

ALL I CAN DO... FREE THE OTHERS... USE THESE DIALS TO SLIDE OPEN THE PIT DOOR...

AZAR PROTECT ME!??-- WHAT?

BLOOD'S TURNING... THIS IS MY CHANCE.
GOTTA HIT 'IM WITH EVERYTHING I'VE GOT!

WELL, WELL... LOOKS LIKE I CAME TO JUST IN TIME.
ROBBIE, YOU AND WONDER GIRL ALL RIGHT?
SHE'S REVIVING, FLASH. THANKS FOR THE LIFT.

X'HAL! HE DIDN'T HEAR ME COMING!
THIS TIME I'VE GOT YOU, BLOOD!
SKREEEE!
18

HE'S NOT DOWN, KORY.
YOUR STARBOLT DIDN'T STOP HIM, BUT MAYBE A FEW SUPER-SPEED PUNCHES WILL DO THE TRICK.
THUD!

KEEP HIM OFF BALANCE.
WE'RE TRYING OUR BEST.
BUT, FOR SOME REASON, HE WON'T STAY DOWN.
SPTOOMM!

I DON'T UNDERSTAND! WE'RE HITTING HIM WITH EVERYTHING WE'VE GOT!
WHY CAN'T WE STOP HIM?
BECAUSE BROTHER BLOOD HAS SURVIVED MORE THAN SEVEN HUNDRED YEARS, GIRL!
DO YOU TRULY BELIEVE YOU CAN DESTROY AN IMMORTAL?

WHAMMMM!

HE'S RUNNIN!
SOMETHIN' TELLS ME HE'S NOT WHAT HE'S PRETENDIN' TO BE.

HE WOULDN'T RUN IF HE WAS REALLY IMMORTAL.
DON'T KNOW WHY GOLDIE'S STARBOLTS DIDN'T STOP 'IM, BUT IT'S NOT 'CAUSE A' SOME MAGIC!

GODS DON'T HAFTA HIDE!
SLAM!
19

CYBORG TOOK OFF AFTER BLOOD.
I WORRY ABOUT HIM. HE CRAVES VENGEANCE.
YOU THINK HE'LL KILL BLOOD?
GOD, I HOPE NOT!
ROBIN, YOU SUFFER FROM THIS FALSE MORALITY. PEOPLE ON YOUR WORLD KILL ALL THE TIME.

WHY NOT SIMPLY RETURN BLOOD'S VIOLENCE WITH VIOLENCE?
SAY, I JUST REALIZED-- I HAVEN'T SEEN GAR. WHERE IS HE?
HMMM. MY QUESTION'S BEEN ANSWERED, I THINK.

HELP! GUYS, I NEED HELP!
THERE'S TOO MANY OF 'EM!
BAM
GUYS!

WE'RE COMING, CHANGELING... HOLD ON.
WONDER GIRL, SEE IF YOU CAN STOP VIC.

SCRATCH ONE TITANIUM STEEL WALL!
SKR-THOOOOM!

SONIC BLASTER RIPPED IT TO SHREDS!
ONLY I'M TOO LATE. HE'S HIGHTAILIN' IT OUTTA HERE!
BUT THAT PROVES I'M RIGHT!

AN IMMORTAL WOULDN'T RUN!
SO WHAT'S HIS BLASTED SECRET?
20

MEBBE I CAN'T FLY LIKE KORY--
--BUT WHEN MY LITTLE HYDRAULICS ARE REALLY PUMPIN'--
--I CAN CERTAINLY LEAP WITH THE BEST OF 'EM.

I'LL WORRY 'BOUT GETTING DOWN WHEN I GOTTA-- BUT FIRST THINGS FIRST...
...I WANT-- NO!

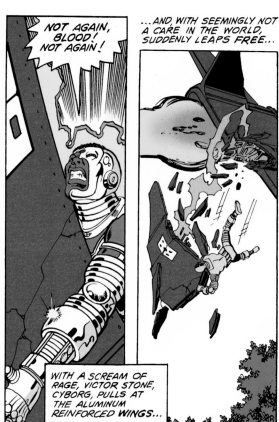

NOT AGAIN, BLOOD! NOT AGAIN!
WITH A SCREAM OF RAGE, VICTOR STONE, CYBORG, PULLS AT THE ALUMINUM REINFORCED WINGS...
...AND, WITH SEEMINGLY NOT A CARE IN THE WORLD, SUDDENLY LEAPS FREE...

SPA-BAMM!

DID YOU HEAR THAT?
I--I COULDN'T STOP VIC ...HE'S DONE IT.

BROTHER BLOOD'S PLANE WENT DOWN.
NO ONE COULD HAVE SURVIVED!
21

AT LEAST NO ONE MORTAL.
BUT, BROTHER BLOOD HAS DIED BEFORE AND ALWAYS HAS HE RISEN FROM THE GRAVE.
HIS CAUSE IS NOT DEAD.

YOU SAW IT LIVE--THESE TEEN TITANS STALKED BROTHER BLOOD AND KILLED HIM...
...KILLED THIS MAN WHO ONLY MINUTES AGO PREACHED FOR PEACE AND HOPE FOR ALL MANKIND.

PARDON ME, BETHANY, BUT PLEASE DO NOT BLAME THESE CHILDREN. BROTHER BLOOD WOULD HAVE ASKED FORGIVENESS.
EVEN FOR HIS KILLERS.

OUR LEADER WILL RISE AGAIN, AS HE HAS ALWAYS DONE.
HE WILL LEAD US INTO A NEW WORLD OF HOPE.
BROTHER BLOOD! BROTHER BLOOD! BROTHER BLOOD!

MAN, SHE COULD SELL USED CARS WITH THREE BROKEN WHEELS!
BUT SHE'S LYING THROUGH HER CAPPED TEETH!

UNFORTUNATELY WE'RE IN A BAD POSITION. HOW DO WE DEFEND OURSELVES?
AND WHAT DO WE DO ABOUT VICTOR?

DURING OUR FIGHTS PEOPLE MAY DIE-- BUT THAT WAS COLD-BLOODED MURDER.

MURDER? NO, ROBIN. I SENSE THERE WAS NO MURDER HERE.
AND FURTHERMORE, I SENSE VICTOR KNEW WHAT HE WAS DOING.

BLOOD WAS NEVER ABOARD THAT PLANE.
BROTHER BLOOD IS STILL ALIVE!
22

THIS IS BETHANY SNOW FOR WUBS NEWS. YOU'VE SEEN THE FACTS--YOU DECIDE WHAT IS THE TRUTH.
SHE'S DONE A GOOD JOB.

IF THIS DOESN'T CONVINCE THOSE AMERICAN POLITICIANS, NOTHING COULD.

THEY WILL BE CONVINCED. ZANDIA WILL RECEIVE OFFICIAL RECOGNITION.
AND MY CHURCH WILL BE ACCEPTED INTO THE AMERICAN MAINSTREAM.
FURTHERMORE, THE PUBLICITY WILL HINDER THOSE CHILDREN. THE TITANS WILL PROVE NO FURTHER THREAT TO MY PLANS.

YES, EVERYTHING IS EXCEEDING EXPECTATIONS!
I WILL NOT ONLY SURVIVE--
I WILL TRIUMPH!!

THE SUB DIVES INTO WATERS OF BLUE...

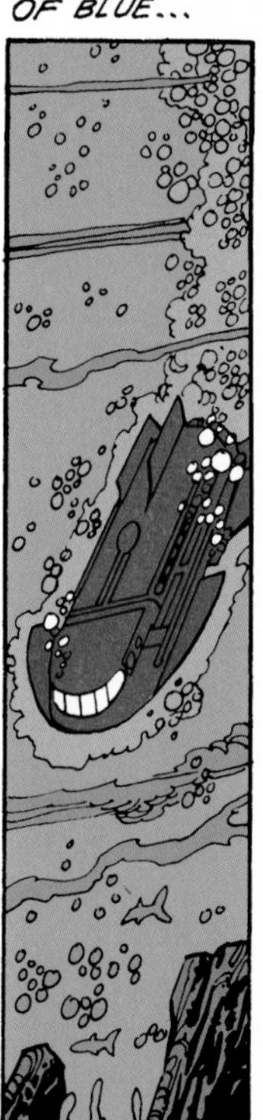

...BLUE AS THE CLEAR SKIES...

...SKIES WHICH SURROUND OUR FRAGILE LITTLE WORLD...

...SUSPENDED IN THE BLACKNESS OF ENDLESS SPACE.

WE ARE BUT ONE WORLD OUT OF BILLIONS...

...ONE WORLD ABOUT TO BE VISITED.

THE SLAVE-SHIP TRAK'R, SLIGHTLY BEYOND THE ORBIT OF NEPTUNE...
GORDANIAN, YOU ARE A DAMNED FOOL!

WE'RE MONTHS LATE IN REACHING THE EARTH-- ALL BECAUSE OF YOUR STUPIDITY!
NOT MINE, COMMANDER-- THE CITADEL COUNCIL REROUTED US TO THE PRISON PLANET...

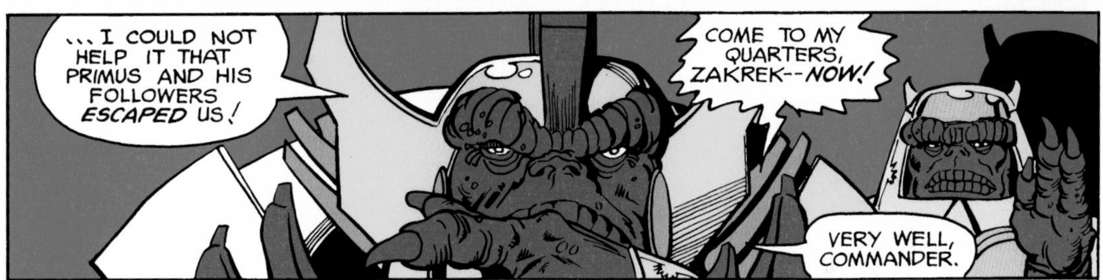
...I COULD NOT HELP IT THAT PRIMUS AND HIS FOLLOWERS ESCAPED US!
COME TO MY QUARTERS, ZAKREK--NOW!
VERY WELL, COMMANDER.

DAMNED HUMAN. SHE KNOWS WE WERE DAMAGED IN BATTLE.
SHE WAS THE ONE WHO INSISTED ON OUR JOINING THE WAR--DESPITE THE FACT THAT SHE KNOWS SLAVESHIPS ONLY CARRY LIGHT WEAPONS.

I AM HERE, COMMANDER.
GOOD, ZAKREK. WE HAVE BEEN DISPATCHED TO EARTH BECAUSE THAT PLANET HARBORS ONE OF OUR ESCAPED SLAVES.
THE POOR, DELUDED FOOL. PRINCESS KORIAND'R OF TAMARAN THOUGHT SHE COULD ESCAPE THE CITADEL'S LONG AND DEADLY ARM.

SHE ALWAYS WAS A WIDE-EYED INNOCENT. WELL, SHE WILL LEARN WHEN SHE DIES ALONG WITH HER PROTECTORS--
--OH, HOW SHE WILL SUFFER WHEN SHE LEARNS THAT--
24

--HER SISTER SHALL BE HER SLAYER!
NEEDLESS TO SAY -- TO BE CONTINUED!

THE NEW TEEN TITANS
ALL NEW! 60¢
NO. 23 SEPT.
APPROVED BY THE COMICS CODE AUTHORITY
HER NAME IS BLACKFIRE! SHE'S PRINCESS KORIAND'R'S SISTER--
--AND SHE'S CROSSED A UNIVERSE TO DESTROY THE TEEN TITANS!
PEREZ + GIORDANO

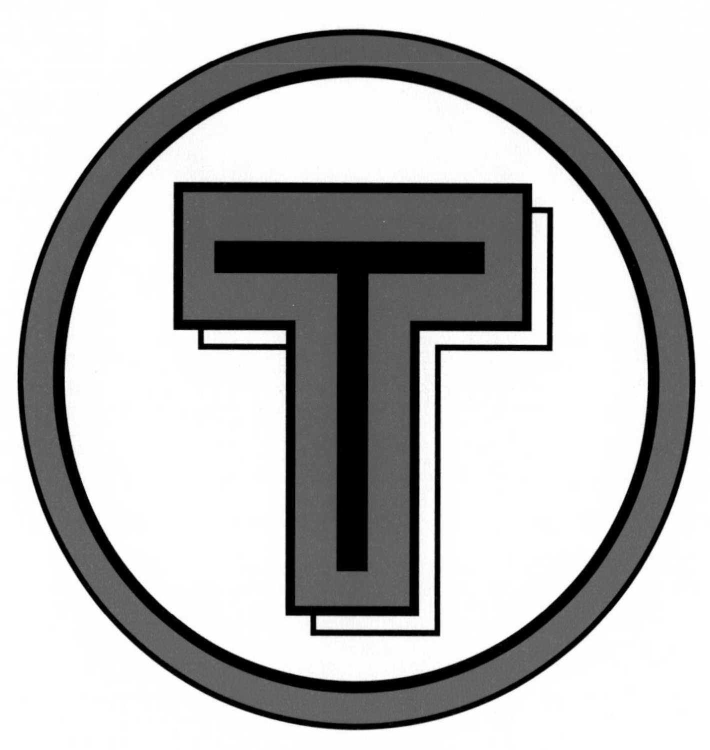

THE NEW TEEN TITANS®
THE SLAVE-SHIP TRAK'R, SLIGHTLY BEYOND THE ORBIT OF MARS...
ZAREK, WE'RE NEARING THE EARTH. GET YOUR GORDANIAN SLAVERS TO THEIR POSTS.
THEY ALREADY ARE, COMMANDER.
AND WE'LL LAUNCH WHEN YOU GIVE US THE WORD!

EXCELLENT, ZAREK. THIS PLANET HARBORS ALL TOO MANY OF THE CITADEL'S *ENEMIES*...
...AND THOUGH I CARE *NOTHING* ABOUT PRIMUS AND HIS FOLLOWERS, I WANT *KORIAND'R* OF *TAMARAN* AS MY OWN!
THAT INNOCENT FOOL HAS PLAGUED ME SINCE THE DAY SHE WAS *BORN*. BUT SHE WILL UPSTAGE ME NO LONGER! THAT I SOLEMNLY *SWEAR*.
SHE IS MY *SISTER*, BUT I SHALL *SLAY HER*.
2

KIDNAPPED!
AND THEN SHE WILL KNOW AT LAST THAT PRINCESS KOMAND'R CAN NEVER BE STOPPED.
NOW, ZAREK, LAUNCH YOUR TROOPS. LAY WASTE TO THAT PLANET. KILL WHOMEVER YOU WISH --
-- BUT BRING MY STUPID SISTER TO ME. MY DAY OF VENGEANCE IS AT HAND.
MARV WOLFMAN & GEORGE PÉREZ
WRITER -- CO-PLOTTERS -- ARTIST
ROMEO TANGHAL — EMBELLISHER
BEN ODA — LETTERER
CARL GAFFORD — COLORIST
LEN WEIN — EDITOR

HEEDLESS OF THE APPROACHING ARMADA, NEW YORK CITY BASKS UNDER A WARM SUMMER SUN...
...THAT IS MOMENTARILY ECLIPSED BY A SPEEDING AIRSHIP OF ANOTHER KIND.

SARGE, I DON'T LIKE THIS NO HOW.
YOU KNOW WHAT'LL HAPPEN IF THEY TURN ON US?
YEAH, I KNOW, HEYBACK.
BUT THEY AIN'T GONNA DO NOTHIN'.

THEY AIN'T EVEN GONNA BUDGE.
THEY'RE GONNA SIT THERE, STARIN' AT OUR RIFLES, AN' THINK TWICE BEFORE MAKIN' ANY MOVE.

THEN THEY'RE GONNA LOOK DOWN AN' SEE HALF THE NEW YORK POLICE JUST WAITIN' FOR THEM TO BREATHE FUNNY.

NAH, THEY AIN'T GONNA DO NOTHIN' IF THEY KNOW WHAT'S GOOD FOR 'EM.

ALL RIGHT, STEP OUT. I'M FRANK FITZSIMMONS, ASSISTANT DISTRICT ATTORNEY.
I PROMISE YOU SAFE CONDUCT.

I'M NOT WORRIED ABOUT US, MR. FITZSIMMONS. IF WE HAD WANTED TO, WE COULD HAVE DESTROYED EVERY ONE OF YOUR WEAPONS--
--EVEN BEFORE WE HAD LANDED.
WE DON'T WANT ANY OF YOUR MEN HURT.
4

I DON'T LIKE THEM POINTING THEIR GUNS AT ME, ROBIN! TELL THEM TO AIM THEM ELSEWHERE...
...BEFORE I GET ANGRY.
YOU HEARD STARFIRE, MR. FITZSIMMONS.

WE'LL GO WHERE YOU WANT US TO--
--BUT NOT AS YOUR PRISONERS.
YOU KNOW AS WELL AS WE DO-- WE DIDN'T KILL BROTHER BLOOD.
SO TELL YOUR MEN TO STOP STARING AT US LIKE WE'RE MURDERERS... OR EVEN WORSE.

DON'T THREATEN US, ROBIN. WE'VE GOT A JOB TO DO.
FACE IT. YOU WERE SEEN ON TELEVISION, SMASHING UP BLOOD'S CHURCH AND GENERALLY CREATING CHAOS.
IF WE DIDN'T HAUL YOU IN HERE, THE PUBLIC WOULD HAVE OUR BUTTS IN A SLING.
ALL RIGHT, I'LL GO. BUT DON'T DARE PUT THOSE HANDCUFFS ON ME.
I'LL NEVER ALLOW MYSELF TO BE CHAINED UP AGAIN.

THIS IS BETHANY SNOW FOR WUBC NEWS AT THE OFFICE OF DISTRICT ATTORNEY ADRIAN CHASE.
THE HELICOPTER BEARING THE TEEN TITANS HAS FINALLY ARRIVED HERE AND THE OFFICIAL INQUIRY BEGINS.

BUT THIS REPORTER HAS LEARNED THAT THERE WILL BE A WHITEWASH OF THE EVENTS LEADING TO THE INVASION OF BROTHER BLOOD'S CHURCH.
WE PREDICT THESE TEEN TITANS WILL BE RELEASED... DESPITE OVERWHELMING EVIDENCE OF THEIR GUILT.
PRESS

THERE! THEY'RE COMING. THEY LOOK MAD, OUT FOR BLOOD.
LET'S HOPE THEY DON'T ATTACK THE PRESS AS THEY DID AN INNOCENT CHURCH.
5

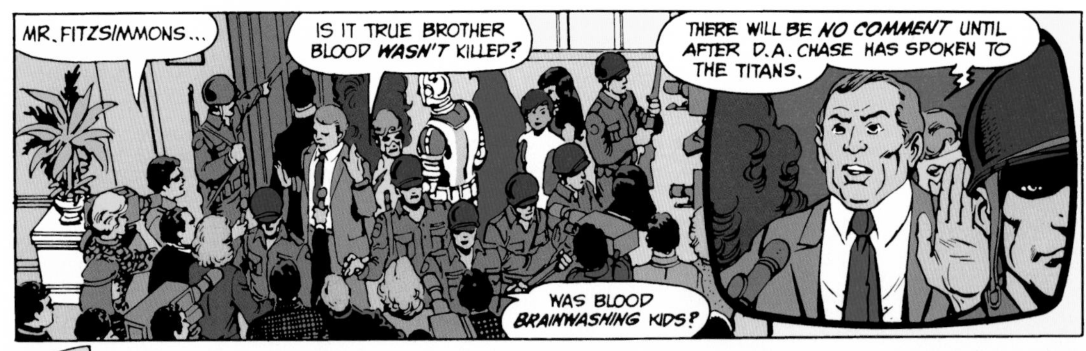
MR. FITZSIMMONS...
IS IT TRUE BROTHER BLOOD WASN'T KILLED?
THERE WILL BE NO COMMENT UNTIL AFTER D.A. CHASE HAS SPOKEN TO THE TITANS.
WAS BLOOD BRAINWASHING KIDS?

AND...
YOU KIDS REALLY BLEW IT.
BLOOD HAD EVERYTHING GOING AGAINST HIM, AND NOW HE'S MADE YOU LOOK LIKE THE VILLAINS.

I THOUGHT YOU KIDS WERE PROS. HOW DID YOU GET SO FAR SCREWING UP LIKE THIS?
BLOOD WAS TRICKY. HE HAD THE PRESS ON HIS SIDE.
THEY DISTORTED THE FACTS.

JUST ONE MEMBER OF THE PRESS: BETHANY SNOW. SHE'S EVEN A MEMBER OF BLOOD'S CHURCH, BUT WE CAN'T TELL ANYONE THAT.
IT WOULD MAKE IT SEEM LIKE WE'RE OUT TO GET HER.
LISTEN, WE KNOW THAT BROTHER BLOOD STAGED HIS "MIRACULOUS" RESURREC-TION LAST NIGHT...

...TO GAIN PUBLICITY AND MONETARY CONTRIBUTIONS.
WE ALSO KNOW BLOOD'S PROBABLY GUILTY OF EVERY CRIME FROM MURDER TO NOT CURBING HIS DOG--

--BUT WE CAN'T PROVE IT. NOW YOU KIDS MADE IT EVEN HARDER FOR US TO DIG OUT THE FACTS.
PROVE IT? MAN, THAT CREEP OFFED A GIRL I KNEW. HE KILLED ANOTHER ONE -- RIGHT IN FRONT'A US.
AND WE SAW YOU ON TV ATTACKING HIM ON PRIVATE PROPERTY.

YOUR WORD DOESN'T HOLD, MISTER.
BUT SIR, WHAT ABOUT THE ONES WHO LEFT HIS CHURCH. WON'T THEY TALK?
C'MON, RAVEN, YOU SAW THOSE KIDS. THEY BELIEVED BLOOD WAS A GOD.
HIS COMIN' BACK TO LIFE AGAIN WILL ONLY PROVE THAT POINT.
6

I WANT BLOOD'S BUTT. FILTH LIKE HIM TAKE ADVANTAGE OF EVERY BLASTED LEGAL LOOPHOLE THEY CAN FIND.
LOOK, THIS FILE IS FILLED WITH MORE THAN ONE HUNDRED CRIMES WE SUSPECT HE'S COMMITTED BUT CAN'T PROVE--
--OR CRIMES HE'S LEGALLY SQUIRMED HIS WAY FREE FROM.

DO YOU KIDS UNDERSTAND ME? I WANT HIM NAILED!
I WANT HIM TO GO ON TRIAL. I WANT HIM TO PAY. I WANT HIM TO GET THE CHAIR.
BROTHER BLOOD

BUT WHEN PEOPLE LIKE YOU FALL INTO HIS TRAP, TURN HIM INTO SOME BLASTED MARTYR--
--IT DESTROYS EVERYTHING I WORK FOR.

LISTEN, WE TRY TO COÖPERATE, BUT--
NO BUTS! THERE'S NO EXCUSE.
NOW, WE'RE GOING OUT THERE. YOU'RE GOING TO SAY ABSOLUTELY NOTHING!

HOLD ON. THE PRESS HAS A RIGHT TO KNOW.
I SAID SAY NOTHING.
BLOOD MAY HAVE DROPPED CHARGES ON YOUR TRESPASSING, BUT I'M CERTAIN I COULD FIND SOMETHING TO HOLD YOU ON.

AND NOW--LADIES AND GENTLEMEN, QUESTIONS, PLEASE.
YES, MISS SNOW. YOU FIRST.
I DON'T LIKE THIS, GUYS. I DON'T LIKE THIS AT ALL!
7

LIKE SILENT SCYTHES, THEY CUT ACROSS THE MANHATTAN SKIES...
SEARCHING... SEARCHING...

SHE'S HERE.
BELOW US.

SALKAS, I FOR ONE WILL BE GLAD WHEN THIS MISSION IS OVER.
I CANNOT STAND THAT SHE-WITCH'S COMPLAINING!

I TELL YOU, I'D SOONER BE DISSECTED BY A PSION THAN SERVE ANOTHER TERM WITH THAT TAMARAN MADWOMAN.
DO WELL, SALKAS, BEGIN THE MENTAL GRAPPLER PROBE -- NOW!

WHILE...
ONE THING BLOOD WASN'T JOKING ABOUT. ACCORDING TO THIS, HE'S BEEN ALIVE FOR MORE THAN 700 YEARS.
YOU BELIEVE THAT, SHORT-PANTS?

I BELIEVE HE'S GOT A GOOD RACKET GOING.
HE COMES FROM ZANDIA, WHICH IS AN ISLAND MANNED BY TERRORISTS. IF HE'S THE HEAD OF THEIR RELIGION--

--HE'S REALLY BAD NEWS--
X'HAL!!

KORY? WHAT'S WRONG?
I--I DON'T KNOW... THERE WAS THIS THING... ALMOST LIKE A SOUND.
I-IT HIT ME AND IT HURT... IT HURT SO MUCH.
8

...BROTHER BLOOD ISN'T DEAD, MISS SNOW, AND HE'S DROPPED HIS CHARGES. SO YES, THE TITANS WILL BE SET FREE.

ARE YOU GOING TO CONDONE THOSE SEVEN CHILDREN GOING OUT VIGILANTE STYLE TO DESTROY A CHURCH?
THEY'RE EVIL. AS DISTRICT ATTORNEY, YOU SHOULD STOP THEM.

TRUST ME, MISS SNOW. THE ONES WHO DESERVE PUNISHMENT WILL GET IT.
YOU CAN QUOTE ME ON THAT.

SKRASSSKK

THE TITANS WERE IN THERE, MR. CHASE. IS THIS THE WAY YOU MAKE THEM PAY?
WHAT'S GOING ON?
WHY DON'T YOU SEND THE NATIONAL GUARD IN THERE AND FIND OUT?

ALL RIGHT, COME ON--BUT NO ONE FIRES. GOT THAT? NOBODY USES THEIR RIFLE.
ROBIN, WHAT'S GOING ON HERE?

STARFIRE FLIPPED OUT!
SHE WAS IN PAIN--
--THEN SUDDENLY WENT BERSERK!
WHAT CAUSED IT?
I DON'T KNOW. BUT LOOK--THERE SHE IS!
9

AND SHE'S NOT IN CONTROL OF HERSELF!
SKRAAKK
HELP ME, PLEASE. I CAN'T STOP!
SKREEEEEE
SKREEEEE
SOMEONE-- HELP!!

YOU SEE, CHASE, THEY'VE GOT THESE POWERS AND THEY CAN'T CONTROL THEM.
AND YOU CAN'T HIDE IT ANY LONGER. WE'VE GOT ALL THIS ON FILM.
THE AMERICAN PEOPLE WILL SEE THE TRUTH.
WE GOTTA HELP STARFIRE...

I'M ALREADY ON MY WAY, VIC.
WHERE YOU GO, BEAUTIFUL, I GO, TOO.
GOOD. I MIGHT NEED YOUR HELP, GAR.
KORY'S POWER COULD PROVE DIFFICULT TO HANDLE.

KORIAND'R, CAN YOU HEAR ME?
RAVEN, DO SOMETHING, WILL YOU?
I-- I CAN'T CONTROL MY STARBOLTS!
EVERYTHING HURTS!
10

BETHANY SNOW WAS RIGHT! THOSE TITANS ARE DANGEROUS.
SSKREEEEEEEKKK
LOOK AT WHAT SHE'S DOIN'!
HEY, I'VE SEEN HER LAST WEEK AT YANKEE STADIUM. SHE RISKED HER OWN LIFE TO SAVE US.
SOMETHING'S GOT TO BE WRONG WITH HER.
I TELL YOU, THOSE KIDS ARE GOOD!
AZAR HELP US ALL. SO THAT IS WHAT'S CAUSING KORIAND'R'S MADNESS.

I RECOGNIZE THOSE SHIPS-- FROM OUR FIRST ADVENTURE.
THEY ARE THE SAME ONES WHO PURSUED KORIAND'R BEFORE.
AND NOW THEY MUST BE CONTROLLING HER.

WE'VE BROUGHT HER TO US.
NOW, LOCK ON THE MIND DAMPENER!

THEN SHE WILL BE OURS!
OUR JOB WILL BE OVER!
AND THEN HER SISTER CAN REND HER LIMB FROM LIMB FOR ALL I CARE!

IT'S THE GORDANIANS! THEY'VE COME BACK FOR KORY!
HOOBOY, DONNA, THOSE CREEPS SORTA OUTPOWER US!
WE'RE NOT SET UP FOR A DOWN-HOME "STAR WARS!"
11

BUT THEY'RE NOT GOING TO GET KORY WITHOUT A FIGHT.
REMEMBER, GAR, WE WON OUR LAST BATTLE.
YEAH, BUT I DIDN'T HAVE ANY SKIN LEFT ON MY TEETH.

SKRAK!
DONNA! WATCH OUT!
NUTS! THAT KERMIT-THE-FROG LOOK-ALIKE GOT HER!

WELL, SHE'LL BE OKAY...
...MEANWHILE, OCTY OCTOPUS HERE SAYS "YOU'VE COMMITTED A DEFINITE NO-NO!"
"OCTY-OCTOPUS"? HMM. WONDER IF I COULD SELL THAT TO THE ZOO CREW?
I COULD MAKE AT LEAST HALF A BUCK FROM THE RESIDUALS!

AND, AS THE SHAPE-CHANGER PUTS THE ARMS ON THE ALIEN SLAYER...

HEY, RED, MOVE THEM FEET AND HELP OUT WONDER GIRL!
I GOTTA GET RIDDA SOME EXCESS GARBAGE!
I DON'T NEED MY FEET TO HELP HER, LOGAN.
REX RAFFY

LOOK! MY HAND IS FASTER THAN THE EYE!

AS KID FLASH'S SUPER-SPEED WIND TUNNEL LOWERS THE YOUNG AMAZON TO THE GROUND...

THUMP!

... THE CHANGELING'S ALIEN CHARGE FINDS HIS LANDING NOT QUITE SO PLEASANT.

12

HIS HYDRAULIC LEGS PUMPING, THE MOLYBDENUM STEEL-AND-FLESH TITAN KNOWN AS CYBORG LEAPS HIS WAY ACROSS THE FIERY SKIES...

PUT THAT WARPER DOWN, FROG!

I AIN'T FORGOTTEN WHAT IT DID TO ME THE LAST TIME!*
THOOM!
*TNT #1.--Len.

JUST GOTTA KEEP 'EM OFF MY TAIL WHILE I FIGGER OUT THESE COMPUTER CONTROLS...
...WHICH SHOULDN'T TAKE TOO LONG.
SKROOOM!
I PLUGGED INTA THEIR MASTER COMPUTER BACK WHEN WE FIRST BATTLED, AND MOST OF THAT INFO'S STILL STORED IN MY MINI-COMPUTER.

YEAH, SOMETIMES BEING A STEEL FRANKENSTEIN AIN'T TOO BAD.
AS LONG AS YOU DON'T LOOK AT MIRRORS, THAT IS.

CALL OFF YOUR FORCES, EARTHLING. RESISTANCE IS FUTILE.
OUR ORDERS ARE TO DESTROY THIS WORLD.

THEN WE SIMPLY HAVE TO STOP YOU...
...ANY WAY WE MUST.
13

RAVEN'S SOUL-SELF ENVELOPS THE SUDDENLY FRIGHTENED GORDANIAN, WHILE ANOTHER OF HIS SPECIES FINDS HIMSELF IN A STRUGGLE OF A DIFFERENT KIND...
STAND BACK, YOU FOOLS, AND LISTEN TO ME. DURING THESE PAST MONTHS WE HAVE LEARNED YOUR LANGUAGE...
...SO THAT WE CAN OFFER YOU YOUR ONLY HOPE.
SURRENDER TO THE CITADEL EMPIRE, OR YOUR PLANET WILL BE DISINTEGRATED.

HOLD IT, LISTEN TO US.
THERE ARE MANY HEROES HERE-- EVEN STRONGER THAN WE ARE.
SO WE MAKE THIS OFFER TO YOU. GIVE US BACK STARFIRE, OR YOUR ENTIRE FLEET WILL BE DESTROYED.

YOU DARE THREATEN US? VERY WELL, YOU'VE SEALED YOUR DOOM.
I WILL DISINTEGRATE YOU MYSELF!

YOU HEARD HIM!
FIRE!
BAM BAM

GOOD GOD. YOU'VE KILLED HIM.
KID FLASH, HE HAD A WEAPON IN HIS HAND. HE WAS READY TO USE IT.
I KNOW. I KNOW. IT'S JUST THAT I'M STILL NOT USED TO THINGS LIKE THIS --HOLD IT.
SOMETHING'S GOING ON.
GET BACK!
FOOOMFF!

H-HE'S GONE? JUST LIKE THAT?
B-BUT HOW?
14

MEANWHILE...
SOMETHING IS WRONG... I NO LONGER SENSE THE ALIEN.
RAVE, YOU SEE WHAT HAPPENED DOWN THERE?
AZAR PROTECT ME! THE ALIEN--WAS DESTROYED!
I-- I'VE TAKEN A LIFE.
I'VE KILLED HIM.
NO, RAVEN -- LISTEN...
FLASH'S GORDANIAN ALSO MADE AN ASH OF HIMSELF.
THESE GUYS GO POOF IF THEY'RE CAPTURED. YOU DIDN'T DO IT.
YES I DID, CHANGELING. BECAUSE OF ME HE DIED.
DO YOU UNDERSTAND, CHANGELING? I'VE KILLED. I'VE KILLED!!
WELL, "ALLSTATE" CERTAINLY WON'T GIVE ME A GOOD-DRIVER'S DISCOUNT.
BUT THEN, I DON'T THINK I'M GOING ANYWHERE. NOT IF YOU TWO--
FUMP!
NUTS!
THEY'VE TAKEN STARFIRE, AND THIS SHIP'S DESTROYED. WE CAN'T POSSIBLY USE IT TO FOLLOW THEM.
I KNOW. I KNOW. I'M TRYING THE J.L.A. SATELLITE, BUT I'M NOT GETTING THROUGH.
THEY MUST BE OUT ON A MISSION, TOO.
CYBORG TO ROBIN. I GOT ME ONE OF THE GORDANIAN SHIPS. WHAT DO YOU WANT DONE WITH IT?
VICTOR, I COULD ALMOST KISS YOU.
HEY, BATBOY, COVER UP YOUR LEGS OR SOME-BODY MIGHT START ASKIN' QUESTIONS.
HOW BIG'S THE SHIP? HOW MANY OF US COULD IT CARRY?
THREE MAXIMUM. WHY?
C'MON BACK TO THE TOWER. I HAVE AN IDEA.
15

TITANS' TOWER, ON A SMALL ISLAND IN NEW YORK'S EAST RIVER...
WE NEED TWO SPACE-SHIPS IF WE WANT TO RESCUE KORY.
NOW, CYBORG GOT US ONE, AND I REMEMBERED WHERE ANOTHER'S BEEN.

WE NEVER BOTHERED TO SALVAGE THE SHIP THAT BROUGHT KORY TO EARTH.
BUT IT IS BENEATH THE OCEAN. HOW CAN WE REACH IT?

WELL, RAVEN, THAT'S NOT REALLY SO DIFFICULT, WHEN YOU KNOW THE SECRET.

YOU WEREN'T WITH US WHEN WE RAN ACROSS AN OLD FRIEND A FEW MONTHS BACK.*
*AS SHOWN IN THE TITANS DIGEST. -- Len.

WHICH MIGHT BE THE REASON YOU'RE NOT AS FAMILIAR WITH --

--AQUALAD!
HI, WERE YOU LOOKING FOR A SPACESHIP, ROBIN?
JUMBO AND I JUST HAPPENED TO FIND ONE.
16

THANKS, WE REALLY NEEDED YOU.
NO PROBLEM, PAL. GLAD TO HELP.
BESIDES, I WASN'T DOING MUCH WHEN I GOT YOUR MESSAGE.
YOU WANT TO JOIN US?
IN SPACE? DON'T YOU REMEMBER MY STANDARD PROBLEM?
I NEED WATER EVERY HOUR. IT MIGHT GET DRY OUT THERE.
MAYBE SOME OTHER TIME, PAL-- I THINK I'LL STICK TO THE OCEANS AND LET LUKE SKYWALKER SOAR THROUGH THE STARS.
OKAY, AQUALAD, BUT WE REALLY WANT YOU TO CONSIDER REJOINING US SOMETIME-- EVEN IF YOU'RE NOT A REGULAR.
HEY, SHORTPANTS...
YOU GOT THE OTHER SHIP?
YEAH, VIC. AND IT LOOKS LIKE IT'S IN WORKING ORDER.
OKAY, LET'S GET IT OVER HERE AND MAKE CERTAIN ABOUT IT.
MEANTIME I'M TEACHIN' DONNA HOW TO FLY THE THING.
SEVERAL HOURS PASS, AND...
YOU GOT EVERYTHIN' SET, DONNA?
I CERTAINLY THINK SO, VIC.
THEN LET'S GO DO IT!
LET'S GO GET KORIAND'R.
17

THIS BABY HANDLES LIKE A *DREAM*. HOW'S IT WITH *YOU*, DONNA?
LITTLE ROUGH GETTING USED TO IT, VIC. BUT I'LL *MANAGE*.

HATE TO BE A *PARTY POOPER*, BUT WHERE ARE WE *GOING*?
GOOD QUESTION, GAR. THE ANSWER IS -- *STRAIGHT UP!*
THERE'S *GOTTA BE* A *MOTHER SHIP* HERE SOMEWHERE...

YEAH, BUT WE DON'T PICK UP ANYTHING ON THE *RADAR!*
WE DON'T *NEED* TO, WALLY. LOOK STRAIGHT AHEAD.

MAN, THAT MAKES THE STARSHIP ENTERPRISE LOOK LIKE A *MATTEL TOY!*
YOU SURE THAT THING IS *REAL* AND NOT SOME KINDA *SPECIAL EFFECT?*
IT'S *REAL* ALL RIGHT, GAR. OKAY, WE'VE *FOUND* IT--
NOW WE HAVE TO FIGURE OUT HOW TO GET *INSIDE!*

I GOT IT, ROBBIE -- "SCOTTY, *BEAM* US ABOARD!"
OH WELL, SO MUCH FOR *WISHFUL THINKING*.

MEANWHILE...
MY SISTER'S FRIENDS HAVE *FOLLOWED* HER HERE.
EXCELLENT.

THEY WILL *DIE* ALONG WITH THEIR STUPID *PLANET*.

COME WITH ME. I WISH TO LET KORIAND'R KNOW THAT A *RESCUE MISSION* HAS COME TO SAVE HER...
I WILL ENJOY WATCHING HER FACE AS HER FRIENDS ARE *DESTROYED*.
18

WELL, WELL, KORIAND'R. HOW *ARE* YOU?

KOMAND'R? THEN IT'S *TRUE?* THE GORDANIANS *WEREN'T* LYING WHEN THEY SAID *YOU* WERE HERE.

LET ME *FREE*, SISTER, AND I'LL *CRUSH* YOUR STINKING BONES FOR WHAT YOU DID TO *TAMARAN*.

NOW, NOW, SWEET ONE. IS *THAT* ANY WAY TO GREET YOUR LOVING *SISTER* AFTER ALL THESE YEARS?

YOU'RE *SLIME*, KOMAND'R. I WOULD *KILL* YOU IF I HAD THE CHANCE.

BUT YOU *DON'T*, LITTLE SISTER. AND YOU NEVER *WILL*.

BESIDES, I'VE ALWAYS BEEN YOUR *BETTER*. I ALWAYS *WON* OUR LITTLE FIGHTS.

NOW, EXCUSE ME WHILE I PUNISH THESE LOUD-MOUTHED GORDANIANS.
I SHOULD HAVE BEEN THE ONE TO TELL YOU I WAS HERE. THEY HAD NO RIGHT TO SPOIL MY SURPRISE.
I TELL YOU, THESE GORDANIANS ARE SUCH BOTHERS! THAT'S WHY I'VE HAD TO PROGRAM THEM TO DIE RATHER THAN BE DEFEATED.

YOU'D THINK BY NOW THE CITADEL WOULD ASSIGN ME WARRIORS AND NOT SLAVERS TO--

I PRATTLE ON, DON'T I, SWEET SISTER? WELL, DON'T WORRY, DEAR KORIAND'R, YOU WON'T HAVE TO HEAR ME MUCH LONGER.
19

I'VE SEVERAL EXQUISITE TORTURES IN MIND FOR YOU THAT I'VE BEEN PLANNING FOR MONTHS NOW.
IT WILL BE FUN WATCHING YOU SQUIRM...

...AND SUFFER BEFORE YOU EVENTUALLY DIE.
AH, ENOUGH OF THAT. I WOULDN'T WANT YOU UNCON-SCIOUS EVEN BEFORE THE FUN BEGINS.

DO YOU HEAR ME, SISTER?

SPEAK UP, YOU DOG! DO YOU HEAR ME?

GO TO HELL, KOMAND'R.

OH, I'M CERTAIN I WILL... BUT NOT FOR A LONG TIME.
AND CERTAINLY NOT BEFORE YOUR FRIENDS SUFFER FOR KNOWING YOU.
THE TITANS?

YOU SEE ANY WAY IN?
NOT EVEN A MOUSE HOLE, ROBIN.
WHY DON'T WE JUST BLAST OUR WAY IN? WE'VE GOT THE POWER!
BUT WE DON'T HAVE THE PROTECTION, WALLY.

WE NEED SPACE SUITS, REMEMBER, FLASHER?
UNLESS YOU WANNA GO BOOM FIRST TIME YOU TRY TO BREATHE IN A VACUUM.
20

HOLD IT. SOMETHING'S GOIN' ON.
WE'RE TRAPPED IN SOME KINDA LIGHT.
ROBIN, I THINK IT'S A TRACTOR BEAM. MY SHIP'S SUDDENLY FROZEN IN SPACE.

IF DARTH VADER'S IN THAT SHIP--
THIS ISN'T ANY TIME FOR HUMOR, GAR--
VIC, CAN YOU GET US OUT OF HERE?
I'M TRYIN', MAN...
...BUT I CAN'T BREAK US FREE.

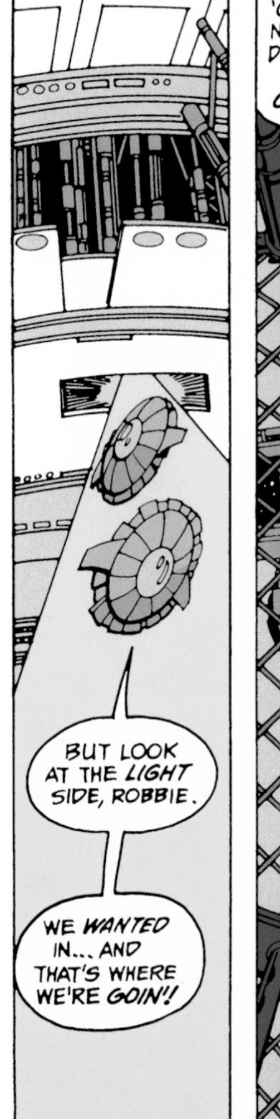
BUT LOOK AT THE LIGHT SIDE, ROBBIE.
WE WANTED IN... AND THAT'S WHERE WE'RE GOIN'!

'COURSE, WE'RE NOT EXACTLY DEALIN' THIS HAND OURSELVES.

COMMANDER, WHAT IS IT?
WE HAVE VISITORS. SET UP A BIO-SCAN AND LINK IT IN WITH THE DRONES.
THEY WILL ADAPT TO GREET OUR STARFARERS....
...AND TO DESTROY THEM.

THIS SHIP HAS AN EVIL AURA ABOUT IT.
DO YOU SENSE KORIAND'R HERE, RAVEN?
I AM SORRY, DONNA. MY POWERS DO NOT HAVE ANY GREAT RANGE.

YET, I DO SENSE EVIL... TERRIBLE EVIL...
...COMING EVER CLOSER.
21

BUT BEFORE THE EMPATH CAN BUDGE...
HOLY COW! THAT THING GOT RAVEN!
ZZAKKKK!

THEY'RE LIKE LITTLE GNATS OR DRAGONFLIES... ONLY A HECKUVA LOT MORE DANGEROUS.
KEEP OUTTA THEIR WAY!
RAVEN'S BREATHING. SHE'LL BE ALL RIGHT.

FINE FOR HER. WHAT ABOUT US?
THEY ONLY SEEM TO BE THROWING LASERS AT US. WE CAN AVOID THEIR BLASTS.

BUT FOR HOW LONG, WONDY?
I TRY CATCHIN' 'EM AND THEY EXPLODE ON CONTACT.
ONE OF 'EM'S BOUND TO GET US.

BUT THEN...
WATCH OUT, NOW THEY'RE SHOOTING OUT CABLES AT-- WONDER GIRL!?!
DICK, THEY'RE TOO STRONG TO SNAP!
MOVE BEFORE--

TOO LATE, DONNA...

TROUBLE IS, THEY'RE SPEEDING UP. IT TAKES EVERYTHING I'VE GOT TO AVOID 'EM.
AGHHH!

IT GOT GAR! HIT HIM POINT BLANK.
AND ANOTHER ONE'S SHOOTING OUT THAT OOZE.
22

GROWING TOO FAST... SPREADING ALL OVER.
CAN'T FREE MY LEGS.

I NEED SOME HELP OVER HERE --MFMFMMMM
THE DRONES NOW TWIST IN MID-AIR AS THEY ANALYZE THEIR FINAL OPPONENT.
THEY ARE READY TO MOVE...

AND THEY DO...
SWIFTLY...
SKREEEEEK
WITH FINALITY.

OH, WELL, SO MUCH FOR YOUR RESCUE.

AND SO MUCH FOR YOUR FRIENDS.
PLEASE, DON'T HURT THEM.
HURT THEM? DON'T WORRY, SWEET SISTER.
I PROMISE YOU THEY WILL DIE LONG BEFORE THEY CAN FEEL ANY PAIN.
WITH A SUDDEN ACTION, PRINCESS KOMAND'R, LATE OF TAMARAN, PROPELS THE UNCONSCIOUS TITANS INTO THE INKY BLACKNESS OF AIRLESS SPACE.

NOOOOO!!
IN A MOMENT IT WILL ALL BE OVER.
23

THEY'RE DONE FOR, KORIAND'R. AND NOW WE'LL DEAL WITH YOU.
I'LL KILL YOU FOR THIS, KOMAND'R.
THAT, MY DEAR, I RESPECTFULLY DOUBT!

COMMANDER, CITADEL HIGH COUNCIL WANTS YOU ON THE HOME WORLD NOW.
OH, VERY WELL. WE'LL JUST HAVE TO DESTROY THIS PLANET ANOTHER TIME.

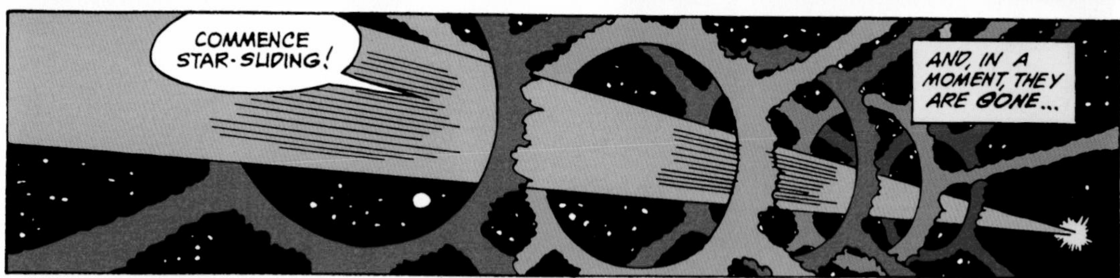
COMMENCE STAR-SLIDING!
AND, IN A MOMENT, THEY ARE GONE...

BUT...
I HAVE YOU, BUT I DO NOT KNOW HOW LONG I CAN PROTECT US.

MY SOUL-SELF CANNOT WITHSTAND THE RAVAGES OF SPACE FOR LONG.

THE JUSTICE LEAGUE SATELLITE, 23,300 MILES OVER THE PLANET EARTH...
THIS IS THE HOME OF THE WORLD'S GREATEST SUPER-HEROES...
...ASSUMING THEY'RE HOME, OF COURSE.
WHICH, IN THIS CASE, THEY AREN'T.*
BUT...
EMERGENCY KLAXONS WEREN'T KIDDING...
*FOR REASONS YOU CAN SEE IN J.L.A #207.--Len.

THERE'S SOMEONE TRAPPED OUT THERE.
I JUST HOPE I'M IN TIME.

A POWERFUL FINGER STABS AT THE COMPUTER CONSOLE...
...AND A J.L.A. TRACTOR BEAM PULSES THROUGH THE INKY BLACKNESS OF SPACE...
SOMETHING'S HAPPENING. WE'RE BEING DRAWN TO THE JUSTICE LEAGUE SATELLITE!

AND, MOMENTS LATER...
I DO NOT BELIEVE THIS. I COULD NOT HAVE HELD ON FOR A MOMENT MORE.
HEY, RAYE, YOU'RE ONE COLD LADY, YOU KNOW THAT?

WELL, VIC, THAT'S YOU ALL OVER.
FUNNY, LOGAN. WANT TO EAT MY FOOT?
NOT EVEN FOR DESSERT, BUDDY.

YOU'RE ALIVE. GOOD. I WAS AFRAID YOU WEREN'T GOING TO MAKE IT.
YOU!
I SHOULDN'T BE SURPRISED. WHO ELSE COULD HAVE SAVED US--

--BUT SUPERMAN!
IT WAS MY PLEASURE, ROBIN.
MIND EXPLAINING WHAT YOU WERE DOING OUT THERE?

I'D LOVE TO, SUPERMAN, BUT AFTER YOU'VE STOPPED THAT SPACESHIP THAT LEFT US HERE.
WITH YOUR POWERS THAT SHOULD PROVE A SNAP!
BUT I CAN'T, ROBIN.
WHAT? WHY?

I DON'T HAVE MY POWERS RIGHT NOW... AT LEAST NOT ALL OF THEM.

QUITE LITERALLY, ROBIN, I'M HALF THE SUPERMAN I ONCE WAS.*
THEN WE'RE DEFEATED EVEN BEFORE WE START.
*FOR THE FULL STORY, SEE ACTION COMICS, ON SALE NOW. --Len.

AND KORY'S GONE ... PROBABLY BEING TAKEN TO HER DEATH.
I HATE FEELING SO HELPLESS, ROBIN. I SIMPLY HATE IT.
KORIAND'R, WE'LL FIND YOU... SOME-HOW, IN SOME MANNER, WE'LL GET YOU BACK...

...WE'LL GET YOU BACK.

NEXT ISSUE: THE OMEGA MEN!

THE OMEGA MEN™ JOIN FORCES WITH...
THE NEW TEEN
TITANS
ALL NEW! 60¢
NO. 24 OCT.
APPROVED BY THE COMICS CODE AUTHORITY

THE SATELLITE HEADQUARTERS OF THE JUSTICE LEAGUE OF AMERICA. ONLY MOMENTS AGO SUPERMAN SAVED THE LIVES OF THE NEW TEEN TITANS. NOW...
DOES IT HURT, VIC?
NAH, DONNA. I LOVE GETTIN' MY MECHANICAL LEGS AMPUTATED.
YOU KNOW HOW MUCH I DIG BEIN' REMINDED THAT I'M NOT ALL HUMAN.
I STILL DON'T UNDERSTAND. YOU ONLY HAVE HALF YOUR POWERS?
THAT'S WHAT I SAID, ROBIN.
AND IF IT WEREN'T FOR THE HELP OF SOME NEW-FOUND FRIENDS, I MIGHT HAVE DIED BECAUSE OF MY LOSS.
THE NEW TEEN TITANS
CREATED BY MARV WOLFMAN & GEORGE PÉREZ
1

AND FROM WHAT YOU TOLD ME OF STARFIRE'S KIDNAPPING, MY FRIENDS MIGHT BE ABLE TO HELP YOU, TOO.*
YOU SEE, THEY'RE FROM THE VEGAN STAR SYSTEM--THE SAME AS KORIAND'R.
TITANS, LET ME INTRODUCE YOU TO--
THE OMEGA MEN
*SEE ACTION COMICS #'S 535 & 536.--LEN.
2

THIS IS NIMBUS, AND KALISTA ALONG WITH HER HUSBAND, PRIMUS.
HARPIS, BROOT AND TIGORR ARE THE OTHERS.
PRIMUS, WHY ARE WE DELAYING OUR DEPARTURE?
WE HAVE THE FUEL TO RETURN HOME.
FOR ONCE I AGREE WITH HARPIS. WE ARE IN A RUSH.
CITADEL STRIKE!
MARV WOLFMAN & GEORGE PÉREZ WRITER-CO-PLOTTERS-ARTIST
ROMEO TANGHAL, EMBELLISHER
TODD KLEIN, LETTERER
CARL GAFFORD, COLORIST
LEN WEIN, EDITOR
3

I KNOW YOU ARE, BUT THIS MIGHT NOT DELAY YOU.
PRIMUS, THESE ARE THE TEEN TITANS, AND ONE OF THEM HAS BEEN KIDNAPPED--BY THE CITADEL.
X'HAL'S BLOOD! THAT IS IMPOSSIBLE!
BUT IT'S TRUE, PRIMUS. HER NAME IS KORIAND'R OF TAMARAN. THAT'S A PLANET IN--
I KNOW WHERE TAMARAN IS, ROBIN. AND I KNOW YOUR PRINCESS KORIAND'R.
SHE AND HER SISTER TRAINED WITH KALISTA AND ME ON OKAARA WHEN WE WERE CHILDREN.*
I HAD HEARD THAT KORIAND'R WAS SLAIN BY THE CITADEL.
* TALES OF THE NEW TEEN TITANS #4.--LEN.
SHE WASN'T, PRIMUS. SHE'S ALIVE...OR AT LEAST SHE WAS BEFORE HER SISTER KID-NAPPED HER.
WE WANT TO RESCUE HER, BUT WE DON'T KNOW HOW TO GET THERE.
WHAT SHE'S SAYIN', MISTER, IS THAT IT AIN'T EASY THUMBIN' A RIDE THROUGH THE STARS--
--EVEN WITH A COPY OF THE "HITCHHIKER'S GUIDE TO THE GALAXY."
I HELPED MAKE IT POSSIBLE FOR YOU TO RETURN TO YOUR STAR SYSTEM. DO YOU THINK YOU CAN TAKE THE TITANS WITH YOU?
WE ARE FIGHTING FOR FREEDOM, SUPERMAN. FREEDOM FROM THE TYRANNY OF CITADEL RULE.
IF THE CITADEL IS HOLDING KORIAND'R, THEN WE WILL RESCUE HER...
...OR THERE WILL BE HELL TO PAY.
STOP THAT, KID. OR ELSE.
HEY, NOT BAD... NOT BAD AT ALL.
WE WON'T FORGET THIS, PRIMUS. ANYTHING WE CAN DO TO HELP, WE WILL.
THEN LET US GO, MY FRIEND.
THERE IS LITTLE TIME TO WASTE.
4

WORLDS WHIZ BY AT IMPOSSIBLE SPEEDS AS THE GORDANIAN SLAVE-SHIP STAR-SLIDES THROUGH THE DARK REACHES OF SPACE, CUTTING A CENTURIES-LONG JOURNEY TO LESS THAN FIVE DAYS.
SUNS BECOME MOMENTARY FLASHES OF LIGHT THAT COME AND GO WITH EACH BLINK OF AN EYE, GALAXIES ARE MERE BLURS...

...BUT, FOR PRINCESS KORIAND'R OF TAMARAN, THE JOURNEY TO HER HOME SYSTEM IS EXCRUCIATINGLY LONG...
WELL, SISTER, IT WON'T BE LONG BEFORE YOU'RE ON THE CITADEL HOMEWORLD.
DO YOU KNOW WHAT SPECIAL TREAT IS IN STORE FOR YOU?

WE'RE ALTERING THE RULES FOR SLAVE-HOLDING, MY DEAR...
...NO MORE ONE YEAR TENURES FOR YOU.
YOU SEE, SWEET ONE, YOU'RE MINE NOW... MINE FOR AS LONG AS YOU LIVE--
--BUT, IF YOU PLAY YOUR CARDS RIGHT, MY DEAR --YOUR LIFE WILL NOT BE A LONG ONE.

K...KOMAND'R...
...I-- I WANT TO KILL YOU!!
5

GET OUT OF MY WAY, GORDANIAN. IT'S YOUR MISTRESS I'M AFTER.
SKREEE

WHY DO YOU DO THIS TO YOURSELF, SISTER? YOU KNOW I CAN EASILY DESTROY YOU.
I'VE ALWAYS BEEN YOUR BETTER.
BRAKK
NO YOU HAVEN'T, KOMAND'R. NOT IN ANY FAIR BATTLE.
I'VE ALWAYS BEEN YOUR EQUAL, BUT WE'VE NEVER FOUGHT AS SUCH.
SKREEE

COMMANDER, SHALL WE--?
BACK, YOU WORTHLESS SLUGS. DO YOU THINK ME INCAPABLE OF HANDLING THAT WEAK FOOL?

ALL MY LIFE YOU'VE DONE EVERYTHING YOU CAN TO RUIN WHATEVER I'VE LOVED!
SKRE
BUT THIS I TELL YOU, KOMAND'R --WHEN YOU TURNED TRAITRESS TO TAMARAN, WHEN YOU REVEALED OUR DEFENSE SECRETS TO THE CITADEL--
--THEN I SWORE YOU WOULD DIE!
YES, YES, SISTER, GROW ANGRIER AND MORE CARELESS. YOUR BLASTS ARE WILD NOW...
BRAKK
6

...BUT MINE, SWEET ONE, NEVER MISS!
BRAAAKKKKKK

YOU'VE ALWAYS BEEN THE CARING ONE, SISTER, THE ONE WHO TENDED THE WOUNDED CREATURES--
--WHO SEARCHED FOR LOVE INSTEAD OF HATE TO URGE HER ON.
YOU WERE THE ONE EVERY-ONE CARED FOR. I WAS THE ONE EVERYONE FEARED...
...BUT I LEARNED TO TAKE THAT FEAR AND USE IT AS MY STRENGTH.

AND THAT, DEAR ONE, IS WHY I AM YOUR BETTER.
I'VE MONITORED YOU, KORIAND'R. ON THAT PLANET YOU TOOK THE NAME STARFIRE. WELL, I SHALL TAKE A SECOND NAME AS WELL.

BUT, WHERE YOUR HEART BURNS AS BRIGHTLY AS THE STARS...
...MINE IS AS BLACK AS THE DEEP PITS OF HELL.

MEN FEAR HELL, AND ALL MEN SHALL FEAR THE POWER OF--

--BLACKFIRE!

COMMANDER, WE ARE ENTERING CITADEL SPACE.
THE HOMEWORLD IS BEFORE US!
7

CITADEL HOMEWORLD! THE MOST FEARSOME PLANET THIS ALIEN GALAXY HAS EVER KNOWN.
MANY YEARS AGO THE CITADEL WAS ATTACKED BY THEIR MORTAL ENEMIES, THE PSIONS, AND DURING THAT WAR THE HOME-WORLD'S MOON WAS SHATTERED AND TURNED INTO A RING OF FREE-FLOATING BOULDERS.
BOULDERS WHICH THE CITADEL HOLLOWED OUT, BUILT UPON AND THEN FINALLY ARMED. NOW, THE HOMEWORLD IS RINGED BY AN IMPENETRABLE FORTRESS THAT NO ONE, NOT EVEN THE PSIONS, HAVE BEEN ABLE TO BREACH.
8

A SMALL FLIER DESCENDS FROM THE SLAVE-SHIP TRAK'R...

...CONSTANTLY EMITTING A SPECIAL CODE WHICH PERMITS IT TO ENTER CITADEL SPACE.

IT CIRCLES THE HOME-WORLD, PASSING OVER OCEANS OF FROZEN METHANE, PAST MOUNTAINS OF ICY SULPHUR...

...UNTIL IT LANDS ON WHAT APPEARS TO BE A BLEAK AND BARREN PATCH OF ICE. EVERYTHING IN ALL DIRECTIONS SEEMS WHITE ...ENDLESS... EMPTY.
BUT...

KOMAND'R, COMMANDER OF THE SLAVE-SHIP TRAK'R?
YOU KNOW I AM. GET ON WITH IT, MAN.

YOU ALSO KNOW I DESPISE THE COLD... OPEN THE GATES AND LET ME INSIDE.

I HAVE MY ORDERS, KOMAND'R. YOU WILL WAIT HERE UNTIL A SHIP COMES TO TAKE YOU TO THE INNER CORE.
AND IF YOU DO NOT LIKE THE COLD... WELL, THAT IS SIMPLY TOO BAD. I'VE SUFFERED A MONTH ALREADY.
9

AH, RELIEF COMES, KOMAND'R... YOU'LL REST IN WARMTH SOONER THAN I.
WRONG, DOG! YOU'LL ROAST IN HELL--NOW!

A DEADLY BLAST OF BLACKFIRE'S STARBOLT ENDS THE GUARD'S LIFE. HIS FAMILY WILL NEVER KNOW HOW HE DIED.

AS THE HEATED LAND-SHIP SPEEDS ACROSS THE HOMEWORLD'S ICY TERRAIN, KOMAND'R SETTLES BACK, THINKING OF THE MEETING TO COME.
SOON SHE WILL BE STANDING BEFORE LORD DAMYN, HIGH CHIEFTAIN OF THE CITADEL EMPIRE. LORD DAMYN, WHO PERSONALLY LED THE RAID ON VEGA'S SIXTEENTH PLANET, EUFORIX...
...WHO SINGLE-HANDEDLY EXILED THE LIVING GODDESS, X'HAL; WHO SWEPT THE CITADEL ARMIES THROUGH ALL 22 VEGAN WORLDS AND OUTWORLDS ALIKE...
THERE IS NO ONE HIGHER OR MORE IMPORTANT THAN LORD DAMYN.
PRINCESS KOMAND'R, COMMANDER OF THE SLAVE-SHIP TRAK'R. I HAVE BEEN SUMMONED HERE.
KOMAND'R WONDERS WHAT IT WOULD TAKE FOR HER TO REPLACE HIM.
PLEASE TELL LORD DAMYN THAT I AWAIT.
SPACE: ANOTHER STAR-SHIP SLIDES THROUGH THE EBON GLORIES OF THE UNIVERSE...
...BUT INSIDE, ONE MAN CONTEMPLATES NOT THE BEAUTY THAT SURROUNDS HIM, BUT THE GRIM REALITIES OF THE WARS TO COME...
IF WE ARE TO RECAPTURE PRINCESS KORIAND'R, WE WILL HAVE TO FIGHT FOR HER.
TO FIGHT, WE WILL NEED MORE WARRIORS THAN WE HAVE.
OUR FIRST STOP THEN MUST BE OKAARA, THE WARRIOR-WORLD.
10

Y'KNOW, IT SORTA STUNS ME, LOOKIN' OUT THERE.
YOU GET A WHOLE NEW PERSPECTIVE 'BOUT THINGS.
PAL, I KNOW WHAT YOU MEAN.
SPACE IS SO INSPIRING, SORTA LIKE STARIN' AT GIRLS IN BIKINIS.

YOU TWO FINISHED LOOKING AT THAT MUCK? GET TO WORK!
WE NEED HELP RUNNING THIS SHIP.
GET A LOAD'A TONY THE TIGORR!
WHO APPOINTED YOU SLAVE-DRIVER?

EARTHLING, LISTEN TO TIGORR.
THERE IS NO TIME FOR SIGHT-SEEING IN SPACE.
OUR VERY LIVES DEPEND UPON OUR WORKING TOGETHER.

HARPIS' STINGING WORDS ARE **TRUE**. SPACE TRAVEL, NO MATTER **WHAT** THEY SHOW YOU IN THE MOVES, IS **NOT** ALL FUN AND GAMES. THERE ARE AN INFINITE NUMBER OF TASKS THAT MUST CONTINUOUSLY BE DONE.

CONTROLS MUST BE MONITORED, **COMPUTERS** SET AND RECALIBRATED. **PROBLEMS** SOLVED QUICKLY AND PRECISELY.

ABOARD A STAR-SHIP THERE MUST BE COMPLETE **COOPERATION** BETWEEN A HUNDRED OR MORE BEINGS, FOR EACH LIFE DEPENDS ON THE OTHERS TO SAFELY CARRY THEM TO THEIR **DESTINATION**.

11

AND EVEN THOSE WHO STAND ON THE OUTSIDE AT LEAST WORK BESIDE THEIR FELLOW TRAVELLERS...
SPEAK ENGLISH, DEMONIA, EVEN IF YOU DO NOT APPROVE OF OUR GUESTS. I DEMAND COURTESY HERE.
I FEAR THIS DEMONIA. I SENSE EVIL WITHIN HER. SHE WOULD BETRAY US ALL IF GIVEN THE CHANCE.
MAYBE SO, RAVEN, BUT WE CAN'T MOVE AGAINST HER.

IF THE OMEGANS TRUST DEMONIA, THAT WILL HAVE TO DO.
I UNDERSTAND, BUT I FEEL WE MUST MAINTAIN OUR GUARD.
HEY, GUYS--
MY INNER SOUL TREMBLES AS I NEAR HER.

--YOU GOTTA SEE THIS SHIP!
IT MAKES THE J.L.A. SATELLITE LOOK LIKE A MEGO TOY!

VERY WELL, PRIMUS, I'LL SPEAK SO THEY UNDERSTAND ME.
THESE EARTHLINGS WILL ONLY HINDER OUR MISSION. DESTROY THEM BEFORE THEY DESTROY US.

THEY ARE OUR GUESTS, DEMONIA. DO NOT HARM THEM.

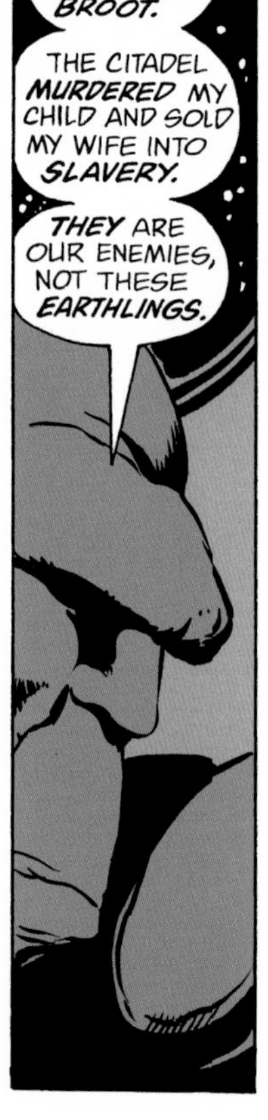
OR, YOU WILL ANSWER TO BROOT.
THE CITADEL MURDERED MY CHILD AND SOLD MY WIFE INTO SLAVERY.
THEY ARE OUR ENEMIES, NOT THESE EARTHLINGS.

SOMETHING TELLS ME, NIMBUS, THAT WE'RE IN THE WAY.
NO. JUST IGNORE DEMONIA. SHE DESPISES ALL RACES BUT HER OWN.
WE WILL HELP YOU FIND YOUR PRINCESS KORIAND'R NO MATTER WHAT DEMONIA ESPOUSES.
12

WE'RE ALMOST HOME, THANK X'HAL. IT HAS BEEN TOO LONG SINCE I BREATHED THE COOL SEA-AIR OF EUFORIX...

...OR GAZED INTO ITS EMERALD SKIES, TO WATCH ITS THREE BRIGHT MOONS.
I PRAY OUR FORCED EXILE IS OVER, DEAR PRIMUS.
AS I PRAY THAT WE MIGHT YET CRUSH THE CITADEL TYRANNY THAT FORCED US TO FLEE.

THE CITADEL...
LORD DAMYN, I BRING YOU A PRIZE.
WAIT. JUST WAIT, KOMAND'R. ME GOT THIS HERE SKRIG TO KILL.
ME LIKE TO TEAR YOU APART, EH. YOU SCRATCHED ME TEETH WHEN YOU BRUSH THEM, YOU DID.

ME NO LIKE SCRATCHED TEETH, SKRIG. ME PROUD OF ME TEETH.
OH, YESSSS, ME LIKE THEM CLEAN, ME DO.
GURGL
HMMM. ME GET IDEA, ME DO. AHH, MAYBE ME TAKE YOUR TEETH AND WEAR THEM ON MINE.
WHAT YOU THINK, KOMAND'R?
UHHH, LORD DAMYN, I WISH TO SHOW YOU THE FRUITS OF MY VICTORIOUS MISSION TO EARTH.
LOOK! IT'S MY SISTER, KORIAND'R OF TAMARAN.
13

OHHHH? REALLY? PRINCESS KORIAND'R? YOU DO NOT PLAY JOKE ON LORD DAMYN, HIGH OF HIGHS, BEST OF BEST?
NO, OF COURSE YOU DO NOT. ME WOULD RIP OFF YOUR ARMS, ME WOULD. HO! WHAT JOKE THAT WOULD BE, EH?
YOU NOT LAUGH, KOMAND'R? BUT ME THINK IT WOULD BE FUNNY. OH YES, ME DO. HAH!
YOU WITH NO ARMS, MAYBE NO LEGS, EITHER. HMMM. YES, BIG JOKE, EH? EH?

HMMM. YOU PRETTY GIRL, KORIAND'R. YOU WANT TO KISS ME BECAUSE ME AM PRETTY, TOO, EH? COME, COME. KISS.
HMMM. WONDER, MAYBE YOU BE PRETTIER WITH NO ARMS AND LEGS.

LET GO OF ME!

OOOH, SHE TRY TO HURT LORD OF LORDS, HIGH OF HIGHS, BEST OF BEST.
KOMAND'R?
SKRAKKK!

I'VE STOPPED HER, LORD DAMYN.
BRAKK

BUT SHE HURT ME, SHE DID. ME SHOULD CUT HER INTO LITTLE PIECES FOR THAT.
MAYBE THEN EAT PIECES.

AND EAT YOU, TOO. WHY YOU LET HER HURT ME? YOU WANT BE CUT INTO PIECES?
OH, NO, NO, LORD DAMYN. YOU WOULDN'T WANT TO DO THAT.

I PROMISE YOU SHE'LL NEVER HURT YOU AGAIN.
OKAY.
14

ME NOT CUT YOU IN LITTLE PIECES THIS TIME.
HMMM. SAY, SINCE ME NOT EAT YOUR SISTER, ME VERY, VERY HUNGRY, ME IS. burp
COME, WE WILL ORDER FEAST. YOU HUNGRY, RIGHT?
OH, YES, LORD DAMYN. VERY HUNGRY.
YOU WANT EAT KORIAND'R, MAYBE, EH?
OH, NO-- DON'T GO TO THE TROUBLE.
OKAY. JUST ASKING. MMMMMMM. STARVED.

SHORTLY...
DO ME KNOW HOW ENTERTAIN, EH? ME SURE DO. COME. SIT.
THANK YOU, LORD DAMYN. ABOUT MY SISTER...
OH, DO NOT THANK ME, KOMAND'R. SHE WILL WIGGLE IN ELECTRICAL CELL UNTIL DINNER FINISHED...

...THEN WE FRY HER FOR DESSERT. SHE TASTE GOOD, EH?

UH, LORD DAMYN, MAY I ASK YOU A FAVOR?
SURE, SURE, KOMAND'R. YOU WANT KISS, RIGHT? ON YOUR HUMAN LIPS. THEY'RE UGLY, BUT SURE. WHY NOT?

NO, AFTER THE KISS, LORD DAMYN. I'D LIKE YOU NOT TO SLAY MY SISTER.
I WOULD LIKE HER FOR MY OWN.
OH, SURE, ME UNDER-STAND, SURELY DO. NO PROBLEM. ME WILL HAVE HANDMAIDEN COOKED INSTEAD.

SAY, YOU LIKE DINNER?
IT WAS DELICIOUS.
YES, SKRIG SURE HAD MORE MEAT ON HIM THAN ME THOUGHT.
GAGK!
15

SIR, CAN I PLEASE WAIT OUTSIDE?
YOU'LL BE SAFE FROM THAT LOUT. I PROMISE HE WON'T REND YOU LIMB FROM LIMB...
...AS HE DID YOUR SISTER. NOW, COME AND BE SILENT.

LORD DAMYN?
PSION? YOU WANT ME? EH? OF COURSE! EVERYONE WANTS ME. MOST POPULAR FELLOW, EH?
LORD DAMYN, WHY IS THAT PSION ALLOWED HERE? THEY ARE OUR ENEMIES!

PERHAPS YOU ARE UNAWARE, MY DEAR, THAT I AM AN EX-PATRIOT, NOW A FIRM BELIEVER IN THE CITADEL WAY.
I SERVE LORD DAMYN AS LOYALLY AS YOU DO.

YEP. HIM SCARED FOR MISERABLE LIFE, TOO. HEY, STUPID PSION, YOU WORK UP GOOD NEW PLAN, EH? PLENTY OF KILLING? HUH?

INDEED, LORD DAMYN. AN INTRICATE PLAN WHICH WILL INSURE THAT ALL THE VEGAN WORLDS ARE YOURS.
WE ARE GOING TO KIDNAP X'HAL, THE LIVING GODDESS.

IMPOSSIBLE! IT CAN'T BE DONE!
HEY, LIKE THAT, SURELY. WHAT YOU SAY, KOMAND'R?
MMM. OH, YES. GOOD PLAN. GOOD.

I THOUGHT YOU'D SEE THINGS MY WAY. WITH X'HAL UNDER OUR CONTROL--
--THE REVOLUTIONARIES WILL HAVE TO THROW DOWN THEIR ARMS...
...LEST WE PLAY HAVOC WITH THEIR GRIM, GOLD GODDESS.

THEN WE EAT THEIR ARMS, EH? HEY, THAT JOKE. LAUGH!
HMMM. QRULL, YOU WANT LEG BONE?
SURE. SURE DO, LORD DAMYN.

VERY GOOD THEN. I SHALL COMMENCE OPERATIONS IMMEDIATELY.
BY TOMORROW THIS TIME, X'HAL WILL BE OURS!
16

...THIS DAMYN IS THE CITADEL LORD? HE SOUNDS LIKE A FOOL!
HE'S A MURDERING BARBARIAN, VICIOUS AND TOTALLY DEMENTED. BUT NEVER UNDERESTIMATE HIM, ROBIN.
HE WRESTED CONTROL OVER THE CITADEL HOMEWORLD FOR HIMSELF AND THEN SYSTEMATICALLY SUCCEEDED IN INVADING ALL THE VEGAN WORLDS.
THE SHUTTLE IS READY.
HE MAY BE NEAR MINDLESS IN MOST THINGS, BUT HE'S DEADLY IN WARFARE.

AN IDIOT SAVANT. GREAT! JUST WHAT WE NEED.
PRIMUS, HOW MANY ARE COMING WITH US TO OKAARA?
ONLY THE BRIDGE CREW, KALISTA ...ALONG WITH THE TITANS.
AURON?
SOMETHING TELLS ME HE ALREADY KNOWS.
OH, ALERT AURON. HE'LL WANT TO BE THERE.

I SENSED OUR APPROACH. I AM READY.
AURON AWAITS HIS MEETING WITH X'HAL.

HEY, DON'T--
IT WON'T HURT, CHANGELING. I AM MERELY FITTING YOU WITH AN INSTANTANEOUS LANGUAGE TRANSLATOR.
WHY DIDN'T I HAVE ONE'A THESE WHEN I TOOK HIGH SCHOOL SPANISH?

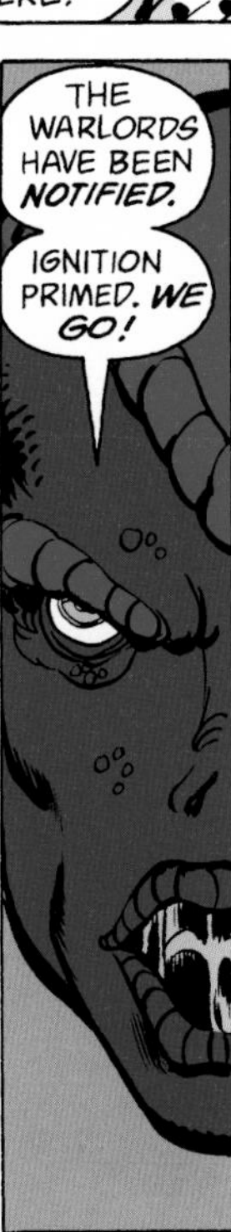
THE WARLORDS HAVE BEEN NOTIFIED.
IGNITION PRIMED. WE GO!

THEY LEAVE, SIX TEEN TITANS AND A HANDFUL OF OMEGA MEN.
TO THE OMEGANS, OKAARA IS THEIR FIRST STEP HOME. TO THE TITANS, IT IS THE BEGINNING OF THEIR SEARCH FOR THEIR FRIEND.
17

OKAARA IS A PLANET UNLIKE ANY OTHER. ITS WONDERS MUST BE BEHELD TO BE BELIEVED.

AN' MY STOMACH MUST BE HELD BEFORE I HEAVE. TAKE IT EASY WITH THOSE SUDDEN DROPS, PRIMUS.

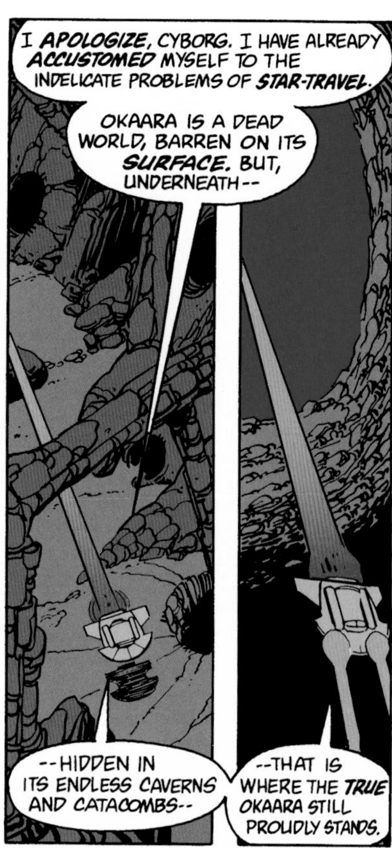
I APOLOGIZE, CYBORG. I HAVE ALREADY ACCUSTOMED MYSELF TO THE INDELICATE PROBLEMS OF STAR-TRAVEL.
OKAARA IS A DEAD WORLD, BARREN ON ITS SURFACE. BUT, UNDERNEATH--
--HIDDEN IN ITS ENDLESS CAVERNS AND CATACOMBS--
--THAT IS WHERE THE TRUE OKAARA STILL PROUDLY STANDS.

KORIAND'R TOLD US ABOUT THIS PLACE, BUT THERE'S NO WAY SHE COULD HAVE DONE IT JUSTICE.*
*TITANS MINI-SERIES #4. WELL WORTH BUYING! --LEN, MARV, GEORGE, ERNIE & TODD.

YOU WEREN'T KIDDIN', RED. WE'RE COMPLETELY UNDERGROUND.
OKAARA IS NOT BATHED IN DARKNESS, YET ITS LIGHT IS A NATURAL ONE.
MERELY THE FIRST OF ITS MANY MIRACLES.
WHERE IS X'HAL? I MUST SEE HER.
YOUR MOTHER HAS BEEN WAITING FOR YOU, AURON. COME WITH ME.

MOTHER? X'HAL'S HIS MOTHER?
IS SOMETHING WRONG, LITTLE ONE?
YEAH. I JUST REALLY REALIZED WE'RE NOT IN KANSAS ANYMORE. I'M STUNNED.
"AND YOUR LITTLE DOG TOTO, TOO."
18

THEY MARCH THROUGH DEEP CATACOMBS CUTTING FAR BENEATH THE PLANET'S SURFACE, YET THEY STILL CAN SEE THE UNFAMILIAR STARS TWINKLING OVERHEAD.

WHAT IS THIS PLACE? IT ALMOST FEELS... HOLY.
IT IS. THIS IS WHERE X'HAL REFORMS.
REFORMS? WHAT DO YOU MEAN?
YOU SHALL SEE.

MOTHER, I CALL UNTO YOU, YOU WHO CONTROL ME HAVE BROUGHT ME THIS FAR. REVEAL YOURSELF TO ME NOW.

APPEAR BEFORE ME, MOTHER! LET ME SEE YOUR FACE AND THEN SLAY ME. LET ME DIE AS I SHOULD HAVE DIED.

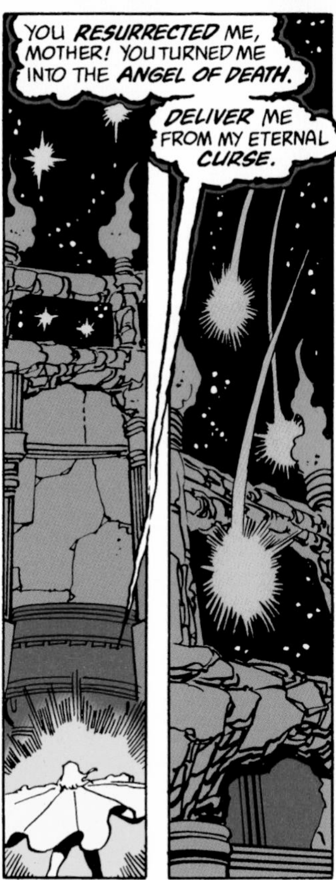
YOU RESURRECTED ME, MOTHER! YOU TURNED ME INTO THE ANGEL OF DEATH.
DELIVER ME FROM MY ETERNAL CURSE.

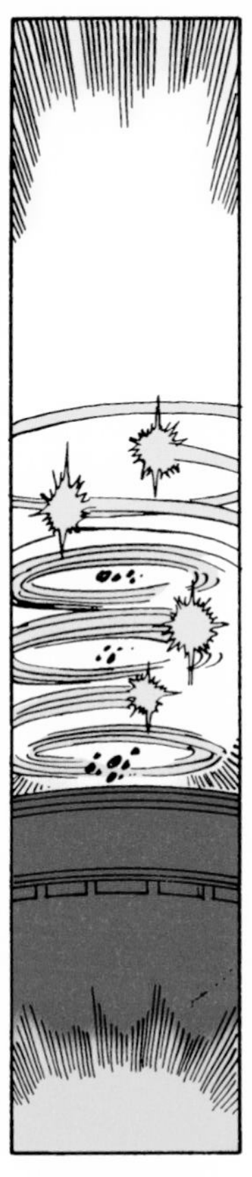

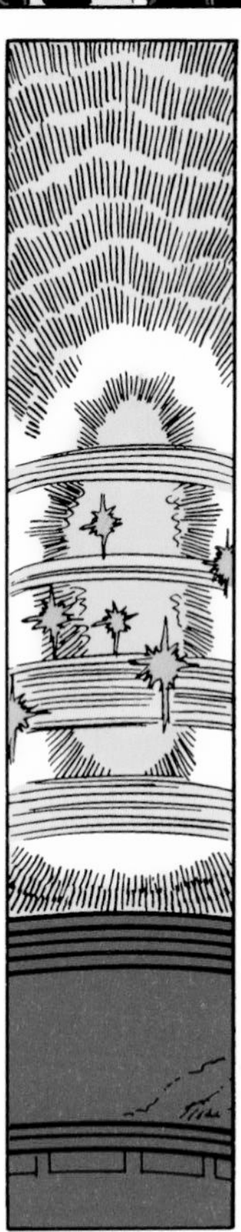

19

I STAND REFORMED BEFORE YOU, AURON--HE WHO WAS ONCE LAMBIEN --MY CHILD.
YOU BESEECH ME TO END YOUR LIFE, YET THAT IS DENIED ME.
I CRY OUT FOR VENGEANCE, AND YOU ARE MY HANDS.
MY INSTRUMENT.
MY WEAPON.
YOU SHALL SUCCEED WHERE I HAVE FAILED.

I--I CAN'T SEE. HER DAMNED LIGHT BLINDS ME.
GET AWAY FROM ME, X'HAL. GET AWAY!

BUT WHY MUST I DEAL DEATH TO OTHERS WHEN THAT IS FOREVER DENIED ME?
WHY DO YOU FORCE ME TO SLAY YOUR ENEMIES? WHY, MOTHER-- WHY?
BECAUSE I NEED A GOD AT MY SIDE.
I'M NOT A GOD. I'VE BECOME A DAMNED DEVIL.
YOU WILL DO WHAT MUST BE DONE.

YOU WILL AVENGE YOUR MOTHER'S DEATH.
AND YOU SHALL DO SO-- NOW!

OKAARA! HEED US! THE CITADEL DEMANDS A HOSTAGE OR YOUR PLANET SHALL BE DESTROYED!

WE WANT X'HAL! GIVE HER TO US NOW!
20

NO! MOTHER, YOU DO IT TO ME AGAIN!
MY ANGER GROWS! MY RAGE SUDDENLY SWELLS!
AND IT CANNOT BE ABATED UNTIL I HAVE KILLED!

I SHALL BE AVENGED! AND YOU, MY SON, SHALL BE MY AVENGER!
DO AS X'HAL COMMANDS!

I SHALL... BECAUSE I MUST.
I RESIST, BUT IT DOES ME NO GOOD.
MY EVERY FIBER FIGHTS OUT, CRIES OUT AND SAYS "NO!" BUT I CANNOT HELP WHAT I DO.

EVEN WITH THESE DEATHS, MY ANGER STILL GROWS. X'HAL WILL NOT RELEASE ME UNTIL HER BLOODY APPETITE IS SATED.
NOT EVEN THE DESTRUCTION OF AN ENTIRE CITADEL SHIP PLEASES HER NOW.

WHEN WILL THIS END? X'HAL, WHEN WILL IT END?

IF THE CITADEL ATTACKS--
--IT IS OUR DUTY TO RESIST!
NOW THE BATTLE BEGINS!

THEY HAVE THEIR FIGHT AND WE HAVE OURS. WE SPLIT UP AS WE SAID EARLIER.
GAR, THIS IS UP TO YOU.
21

THINK YOU CAN HANDLE THIS?
BELIEVE IT, ROBBIE. PRESTO, CHANGE-O

--AND YOU'RE LOOKING AT THE CUDDLIEST GORDANIAN EVER TO BE BORN IN WESTCHESTER COUNTY.

JUST DON'T OVERPLAY YOUR HAND.
WE DON'T KNOW TOO MUCH ABOUT THIS CITADEL.
SURE WE DO, ROB. PRIMUS FILLED US IN ON THE WAY HERE.
I'LL JUST TOSS AROUND A FEW WORDS...

NO! DON'T TALK UNLESS YOU HAVE TO.
SPOILSPORT.
WAR IS NOT A PRETTY THING, NO MATTER IF ON EARTH OR ON SOME DISTANT WORLD.

THE PURPOSE OF WAR IS SINGULAR: TO KILL!
THE SIDE THAT KILLS THE OTHER SIDE WINS...

...NO MATTER HOW FEW SOLDIERS THEY HAVE REMAINING.
AND SO, WAR BEGINS...

...A WAR TO SAVE A GODDESS...
...OR SO SOME THINK.
22

HERE COMES THE FIRST TEST. TAKE IT EASY.
SURE, SURE. LEAVE IT TO ME.
HALT! WHO GOES THERE?

I HAVE PRISONERS TO BE TAKEN TO THE HOME-WORLD FOR QUESTIONING.
ON WHOSE ORDERS? I RECEIVED NO NOTIFICATION.
ARE YOU GOING TO LET ME THROUGH OR DO I BLAST YOU?

IXNAY ON THE LASTERBAY. YOU'RE OVERDOING IT.
WHAT DO I CARE ABOUT OUR ENEMIES? MOVE ON.
ALL RIGHT. ENTER THE TRANSPORT.

Whew!
I DON'T WANT TO GO THROUGH THAT AGAIN.
WHAT ARE YOU COMPLAINING ABOUT? I GOT US THROUGH.
AND NEARLY GAVE ME A CORONARY. DON'T TALK, GAR. PLEASE.
I CAN PROVE MYSELF, ROB! GIVE ME A CHANCE.

THE TRANSPORT RISES TO MEET THE MOTHER-SHIP HIGH OVERHEAD. AND, SOON,...
I'VE GOT PRISONERS FOR INTERROGATION. WE MUST GET TO THE HOMEWORLD IMMEDIATELY.

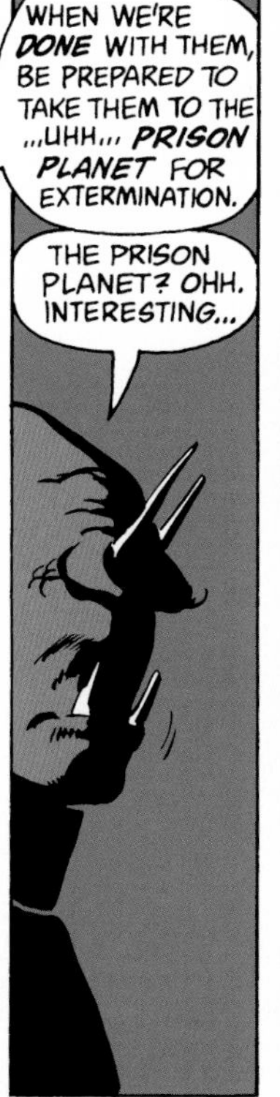
WHEN WE'RE DONE WITH THEM, BE PREPARED TO TAKE THEM TO THE ...UHH... PRISON PLANET FOR EXTERMINATION.
THE PRISON PLANET? OHH. INTERESTING...

...CONSIDERING THE PRISON PLANET WAS LEFT IN RUIN LESS THAN A MONTH AGO. WE'VE ABANDONED THAT WORLD.
YOU ARE A SPY. TELL ME WHO YOU ARE--
--OR YOU SHALL SURELY DIE!
OOPS.
23

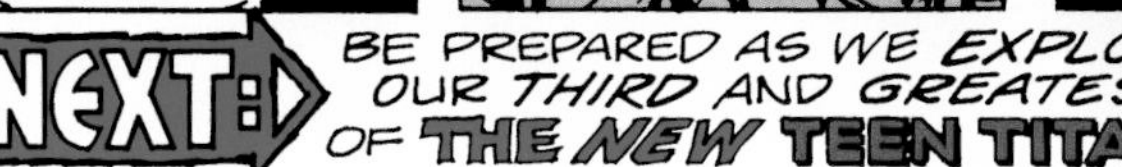
NEXT:
BE PREPARED AS WE EXPLODE INTO OUR THIRD AND GREATEST YEAR OF THE NEW TEEN TITANS WITH...

WAR!

THE NEW TEEN TITANS™

ALL NEW! 60¢

NO. 25 NOV.

APPROVED BY THE COMICS CODE AUTHORITY

SURRENDER, TITANS--OR I'LL UNLEASH THE DEADLY X'HAL!

YOU SURRENDER, BLACKFIRE--OR WE'LL TERMINATE YOUR PRECIOUS LEADER!

LOOKS LIKE WHAT WE HAVE HERE IS A... STAND-OFF!

EXTRA! FREE 16-PAGE COMIC PREVIEW MASTERS OF THE UNIVERSE

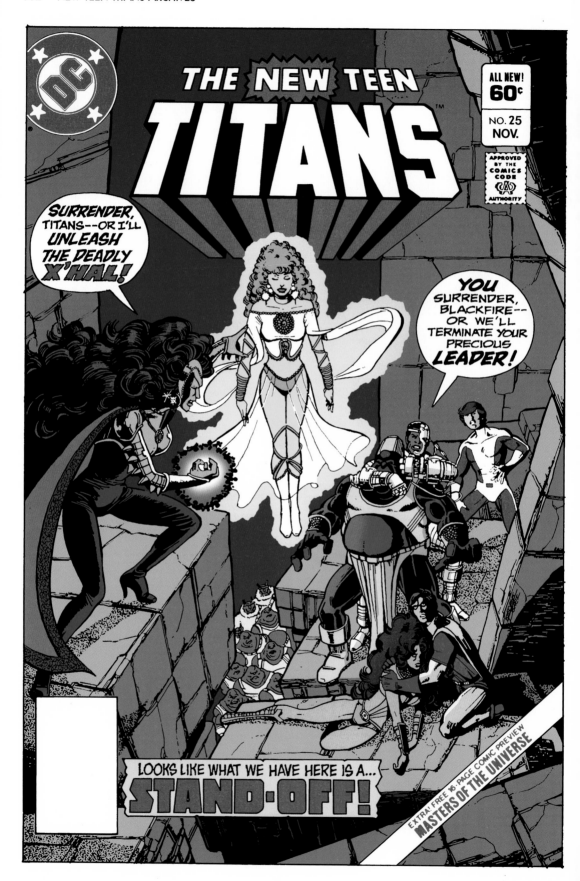

FOR THOSE WHO CAME IN LATE: STARFIRE, ALSO KNOWN AS PRINCESS KORIAND'R OF TAMARAN, HAS BEEN KIDNAPPED FROM EARTH BY HER EVIL SISTER, BLACKFIRE, ALSO KNOWN AS KOMAND'R.

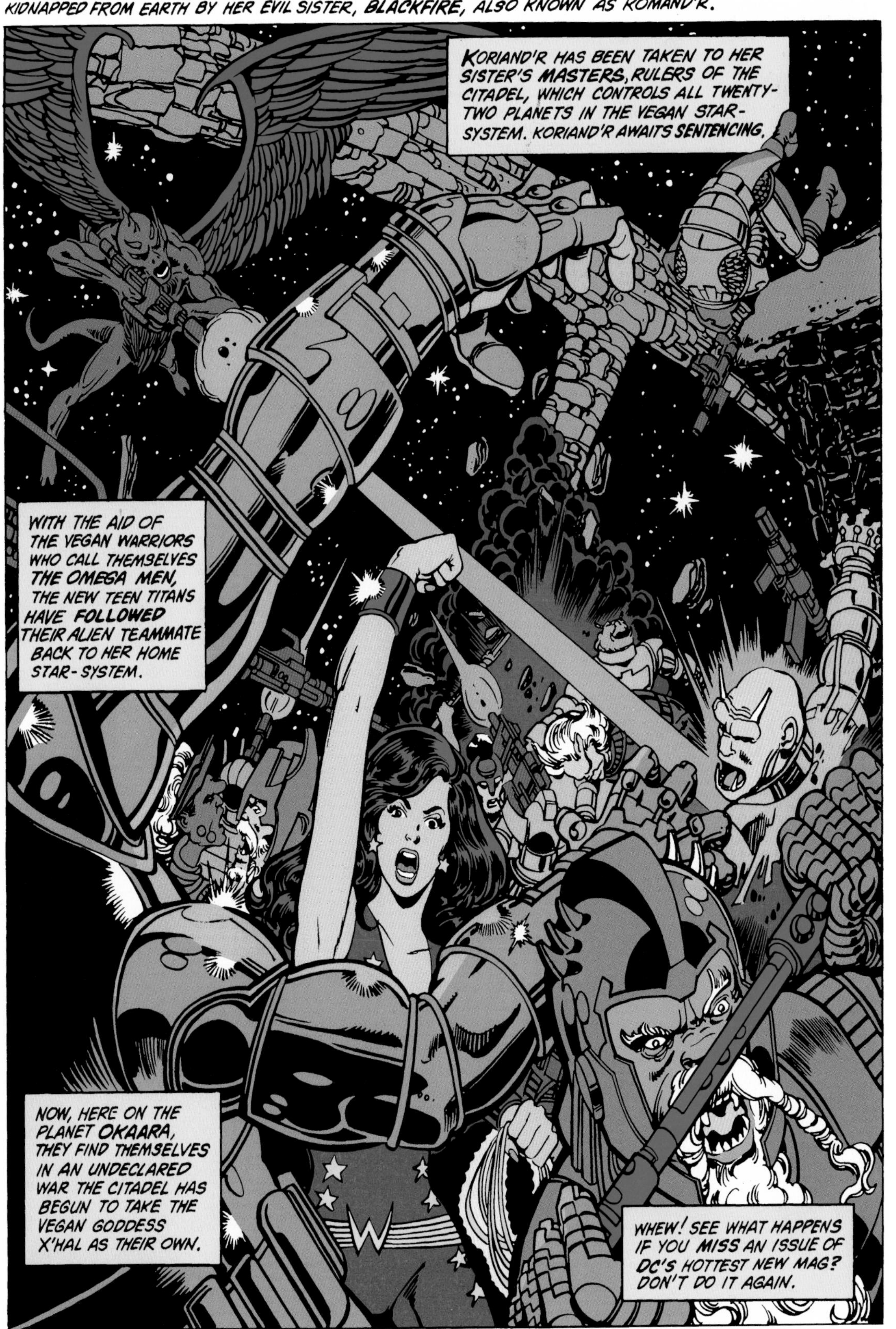

KORIAND'R HAS BEEN TAKEN TO HER SISTER'S MASTERS, RULERS OF THE CITADEL, WHICH CONTROLS ALL TWENTY-TWO PLANETS IN THE VEGAN STAR-SYSTEM. KORIAND'R AWAITS SENTENCING.
WITH THE AID OF THE VEGAN WARRIORS WHO CALL THEMSELVES THE OMEGA MEN, THE NEW TEEN TITANS HAVE FOLLOWED THEIR ALIEN TEAMMATE BACK TO HER HOME STAR-SYSTEM.
NOW, HERE ON THE PLANET OKAARA, THEY FIND THEMSELVES IN AN UNDECLARED WAR THE CITADEL HAS BEGUN TO TAKE THE VEGAN GODDESS X'HAL AS THEIR OWN.
WHEW! SEE WHAT HAPPENS IF YOU MISS AN ISSUE OF DC'S HOTTEST NEW MAG? DON'T DO IT AGAIN.

THE VIOLENCE HERE IS UNENDING AND EVER-ESCALATING. I FEEL IT CUTTING THROUGH MY VERY SOUL.
TO AN EMPATH, ONE WHO LIVES OFF THE EMOTIONS OF OTHERS, SUCH HORROR CAN BE... DEVASTATING.
RAVEN: ONE OF THE NEW TEEN TITANS.
THIS FIGHT WILL END SOON, EARTHLING. BROOT WILL DESTROY ALL THESE KILLERS.
BROOT: ONE OF THE OMEGA MEN. THE CITADEL KILLED HIS CHILD AND SOLD HIS WIFE INTO SLAVERY.
RAVEN, WE'LL GET THROUGH THIS! TRUST ME. WE'VE GOT TO IF WE WANT TO FIND KORY.
KID FLASH: HE LOVES THE EMPATH NAMED RAVEN. HE ALSO FEARS THE SOURCE OF HER POWERS.
WE CANNOT LET THEM TAKE X'HAL FROM OKAARA. ONLY THE FABLED WARLORDS CAN HOLD HER POWERS IN CHECK.
PRIMUS: PSIONIC LEADER OF THE OMEGA MEN...
...AND NIMBUS: WIELDER OF THE DEATH-CLOUD...
THAT IS SIMPLE TO SAY, PRIMUS, BUT THOSE OF THE CITADEL OUTNUMBER US.
WE CANNOT HOPE TO STOP THOSE SAVAGES.
2

THEN, FRIEND NIMBUS, WE SHALL DESTROY THEM.

SO SPEAKS AURON, GOD OF LIGHT, GOD OF DEATH!

REMEMBER, IT IS MY MOTHER THEY WISH TO TAKE. WHO BETTER THAN I KNOWS WHAT DESTRUCTION THEY WOULD UNLEASH?

IT IS X'HAL'S VENGEFUL HAND WHICH GUIDES MY OWN. IT IS HER LUSTFUL WRATH WHICH CONTROLS ME.

I KILL BECAUSE SHE FORCES ME TO.

TO HAVE HER IN THE HANDS OF THE CITADEL WOULD BE TO UNLEASH A POWER UNLIKE ANY THIS UNIVERSE HAS EVER SEEN.

RAVEN DOUBTS AURON'S WORDS. SHE HAS SEEN TRIGON'S POWER. AND IT IS HE WHOM SHE FEARS THE MOST.

STILL, EVEN THIS SEEMINGLY EMOTIONLESS EMPATH TREMBLES WHEN SHE HEARS X'HAL SHOUT TO THE HEAVENS THEMSELVES...

I WILL BE FREE, MY SON. FREE FROM THIS PRISON I HAVE BEEN SENTENCED TO.

I, WHO SAVED ALL VEGA, WILL BE CHAINED NO LONGER.

FREE ME, CITADEL, SO I MAY DESTROY YOU AND ALL YOUR BLOODY KIND.

X'HAL, WE REVERE YOU, BUT YOU MUST NOT LEAVE THIS WORLD.

ONLY ON OKAARA CAN YOU BE CONTROLLED.

ONLY HERE CAN THE PEOPLE WHO WORSHIP YOU BE SAFE.

KALISTA IS A WITCH, AND SHE, TOO, IS AN OMEGAN...

...AS IS TIGORR, WHO SAVAGELY SWEEPS THROUGH THE CITADEL HORDE...

3

WAR HAS BEEN DECLARED, AND THE TITANS MUST SOMEHOW HELP WIN THIS WAR OR THEY MAY NEVER SEE KORIAND'R AGAIN. NOW, BE PREPARED AS WE EXPLODE INTO OUR THIRD AND GREATEST YEAR OF --

THE NEW TEEN TITANS

Co-created by: MARV WOLFMAN and GEORGE PEREZ

THE CHANGELING
CYBORG
KID FLASH
RAVEN
ROBIN
STARFIRE
WONDER GIRL

THE OMEGA MEN

AURON
BROOT
DEMONIA
HARPIS
KALISTA
NIMBUS
PRIMUS
TIGORR

ABOVE THE PLANET OKAARA, A CITADEL WARSHIP PREPARES TO DOCK.

BUT WATCH CAREFULLY. THINGS ARE NOT ALWAYS WHAT THEY SEEM.

WAR!

MARV WOLFMAN & GEORGE PEREZ
writer -- co-plotters -- artist

CARL GAFFORD - colorist
BEN ODA - letterer

ROMEO TANGHAL
embellisher

LEN WEIN
editor

Featuring characters created by MARV WOLFMAN + JOE STATON

4

GORDANIAN, YOU ARE A SPY. TELL ME WHO YOU TRULY ARE OR YOU WILL DIE.
DOES THE NAME RUBY BEGONIA STRIKE A FAMILIAR NOTE?
HOW ABOUT LUKE SKYWALKER? FLASH GORDON? CAPTAIN KIRK? WOULDYA BELIEVE ROCKY JONES?

NEVER HEARD OF THEM, HAVE YOU? WELL, THIS BLOWS THAT THEORY THAT OUR TV SHOWS KEEP PLAYING RERUNS THROUGH SPACE.
SHUCKS, I REALLY WANTED TO SEE IF THEY LIKED "LAYERNE AND SHIRLEY" ON MARS.
GORDANIAN, YOU ARE TALKING LIKE A MADMAN. DO YOU WANT TO DIE?
AHHH, MULTIPLE-CHOICE QUESTIONS. I ALWAYS DID WELL ON THOSE.
I SELECT 'E'--NONE OF THE ABOVE.

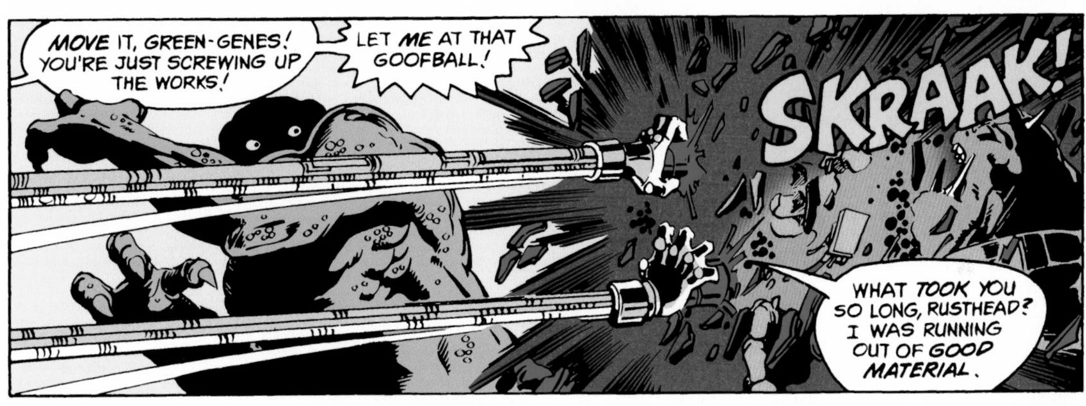
MOVE IT, GREEN-GENES! YOU'RE JUST SCREWING UP THE WORKS!
LET ME AT THAT GOOFBALL!
SKRAAK!
WHAT TOOK YOU SO LONG, RUSTHEAD? I WAS RUNNING OUT OF GOOD MATERIAL.

WE WERE WAITING TO SEE IF YOU'D HANG YOURSELF, GAR.
KLANG!
I TOLD YOU TO KEEP QUIET. YOU ALMOST BLEW EVERYTHING!
OKAY, OKAY, SUE ME. I FOULED UP AGAIN. FIRE ME FROM THE TITANS.
MAKE ME JOIN "THE ZOO CREW." I'D FIT RIGHT IN.
SPOK!
ON THE OTHER HAND, MAYBE I CAN REDEEM MYSELF. HI. GUESS WHO'S GOT MR. BLASTER NOW?
SO, UNLESS YOU WANT SOME LASER-INDUCED CAVITIES, DO WHAT THE KID IN THE SILLY SHORT-PANTS SAYS.
TAKE US TO THE CITADEL. NOW!
OOOK!
5

AS THE CHANGELING'S THREAT URGES THE CITADEL WARRIOR TO HASTEN HOMEWARD...
I WISH THIS WASN'T ALL SO WASTED.
I DON'T WANT TO FIGHT-- I SIMPLY WANT TO LOCATE KORY AND TAKE HER HOME...

HERA! WHY DO I KEEP THINKING THE END OF THAT SENTENCE SHOULD BE--"IF SHE'S ALIVE"?
I'VE GROWN TO CARE FOR HER, TO LOVE HER LIKE A SISTER.
SHE'S AS MUCH "FAMILY" TO ME AS MY MOTHER, OR EVEN DIANA.

OKAARA IS THE PLANET OF WARLORDS. THIS IS WHERE VEGAN KINGS AND EMPERORS SEND THEIR CHILDREN TO LEARN THE ART OF WARFARE.

AND THE OKAARANS ARE MASTERS OF THEIR TRADE, AS THE CITADEL QUICKLY LEARNS.

BUT...
SO, ONE SHIP AVOIDED DESTRUCTION, EH?
WELL, IT SHALL NOT FIND FREEDOM.
AS MUCH AS I FIGHT MY MOTHER'S WILL, STILL SHE CONTROLS MY EVERY MOVEMENT...
I AM FORCED TO REACH OUT, FORCED TO EMBRACE ALL ABOUT ME...
...FOR MY TOUCH BRINGS INSTANT AND TERRIBLE DEATH!
6

FOR ONCE THE WAR GOES OUR WAY, EARTHLING. WE HAVE THEM ON THE RUN.
I WOULDN'T START BUILDING ANY CONDOS HERE, TIGORR--
--WE'RE STILL GREATLY OUTNUMBERED!

BUT NOT FOR MUCH LONGER, EARTHMAN.
SKRUK!

I... DO NOT BELONG HERE...
...TO FIGHT IS NOT MY WAY.

TO SPILL BLOOD SICKENS ME. MINE IS THE POWER TO HEAL, NOT TO KIL--!
AZAR HELP ME! AS FAST AS I HELP THESE PEOPLE, AS QUICKLY AS I HEAL THEIR PAINS--

--ANOTHER FALLS BEFORE ME. ANOTHER DIES!
FOR EACH ONE I SAVE, TWO MORE PERISH.
THIS IS MADNESS! TO HATE IS MADNESS! TO KILL IS MADNESS!

ARRRRHH! THEIR PAIN FLOODS OVER ME. BEFORE I CAN DISPEL THEIR AGONIES, MORE PAIN ASSAILS ME!

I... CANNOT ABSORB ALL THEIR HORROR. I CANNOT FIGHT THE OVERPOWERING TIDE...
OH, LORD AZAR... DEATH IS EVERYWHERE... MY DEFENSES CANNOT ...PROTECT ME...
I HURT, AZAR... THE PAIN... THE BLOOD, THE ANGUISH ...THEY HURT ME... THEY--
AGHHHH!
THE HORROR IS UNBEARABLE! AZAR HELP ME!
7

I...CANNOT FIGHT IT... ALL THOSE SOULS REACHING OUT TO ME...
I AM--AN EMPATH. I HEAL PAIN, BUT NOW THAT PAIN STAYS WITHIN ME... TOO MUCH TO SHUT OUT... TOO MUCH TO ABSORB...

OH, NO... NO! IT CLAWS INSIDE ME NOW...

...CLUTCHING AT ME LIKE SOME DAMNED DEMONIC HAND --REACHING FOR MY SOUL.
NO!!

IT MUST NOT REACH MY SOUL-SELF... MUST NOT RELEASE MY SOUL.

BUT...BUT I CANNOT CONTROL IT ANY LONGER... I CANNOT FIGHT IT...

IT HAS MY SOUL-SELF NOW... IT TEARS THROUGH ALL MY PROTECTIVE BARRIERS...
I CAN FEEL THE EVIL... FEEL THAT WHICH IS TRIGON... I FEEL IT SEETHING... SURGING... DESPERATELY THRASHING TO BREAK THROUGH ALL MY RESTRAINTS...

ARGHHHH!!
SOMETHING IS WRONG, EARTHMAN. DO YOU FEEL THE EVIL?
IT IS OVERPOWERING!
RAVEN? IT'S RAVEN. MY GOD!

PRAY TO YOUR GOD, WALLACE. PRAY THAT THE PART OF ME WHICH IS MY FATHER, TRIGON, DOES NOT BURST FREE!
PRAY, WALLACE... I NEED YOUR PRAYERS... I NEED YOUR PRAYERS!

BUT PRAYERS DO NOT A MIRACLE MAKE. THAT WHICH IS RAVEN'S SOUL IS FELT EVERYWHERE AT ONCE...
...DEEP BENEATH OKAARA'S ROCKY SURFACE...

...AS WELL AS HIGH ABOVE IN STAR-STUDDED SPACE...
...WHERE THE MAN-GOD AURON SENSES AN EVIL GREATER EVEN THAN THAT OF X'HAL. HE SHUDDERS. HE CAN DO NOTHING MORE.
8

I AM YOU, RAVEN. YOU ARE EVIL AS AM I.
NO! NO! I WILL NOT LET YOU BE RELEASED. I WILL NOT BECOME YOUR DAUGHTER OF DEATH!
EVEN IF I MUST PERISH TO STOP YOU, I WILL.

LEAVE ME... LEAVE ME! I... I MUST...

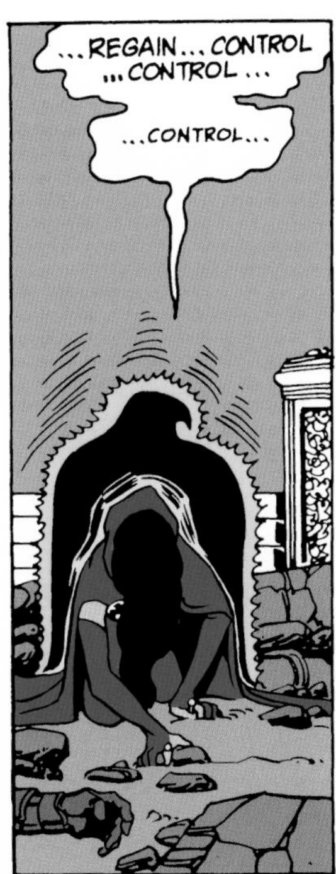
...REGAIN... CONTROL ...CONTROL...
...CONTROL...

RAVEN, ARE YOU ALL RIGHT? WHAT HAPPENED?
...WEAK... SO WEAK... SO DRAINED... I FEEL...
...SHATTERED.
HE IS GONE... TRIGON IS GONE. BUT--
--FOR HOW LONG...? HOW LONG?

WALLY WEST DASHES CLOSER TO THE WOMAN HE LOVES, AS RAVEN TREMBLES AT HIS TOUCH... THEN BURIES HER HEAD IN HIS ARMS.

MEANWHILE, THE WAR CONTINUES...

...BLOODY AND FILLED WITH DESTRUCTION.

THEN...
ENOUGH!
STOP! I COMMAND YOU TO STOP!
9

X'HAL? IS IT POSSIBLE?
THE FIGHTING WILL CEASE, X'HAL.
WHATEVER YOU COMMAND, WE WILL DO.

THE WAR IS OVER AND I WILL VOYAGE TO THE CITADEL.

LET NO MAN OR WOMAN ATTEMPT TO STOP ME.

NO! I WILL NOT ALLOW YOU TO LEAVE OKAARA.
HAVE YOU FORGOTTEN WHAT MADNESS REIGNED WHEN LAST YOU LEFT THIS PLANET?
HAVE YOU FORGOTTEN HOW MANY DIED TRYING TO SUBDUE YOU?
I WILL NOT BE STOPPED, MY SON.

SHOULD I REMAIN, OKAARA WOULD BE DESTROYED.
THAT MUST NOT BE ALLOWED.
NO! ONLY HERE CAN YOUR POWERS BE CONTAINED...

TRUST ME, AURON.
I DO WHAT MUST BE DONE.
AND I PRAY TO WHATEVER GODS A GOD SAYS PRAYERS TO--THAT I MAY CONTROL THE MADNESS THAT FESTERS WITHIN ME.

A SHIP AWAITS!
WE GO!
10

MEANWHILE...
THERE. THAT IS THE CITADEL HOMEWORLD.
IF WE ARE TO PASS THE FORTRESS RINGS, I WILL NEED TO GIVE THE SPECIAL CODE.
WELL THEN, FANGS, GIVE IT--OR YOU'LL BE BLOWING YOUR NOSE OUTTA THE SIDE OF YOUR HEAD.

AND WITHIN THE ARMORED RINGS...

BRANX WARSHIP ON GRID 13, LEVEL 27, PATTERN-B.
ENTRANCE CODE RECEIVED AND ACCEPTED.

THEY'RE LETTIN' US THROUGH.
I VALUE MY LIFE. I WILL DO AS YOU DEMAND.
BESIDES, I WISH TO SEE MY FAMILY AGAIN.

FURTHERMORE, I KNOW THAT EVEN IF YOU SAFELY LAND, YOU CANNOT HOPE TO SURVIVE.
YOU WILL MOST CERTAINLY BE DESTROYED.
WELL, HANDSOME, YOU PAYS YOUR MONEY AND YOU TAKES YOUR CHANCES.

GOTTA TELL YOU, ROBBIE, I DON'T LIKE THIS. I'M SCARED.
I DON'T FEEL IN CONTROL.
I DON'T BLAME YOU, VIC. IT'S ALL GOING A BIT TOO EASILY FOR ME.
JUST KEEP ON YOUR GUARD...

...AND HOPE WE CAN GET KORY OFF THIS LIVING ICEBOX BEFORE ANYONE GETS WISE TO US.
YOU REALLY THINK WE CAN?
NO, BUT SOMEONE'S GOT TO PLAY CHEERLEADER.
11

THOUGH BITTER COLD, THE OXYGEN LEVEL ON THE CITADEL WORLD IS MINIMALLY ACCEPTABLE. BREATHING IS DIFFICULT, BUT THE TITANS PLOD ONWARD...
PRISONERS TO SEE LORD DAMYN.
THEN MOVE ALONG, GORDANIAN.
YIPPEE. HE BOUGHT IT.

IF YOU WISH TO GET INSIDE, YOU WILL HAVE TO LISTEN TO MY EVERY WORD.
SURE THING, SWEET-LIPS. BUT IF YOU SCREW UP EVEN A LITTLE BIT--

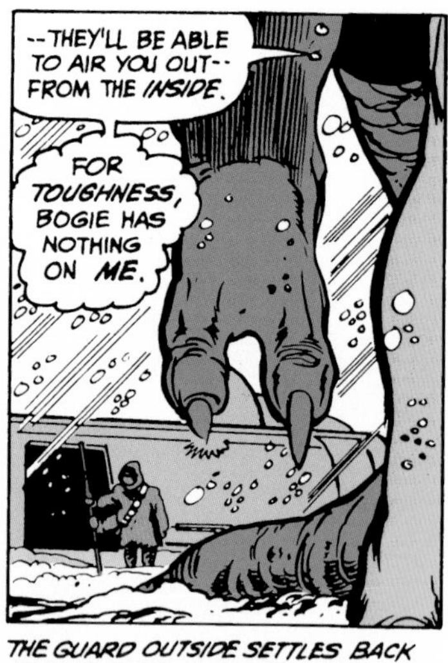
--THEY'LL BE ABLE TO AIR YOU OUT-- FROM THE INSIDE.
FOR TOUGHNESS, BOGIE HAS NOTHING ON ME.
THE GUARD OUTSIDE SETTLES BACK NOW THAT THE GORDANIAN AND HIS PRISONERS HAVE PASSED ON THROUGH.

HE WAITS FOR HIS CURRENT TOUR TO END.
THE COLD BOTHERS HIM, AND HE SHIVERS BENEATH HIS FUR DRESSINGS.

HE'D MUCH RATHER BE AT HOME, WITH HIS MATE AND YOUNG ONES, RESTING BEFORE A FIRE.

BUT HE HAS TWO MORE YEARS OF SERVICE BEFORE HIS OBLIGATIONS TO THE CITADEL ARE OVER.
THEN, HE HEARS A NOISE. BE-GRUDGINGLY, HE INVESTIGATES...
...WISHING HE WERE BACK ON HIS TROPICAL WORLD. WELL, HE THINKS, HE'LL BE GIVEN A LEAVE SOON.

SADLY, HE WON'T BE ABLE TO TAKE IT... NOT EVER AGAIN.
CHONK!

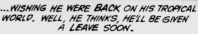

MEANWHILE...
HALT AND IDENTIFY!
THIS IS IT. NOW LISTEN TO ME.
PILOT ARMIAL BORNA-F'EN, THIRD-LEVEL OFFICER.
ARE THESE YOUR PRISONERS?
NO! THESE ARE OKAARAN SPIES. CAPTURE THEM!
NUTS! SOMEHOW I KNEW THIS WAS GONNA HAPPEN.
12

ONE SIDE, BAT-BOY, THIS IS MY KINDA FIGHT.
HAD MY FINGER-LASER IN PLACE EVEN BEFORE WE LANDED.
ZWIPP!

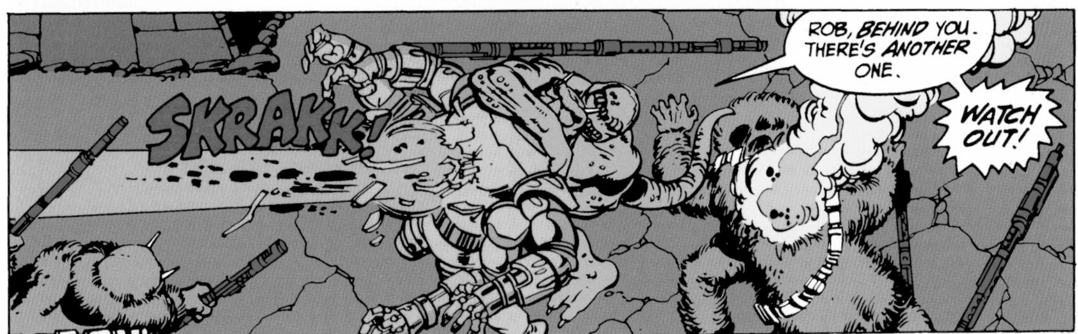
SKRAKK!
ROB, BEHIND YOU. THERE'S ANOTHER ONE.
WATCH OUT!

ALREADY SAW IT, GAR...
... BUT THANKS--
--ANYWAY.
SKREEEK!

WELL, NOW WHAT?
THE REST SHOULD BE EASY. WE GOT THROUGH, DIDN'T WE?
SOMEHOW, PAL, I THINK IT'S GONNA GET WORSE BEFORE IT GETS BETTER!
THAT'S ENCOURAGING. MAKES ME REALLY WANNA MOVE ON.

LOOK, WE GOTTA KNOW WHERE WE'RE GOING, RIGHT? SO LET ME DO A LITTLE SCOUTING.
IT'S WHAT I DO BEST.
MAN, REALLY THOUGHT WE HAD IT MADE. THOUGHT MY TOUGH-GUY ACT HAD THAT ALIEN QUIVERING IN HIS BOOTIES.
I KEEP BLOWING IT, DON'T I?
BLAST!
13

DEEP BENEATH THE FORTRESS THE TITANS HAVE JUST ENTERED...
WELL, PSION, HAVE YOU BROKEN THROUGH MY SISTER'S *RESISTANCE?* OR DOES SHE CONTINUE TO *RESIST* YOUR TORTURES?
SHE IS RATHER AN *AMAZING* SPECIMEN, KOMAND'R.
PRINCESS KOMAND'R, PSION. DO NOT FORGET MY *TITLE*.
WHATEVER. THE TEMPERATURE WITHIN MY CHAMBER IS MORE THAN *200°*.
SHE SHOULD HAVE HAD HER FLESH *BURNED AWAY* BY NOW.
14
OOOOH, KORIAND'R AM REAL *TOUGH*, EH? MAYBE TOO *TOO* TOUGH. MAYBE WE SHOULD CUT HER OPEN AND SEE *WHY*, EH?
UHHH... OH, NO, LORD DAMYN. YOU GAVE HER TO ME FOR MY *PLEASURE*, REMEMBER?
BEFORE SHE DIES, I WANT TO SEE MY SISTER *BEG*.
SIBLING RIVALRY? PASSIONS CONTROL YOU, KOMAND'R. YOU SHOULD BE MORE LIKE US *PSIONS*.
WE LIVE ONLY TO SATISFY OUR SCIENTIFIC *CURIOSITY*. EMOTIONS ARE *MEANINGLESS*.
THEN YOU ARE THE *LOSER*, PSION.
YOU'LL NEVER KNOW THE ECSTATIC PLEASURE OF TRULY HUMILIATING AND *DESTROYING* YOUR FOE.

YOU WON'T GET THE *CHANCE* TO DESTROY HER, TAMARANIAN.

OOOH, LOOK! IT A *GIRL*. OR MAYBE IT A *SNAKE*. ONE OR THE OTHER, *ME AM SURE*.

I *RECOGNIZE* HER, LORD DAMYN.

SHE'S ONE OF PRIMUS' *REBELS* -- THE ONE THEY CALL *DEMONIA*.

I *TRAVEL* WITH THOSE FOOLS, BUT I AM NOT *ONE* OF THEM!

LORD DAMYN, I PLEDGE MY ALLEGIANCE TO *THE CITADEL*.

OH, SHE *GOOD* ONE, SHE TERRIFIED BY ME BIGNESS AND ME CAN SURELY THREATEN HER. SHE *OKAY*. HEY, WANT *KISS*, HUH?

LORD DAMYN, SHE COULD BE A *SPY*. DON'T--

A *SPY?* YES, TAMARANIAN, BUT I *COULD* BE A SPY... FOR *YOU*.

THE OMEGA MEN CANNOT HOPE TO *WIN* THEIR WAR AGAINST YOU, AND DEMONIA DOES NOT SIDE WITH *LOSERS*.

FOR A PRICE, I WILL *WORK* FOR YOU.

OKAY, LADY-SNAKE, WHAT DO YOU *WANT* FROM ME? AND REMEMBER, ME *NOT* VERY GENEROUS. YOU ASK *TOO MUCH*, ME BASH IN YOUR *BRAINS*.

I WANT MY OWN *WORLD*, LORD DAMYN... TO RULE, IN *YOUR NAME*, OF COURSE.

AND SPEAKING OF THOSE SELFSAME TITANS...
JUST MORE TUNNELS AHEAD, GUYS. TUNNELS AND A FEW GUARDS.
WE NEED A ROAD MAP.
WHERE'S THE AAA WHEN YOU REALLY WANT 'EM?

I'D SUGGEST ASKING THOSE GUARDS DOWN THERE, BUT I DON'T THINK THEY'LL BE VERY CO-OPERATIVE.

OKAY, LET ME THINK...
...NEED ANOTHER PLAN IF WE'RE TO GET ANYWHERE.

PAL, TROUBLE WITH YOU IS YOU THINK TOO MUCH.
LEAVE THINGS UP TO ME.

WAIT, VIC... WE HAVE TO WORK THIS OUT THE RIGHT WAY.
BAT-BOY, YOU WORRY TOO MUCH ABOUT FINESSE.

DON'T OWE RON MUCH, BUT I DID LEARN ONE THING WHILE RUNNIN' WITH HIS GANG--

--SOMETIMES YOU GOTTA LET YOUR FIST DO THE TALKIN'.

BTAMM!

NOW THEN, SHORT-PANTS-- YOU WANT INFO--
--YOU GOT IT!
16

OKAARA: A WORLD OF TUNNELS, CATACOMBS AND CAVERNS...
A WORLD ON WHICH THE REMAINING TITANS WAIT...
...I'M STILL WORRIED ABOUT YOU, RAVEN.

SO AM I, WALLACE. FOR A MOMENT I TRULY BELIEVED THE PART OF ME WHICH IS TRIGON WOULD BE RELEASED.
I AM AN EMPATH. I THRIVE ON THE EMOTIONS OF OTHERS...
...EMOTIONS WHICH ARE FOREVER DENIED ME--

--BUT I...I COULD NOT ASSIMILATE ALL THOSE EMOTIONS. THEY ATTACKED ME, HURT ME, MADE ME SO WEAK I WAS AFRAID MY DARK SIDE WOULD COME BURSTING THROUGH.
I JUST WANT YOU TO UNDERSTAND, RAVEN, THAT YOU DON'T HAVE TO FIGHT THIS YOURSELF. I'M HERE...
...I ALWAYS WILL BE.

I STILL LOVE YOU, RAVEN, PERHAPS MORE NOW THAT I KNOW WHAT YOU ARE, AND THE HORRORS YOU HAVE TO LIVE WITH.*
*AS REVEALED IN THE TITANS MINI-SERIES #2. --Len.

I'M SORRY, PRIMUS, BUT I CAN'T UNDERSTAND YOU.
YOU WORSHIP X'HAL, YET SHE WOULD DESTROY YOU.

BECAUSE OF X'HAL, WE ALL LIVE. WHAT HAPPENED TO HER WAS BECAUSE SHE SAVED US. WE CANNOT DISOBEY HER.
IT STILL MAKES NO SENSE.
WE'RE HERE BECAUSE ONE OF OUR FRIENDS WAS BROUGHT TO THIS STAR-SYSTEM.

YOU PROMISED YOU'D HELP US FIND HER.
WE NEED YOUR HELP, PRIMUS, BUT EVEN IF YOU DON'T GIVE IT TO US WE HAVE TO FIND KORY.

WHAT'S IT GOING TO BE?

ARE YOU GOING TO HONOR YOUR PROMISE?
17

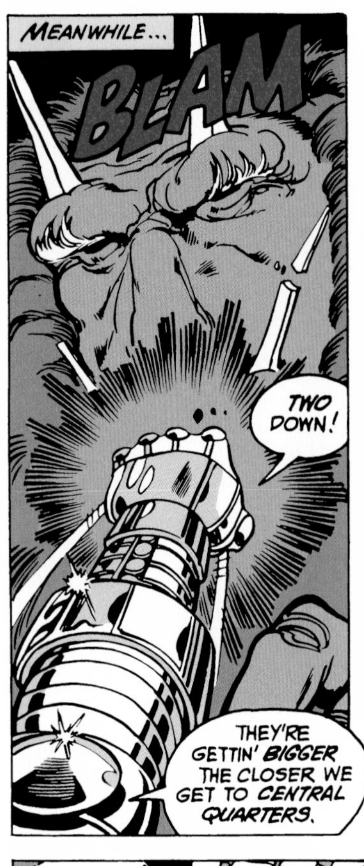
MEANWHILE...
BLAM
TWO DOWN!
THEY'RE GETTIN' BIGGER THE CLOSER WE GET TO CENTRAL QUARTERS.

NOT BAD, TINHEAD. I FORGET SOMETIMES YOU'VE GOT THE STRENGTH OF TEN.
YEAH, THAT'S 'CAUSE MY HEART IS PURE.
AN' IF YOU SAY PURE WHAT-- I'LL WRAP YOU UP INTO A LITTLE GREEN FUR-BALL.

C'MON, I SEE SOMETHING I DEFINITELY DON'T LIKE.
THERE'S NO TIME TO WASTE ON YOUR STUPID JOKES.
YOU'RE GETTIN' TENSE, ROBBIE.
YEAH? SO WHAT?
WORRIED ABOUT KORY?
OF COURSE. SHE'S A GOOD FRIEND.
THAT'S ALL?
VIC, MIND YOUR OWN BUSINESS.

LOOK, IT'S X'HAL, AND SOMEONE WHO LOOKS LIKE KORY.
YOU DID GOOD, KOMAND'R, REAL GOOD. YOU GOT X'HAL.
AND ME NEVER COULD DO THAT.
SO TELL ME, NOW ME GOT GODDESS, WHAT ME GONNA DO WITH HER?
THAT, LORD DAMYN, IS SIMPLE. WE HOLD HER FOR BLACKMAIL PURPOSES.
AS LONG AS X'HAL IS HELD IN THAT STASIS FIELD YOUR PSION TRAITOR CREATED, SHE IS SAFE AND POWERLESS.
BUT, IF THE REBELS FAIL TO LAY DOWN THEIR WEAPONS AGAINST YOU, IF THEY REFUSE TO ACKNOWLEDGE YOU AS THEIR ONLY LEADER--
18

--THEN WE SIMPLY RELEASE THEIR GODDESS.
SHE WILL BE UNABLE TO STOP HERSELF EVEN AS SHE DESTROYS THOSE WHO WORSHIP HER.
EITHER WAY, WE WIN.
CRUSH THE REBELS!
DESTROY THE REBELS!
KILL THE REBELS!
"CRUSH! DESTROY! KILL!" THAT AM MUSIC TO ME EARS, SURE IS.
WE LIKE PLAN, KOMAND'R. THEN ME BE RULER OF EVERYTHING. NOT BAD, EH?

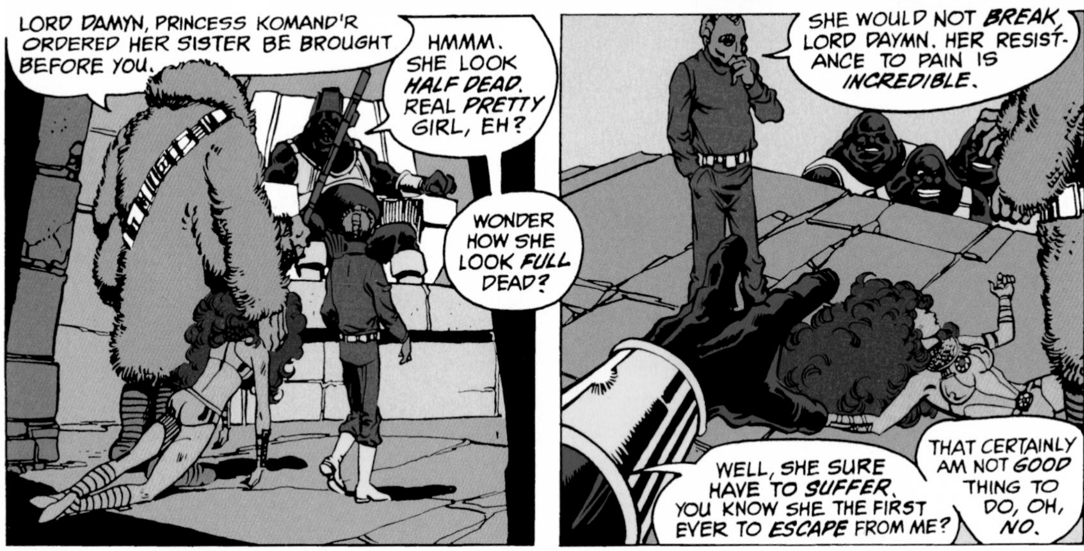
LORD DAMYN, PRINCESS KOMAND'R ORDERED HER SISTER BE BROUGHT BEFORE YOU.
HMMM. SHE LOOK HALF DEAD. REAL PRETTY GIRL, EH?
WONDER HOW SHE LOOK FULL DEAD?
SHE WOULD NOT BREAK, LORD DAYMN. HER RESISTANCE TO PAIN IS INCREDIBLE.
WELL, SHE SURE HAVE TO SUFFER. YOU KNOW SHE THE FIRST EVER TO ESCAPE FROM ME?
THAT CERTAINLY AM NOT GOOD THING TO DO, OH, NO.

VIC, GAR-- IT'S KORY!
SHE LOOKS DEAD.

WHAT HAVE THEY DONE TO HER?

VIC, YOU SAID BEFORE I PLAN TOO MUCH. WELL, I'M NOT DOING THAT NOW.
I WANT THOSE KILLERS!
19

AND I'M GOING TO GET THEM!
SKRAKK
WHEN DICK GRAYSON WAS YOUNG, HE WAS TAUGHT BY THE BATMAN ALL THE ARTS OF COMBAT--
--TODAY THOSE GRUELING LESSONS PROVE WELL-LEARNED.

INCREDIBLY AGILE, THE TEEN WONDER DARTS THROUGH A MAZE OF DEADLY LASERS. NOT ONE GRAZES HIM...

YET GORDANIAN SLAVER AND BRANX WARRIOR ARE NOT QUITE SO LUCKY.
ONE BY ONE, THEY FALL.

NOPE, YOU'RE NOT GETTING AWAY, PAL.
WHAT? YOU'RE NOT A GORDANIAN?
HEY, YOU'RE REAL QUICK, YOU KNOW THAT?

I GOT THEIR BLASTER.
KORY'S BREATHING. SHE'S STILL ALIVE.
WE'VE GOT TO GET HER OUTTA HERE.

NO, EARTHLING, YOU WILL NOT REMOVE MY SISTER...
...UNLESS YOU WISH ME TO UNLEASH X'HAL ON AN UNSUSPECTING GALAXY.

SORRY, SISTER, BUT YOU DON'T HOLD THE UPPER HAND.
GUESS WHAT'S UGLY AND GOT REAL PROBLEMS?
20

WE GO FREE OR SLUG-FACE HERE GETS A SECOND NOSE.
NO, NO. ME LIKE ONE NOSE LIKE ME ALWAYS HAD.
KOMAND'R, YOU SAVE ME, RIGHT? ME GIVE YOU TWO PLANETS, OKAY?

WELL, LADY, WHAT'S THE WORD?
DOES GRUESOME HERE BUY THE FARM?

AHHH. IT SEEMS THAT EVERYTHING IS UP TO ME, DOESN'T IT?
WE HAVE A RATHER INTERESTING DILEMMA.
NOW, WHAT SHOULD I DO?

KORY? CAN YOU HEAR ME, KORY?
D...DICK...?
TH-THEN I'M DEAD...? I... SAW YOU DIE IN SPACE...

RAVEN SAVED US. I'M ALIVE. WE ALL ARE.
OH, X'HAL ...X'HAL...
YOU'LL BE ALL RIGHT, HONEY... YOU'LL BE ALL RIGHT.

HEY, IN CASE YOU DIDN'T NOTICE, WHILE YOU'RE PLAYING 'ROMEO AND JULIET', WE GOT REAL PROBLEMS.

UGLY, YOUR FRIEND SEEMS RELUCTANT. PERHAPS YOU CAN CONVINCE HER.
HEY, COME ON, KOMAND'R, BE GOOD, EH? ME LIKE YOU, REALLY.
SAY, ME MAKE YOU GENERAL. NOT BAD, EH?

YOU'LL MAKE ME A GENERAL? DAMYN, YOU ARE TRULY A DOLT.
WHY TAKE THE TWIG WHEN YOU CAN OWN THE WHOLE TREE?

NO!!
21

UH, ROBBIE, GET KORY AND LET'S SPLIT.
I THINK IT'S ALL GONNA HIT THE FAN NOW.
AND NOW, MY FOOLISH FRIENDS, I DO BELIEVE YOUR BLUFF HAS BEEN CALLED.
AND THOUGH I THANK YOU FOR GIVING ME THE CHANCE TO RID OUR GALAXY OF THAT STUPID BUFFOON--
--MY GRATITUDE SHALL NOT LESSEN MY DESIRE TO SEE YOU ALL DIE.
BUT FIRST-- THE CITADEL HAS A NEW RULER!
KOMAND'R THE FIRST! LORD OF LORDS!
RULER OF ALL I SURVEY!
22

LOOK, YOU GOT THE POWER YOU WANT, YOU DON'T NEED KORIAND'R.
LET US TAKE HER AND GO BACK TO EARTH.
LET YOU GO? EARTHLING, IS THAT YOUR SENSE OF HUMOR?
CAREFUL. SHE'S CRAZY.

KORY ISN'T A THREAT ANY LONGER. YOU'VE GOT EVERYTHING YOU'VE EVER WANTED.
YOU'VE GOT A GALAXY TO RULE. YOU'VE GOT ALL THE POWER YOU NEED.
YOU DON'T HAVE TO WORRY ABOUT YOUR SISTER ANY LONGER.

WORRY ABOUT DEAR, SWEET KORIAND'R? I NEVER HAVE.
I'VE ALWAYS BEEN HER BETTER, DESPITE WHAT OUR DEAR PARENTS MAY HAVE THOUGHT.

NOW, I COULD BE BENEFICENT AND LET YOU ALL GO FREE, BUT I WOULD BE A FOOL TO DO THAT.
THE WARLORDS OF OKAARA ALWAYS SAID TO DESTROY YOUR ENEMIES LEST THEY RISE AGAIN TO DESTROY YOU.
23

AND SO I SHALL...

...BUT FIRST SHE SHALL LIVE LONG ENOUGH TO SEE ME KILL HER PARENTS AND DESTROY HER PRECIOUS PLANET, TAMARAN.

NO! I WON'T LET YOU, KOMAND'R.
I WON'T LET YOU!

EVEN IF I HAVE TO KILL YOU TO STOP YOU!

THIS IS JUST THE *BEGINNING!* JUST WAIT UNTIL YOU SEE OUR HEART STUNNING CLIMAX IN--

THE NEW TEEN TITANS ANNUAL #1! *DOUBLE-SIZED DYNAMITE FROM THE NEW DC!*

NEXT ISSUE: BE HERE FOR MORE THRILLS AS ONLY DC CAN GIVE 'EM!

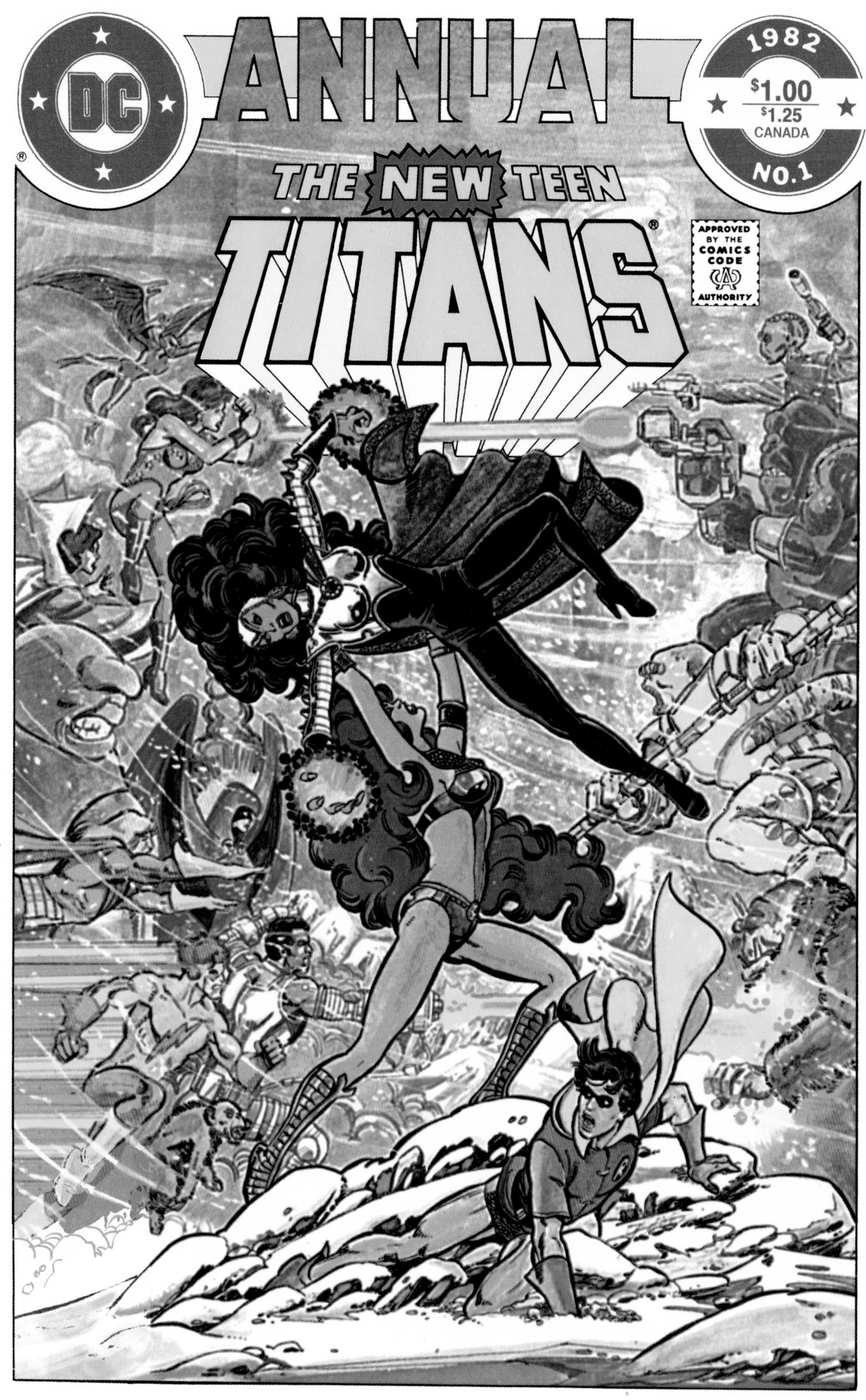
DC
ANNUAL
1982
$1.00
$1.25
CANADA
NO.1
THE NEW TEEN
TITANS
APPROVED
BY THE
COMICS
CODE
AUTHORITY

THEY ARE THE BEST THERE IS: THE CHANGELING, SHAPE-SHIFTER SUPREME; CYBORG, HALF MAN/HALF ROBOT; KID FLASH, SUPER-SPEEDSTER; RAVEN, MISTRESS OF MAGIC; ROBIN, THE TEEN WONDER; STARFIRE, ALIEN POWERHOUSE; AND WONDER GIRL, THE AMAZING AMAZON! TOGETHER THEY ARE...
THE NEW TEEN TITANS
MARV WOLFMAN + GEORGE PÉREZ WRITER -- CO-PLOTTERS -- ARTIST / ROMEO TANGHAL EMBELLISHER / BEN ODA - LETTERER CARL GAFFORD - COLORIST / LEN WEIN EDITOR
FINAL CONFLICT!
YOU HAVE HUMILIATED ME. YOU HAVE TORTURED ME. YOU HAVE DONE EVERYTHING IN YOUR POWER TO DESTROY ME.
BUT YOU FAILED.
NOW, KOMAND'R, NOW I AM GOING TO KILL YOU!!

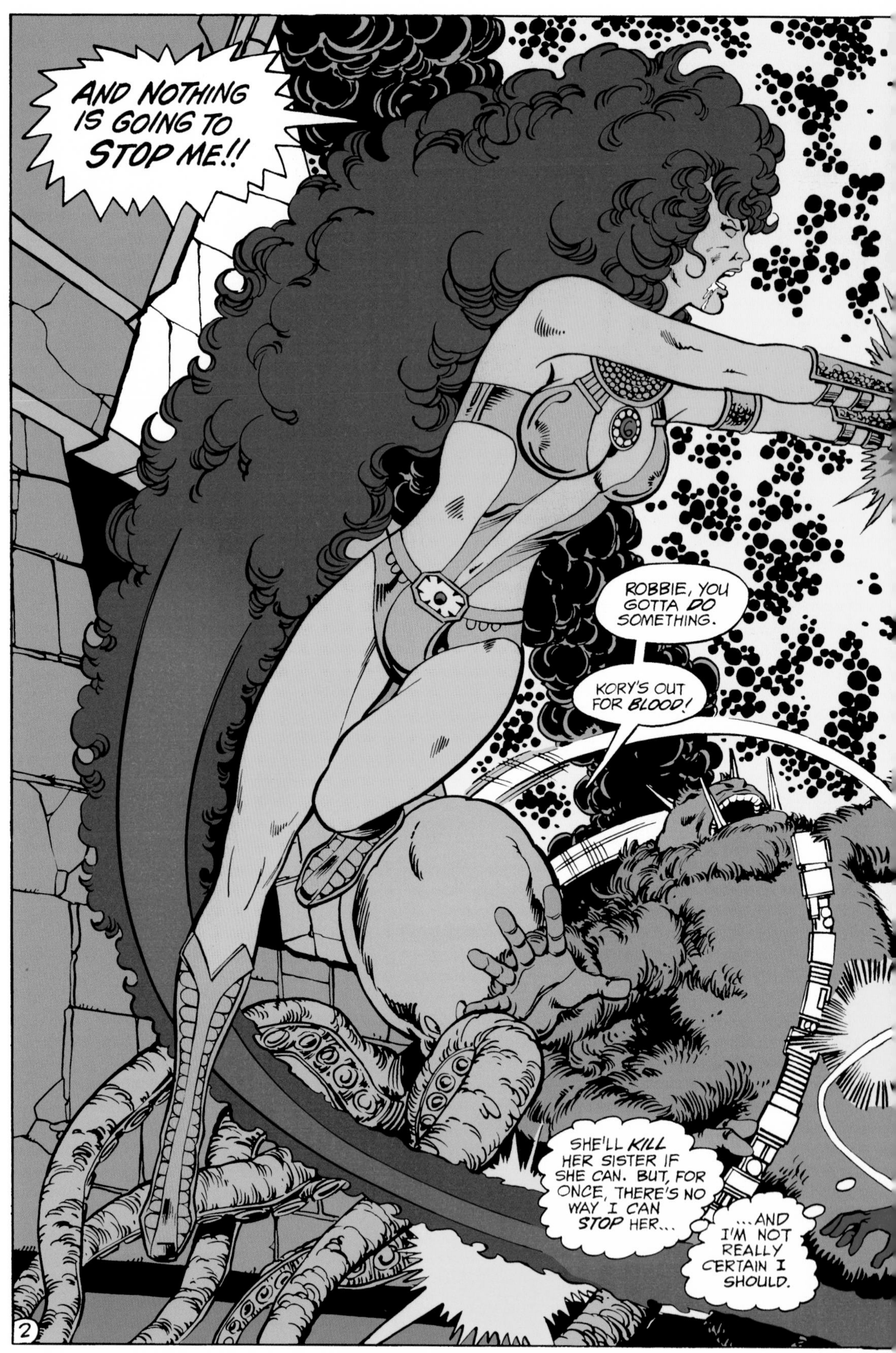
AND NOTHING IS GOING TO STOP ME!!
ROBBIE, YOU GOTTA DO SOMETHING.
KORY'S OUT FOR BLOOD!
SHE'LL KILL HER SISTER IF SHE CAN. BUT, FOR ONCE, THERE'S NO WAY I CAN STOP HER...
...AND I'M NOT REALLY CERTAIN I SHOULD.
2

SKREEEEEEEEEEEEEEEEEEEEEEEE
THIS PASSED BEING A FIGHT LONG AGO. WE'RE IN THE MIDDLE OF A FULL-SCALE WAR--
--AND IN WARS, PEOPLE GET HURT.
NO. KORY'S ON HER OWN. WE ALL ARE, AND MAY GOD FORGIVE US FOR DOING WHAT MUST BE DONE!
HELL, DON'T KNOW IF THIS IS REAL OR A DREAM OR A NIGHTMARE...
...BUT IF I DON'T KEEP FIGHTIN', I'LL NEVER WAKE UP TO FIND OUT.
BEEN IN FIGHTS BEFORE, BUT NEVER NOTHIN' LIKE THIS.
THESE THINGS AREN'T EVEN HUMAN, AND I'M FIGHTIN' ON WORLDS NOT EVEN MY DAD DREAMED EXISTED.
3

GUYS, MEBBE I GOT EIGHT ARMS, BUT I REALLY NEED A COUPLE MORE.
PLEASE, GUYS? GIVE YOUR OLD BUDDY CHANGELING SOME HELP!

COME ON, KOMAND'R... YOU'VE BEEN ATTACKING ME FOR DAYS.
YOU'VE BEEN SWEARING THAT YOU'RE SO MUCH BETTER THAN I AM.
SKREEEEE
LET'S SEE YOU PROVE IT, SISTER.

GOD, MY MUSCLES ACHE, BUT I CAN'T STOP... CAN'T EVEN REST.
GOT TO DO WHAT THE BATMAN ALWAYS TOLD ME... IGNORE THE PAIN, FORGET THE INJURIES... JUST KEEP MOVING AHEAD...
WHUMP!
...ALWAYS PUSH ON AND ON AND ON!

I DON'T BELIEVE IT. IT LOOKSSS LIKE THEY MIGHT ACTUALLY FREE THAT DAMN GODDESSSS, X'HAL.
BUT WHERE WOULD THAT LEAVE ME?
THE OMEGA MEN HATE ME. EVEN HARPISSS, MY SSSISTER, WOULD DEMAND MY DEATH...

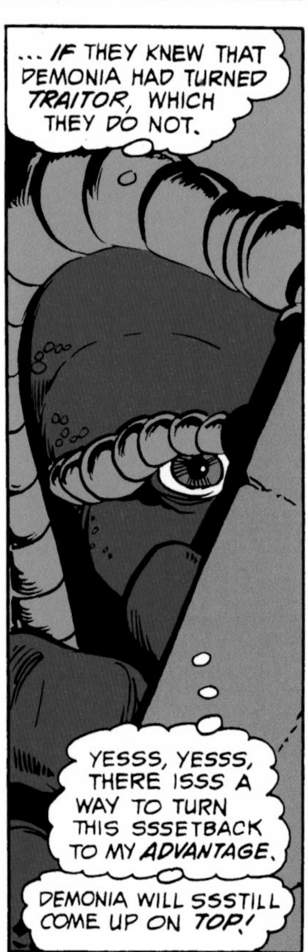
...IF THEY KNEW THAT DEMONIA HAD TURNED TRAITOR, WHICH THEY DO NOT.
YESSS, YESSS, THERE ISSS A WAY TO TURN THIS SSSETBACK TO MY ADVANTAGE.
DEMONIA WILL SSSTILL COME UP ON TOP!

COMIN' AT ME FROM ALL SIDES. NO WAY TO TURN IF I WAS TRYIN' TO GET AWAY -- BUT I'M NOT.
THESE KILLERS DON'T KNOW HOW MUCH STRENGTH MY DAD BUILT INTO MY CYBORG ARMOR.
4

SKRASSHHH!
GOT ALMOST TOO MUCH STRENGTH, AND SOMETIMES THAT SCARES THE HELL OUTTA ME.
COULD CRUSH A SKULL IN MY HANDS WITHOUT EVEN HALF TRYIN'. CRUSH IT JUST AS EASILY AS I CAN BRING DOWN THIS BLASTED WALL!
SO NOW THIS ALIEN BITES IT. OKAY, HE ASKED FOR IT.
BUT WHAT HAPPENS BACK ON EARTH?
WHAT HAPPENS IF I SCREW UP AT HOME?

WE'RE DEFINITELY OUTNUMBERED AND CERTAINLY OUTPOWERED.
EVEN VIC'S STRENGTH ISN'T ENOUGH TO TURN THE TIDE.
BUT THESE GAS GRENADES MIGHT BUY ME A FEW PRECIOUS SECONDS -- THERE!

GOT THIS WARRIOR'S BLASTING ROD!
ONE BLASTER DOESN'T EVEN UP THE SIDES, BUT IT SHOULD HELP...
... I HOPE.

I SHOULD HAVE KNOWN BETTER THAN TO TRUST THOSE CITADEL INFERIORS TO SUBDUE ANY REBELLION.
HOW THEY HAVE MANAGED TO CONTROL THIS GALAXY IS BEYOND ME. BUT--
GENERAL ALERT! WE ARE UNDER ATTACK!

ASSISTANCE IS DEMANDED AT ONCE! ALL PERSONNEL MOVE TO BATTLE STATIONS!
HURRY, GORDANIAN. WE HAVE OUR ORDERS.

ORDERS? THAT CAME FROM THE PSION TRAITOR. I DO NOT LISTEN TO HIS KIND.
HE HAS OFFICIAL SANCTION. I WILL OBEY HIS WORD.
ONLY YOU BRANX WARRIORS MINDLESSLY FOLLOW ORDERS. GORDANIAN SLAVERS ARE TRAINED TO THINK.
5

SHE FIGHTS LIKE A DAMNED *HELLION*, NEVER GIVING ME A MOMENT TO *BREATHE*, LET ALONE RECOUP MY *STRENGTH*.

I'VE SPENT FAR TOO MUCH TIME HONING MY *STARBOLT POWERS* AND NOT ENOUGH ON MY *PHYSICAL* STRENGTH.

SPRAKABAM!

I NEED *TIME*, EVEN A FEW MOMENTS... AND I KNOW HOW TO *GAIN* THOSE PRECIOUS SECONDS.

MY FOOLISH SISTER IS A *COMPASSIONATE* DOLT. I CAN APPEAL TO HER *FAMILY INSTINCTS*...

...CONFUSE HER, TOY WITH HER, AND WHEN HER DEFENSES ARE DOWN, *ATTACK HER*!
I'LL *DESTROY* THAT IGNORANT DOG BEFORE SHE KNOWS WHAT *HAPPENED*.
LISTEN TO ME, SISTER, LET US *TALK*!

NO! I AM *THROUGH* TALKING.
TIME AFTER TIME YOU TAUNTED ME AS TO HOW MY *COMPASSION* WAS MY *UNDOING*.
WELL, KOMAND'R, PERHAPS YOU HAVE FINALLY *SUCCEEDED* IN TEACHING ME.

THE TIME FOR TALK IS LONG *OVER*. I'LL ONLY BE SATISFIED WITH YOUR *DEATH*!
THAT AND *NOTHING LESS*!
6

SHE MEANS IT. SHE'LL KEEP FIGHTING UNTIL SHE BREAKS THROUGH MY DEFENSES.
NO! I CANNOT LET THAT HAPPEN. ALL MY LIFE KORIAND'R WAS HAILED AS THE GREATEST, AS THE IDEAL.
SHE RECEIVED ACCESS TO THE THRONE WHEN THAT SHOULD HAVE BEEN GIVEN TO ME.
SKRAAKK

BUT NOW, AT LAST, I WILL PROVE WHO IS THE TRUE PRINCESS OF TAMARAN!
WHAT IS WRONG WITH YOU, KOMAND'R? I THOUGHT YOU WERE MORE POWERFUL THAN THIS?
I THOUGHT A SINGLE BLAST COULD DISINTEGRATE ME.

HAVE YOU GOTTEN SOFT IN YOUR COMPLACENCY?
SKREEEEEEEEEEEEE
WELL, I HAVEN'T, SISTER. I'VE BEEN TRAINING.

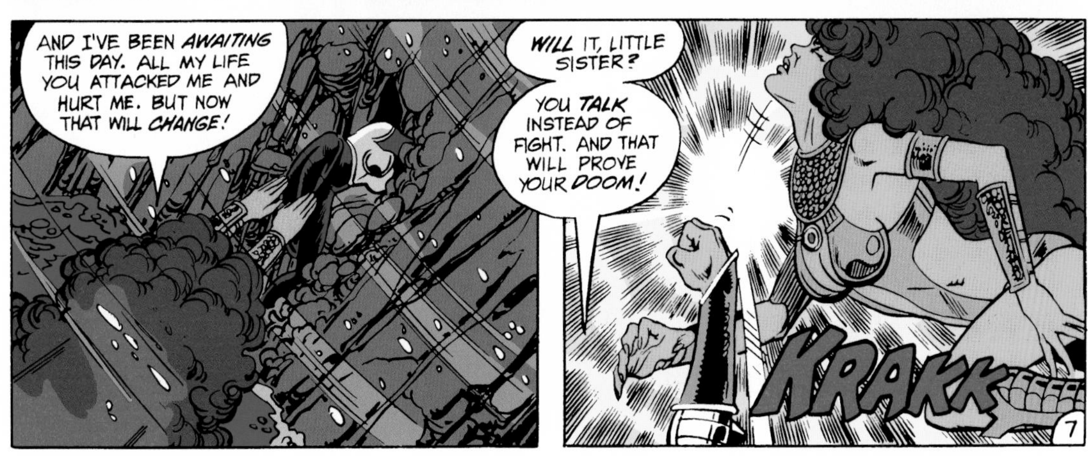
AND I'VE BEEN AWAITING THIS DAY. ALL MY LIFE YOU ATTACKED ME AND HURT ME. BUT NOW THAT WILL CHANGE!
WILL IT, LITTLE SISTER?
YOU TALK INSTEAD OF FIGHT. AND THAT WILL PROVE YOUR DOOM!
KRAKK
7

HER BODY ACHING WITH PAIN, DEEP CUTS SCARRING HER GOLDEN FLESH, PRINCESS KORIAND'R FALLS. DESPERATELY, SHE TRIES TO RISE, BUT HER DAMAGED LEGS STIFFEN. SHE STARES UPWARD BUT ALL SHE SEES IS KOMAND'R'S LEERING FACE. THEN, SUDDENLY, SHE FEELS INTENSE HEAT AS A CRIMSON STARBOLT SEEMINGLY EXPLODES WITHIN HER.

MEANWHILE, THE FIRST BATTALION OF BRANX WARRIORS ARRIVES, ANXIOUS FOR THE BATTLE TO COME.
THEY RECEIVE THEIR NOURISHMENT AND STRENGTH FROM THE DEATH OF OTHERS. THEY ARE THE IDEAL WARRIORS.

THEY LIVE ONLY TO KILL!
DOESN'T MATTER HOW HARD I TRY, THEY KEEP COMING-- AND I'M ALREADY SO TERRIBLY TIRED.
HAVEN'T SLEPT FOR DAYS, NOT SINCE KORIAND'R WAS KIDNAPPED.
SPRAKK!

DIDN'T KNOW HOW MUCH SHE MEANT TO ME.
FIGHTING ONLY FROM REFLEX NOW, SWINGING, DON'T EVEN CARE WHAT I DO...
...JUST KEEP HITTING... JUST KEEP--
ARGHHH!
SPADADAMMMM!

DICK? MY GOD, HE'S BEEN HIT!
HOLD ON, BUDDY--I'M COMING!

POWERFUL HYDRAULICS CARRY CYBORG ACROSS THE DISTANCE IN MERE SECONDS, BUT...

SPADAMM!
8

HELL! FELT THAT ALL THE WAY THROUGH MY ARMOR!
PTAK!
AND NOW IT HURTS TRYING TO LIFT MY ARM. HURTS TRYING TO THROW A PUNCH.
WHOLE SYSTEM'S SHUTTING OFF WHILE IT GOES INTO AUTO-MATIC REPAIR.

BUT I CAN'T GO UNDER... CAN'T LET THE OTHERS DOWN...
DAMN IT, I'M A TITAN! AND IF THAT MEANS ANYTHIN', THEN I GOTTA KEEP FIGHTIN'!
GOTTA KEEP GOING!
POOM!

ROBBIE'S DOWN. VIC'S BEEN HIT. THAT MEANS IT'S UP TO ME!
NO TIME FOR ANY SELF-PITY, NO TIME TO WONDER IF I CAN DO IT. I'VE GOT NO CHOICE NOW.
THEY'RE ALL RELYING ON ME!
KRASH!

KILL HIM! KILL THE EARTHLING!
OH, NO... CAN'T RUN! TOO LATE!

SKRAAK!

HE'S GONE, TOTALLY DISINTEGRATED!
9

GETTIN' IT ON ALL SIDES NOW...
...AND THE PAIN'S UNBEARABLE!
NO WAY OUT, THIS IS IT!
SPOOM!
ONLY THIS IS THE SCUM THAT KILLED GAR.
BEFORE I FALL, HE'S GONNA--
ARGHHHH!
SKKRROOOOOOMM!
THE SSSTUPID EARTHLING FAILED, BUT THAT SSSTILL DOESN'T CHANGE THINGSSS FOR ME.
THE PSION WOULD HAVE ME KILLED. HE'D TRUST ME LESSS THAN I WOULD HIM.
UNLESSS I ACT TO SSSAVE MYSELF FIRST.
AND THERE ISSS A WAY... THERE MOST CERTAINLY ISSS.
YOU ARE THE REMAINING HEADS OF THE CITADEL COUNCIL. LISTEN TO ME.
PLACE ME IN CHARGE OF THIS BATTLE AND I WILL NOT ONLY END THIS FRUITLESS WAR--
--BUT ASSURE CITADEL VICTORY FOREVER!
MEANWHILE...
SPLOOOSHH!
10

KORIAND'R'S BARELY CONSCIOUS. THEN... I'VE WON!
I'M AS SUPERIOR AS I ALWAYS SAID I WAS--
WHAT? SHE STIRS? THEN I'D BEST MOVE QUICKLY, OR--

BUT, AS KOMAND'R STEPS FORWARD, KORIAND'R RISES, ALTHOUGH WITH GREAT UNCERTAINTY.

SHE CAN BARELY FOCUS HER EYES, YET SHE KNOWS WHAT MUST BE DONE...

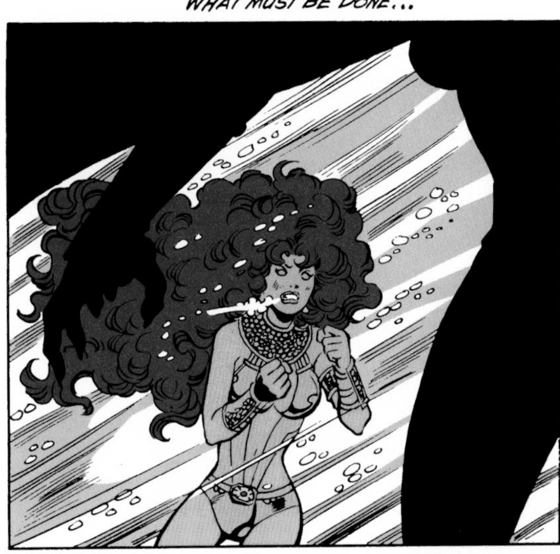

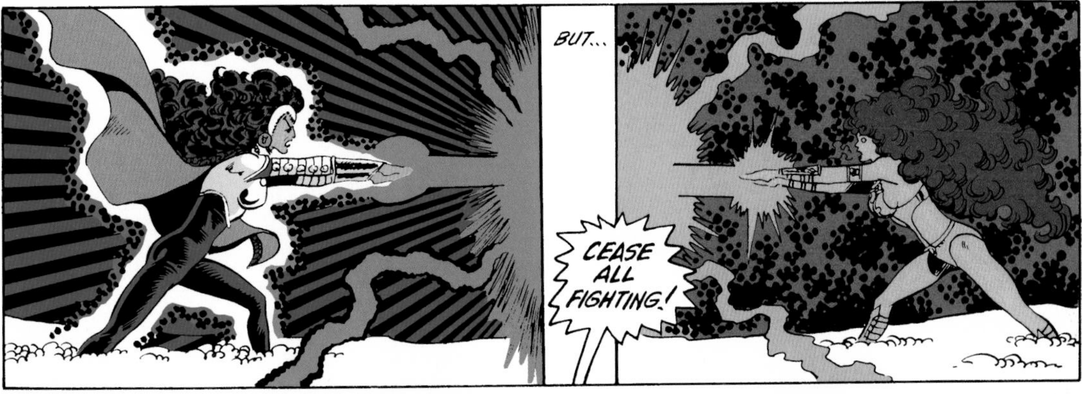

BUT...
CEASE ALL FIGHTING!

A FORCE-FIELD? WHO DARES?

YOU? PSION, WHAT GIVES YOU THE RIGHT TO--?

SILENCE, KOMAND'R, YOU ARE NOT CITADEL LEADER EVEN IF YOU DID SLAY LORD DAMYN.

I HAVE BEEN GRANTED CONTROL OF THIS ENTERPRISE. YOU WILL LISTEN TO ME OR FORFEIT YOUR CLAIM.

ARE YOU READY TO HEAR MY OFFER, KOMAND'R? OR ARE YOU READY TO DIE?

KORIAND'R SQUIRMS. SHE DOES NOT LIKE HER CHOICE AND YET SHE CANNOT AVOID THE PSION'S TERMS. ALSO, SHE IS UNEASY BECAUSE SHE FEARS THE QUESTIONABLE OUTCOME OF BATTLE. ANGRILY, KOMAND'R **GLARES** AT THE SEEMINGLY EMOTIONLESS PSION. INWARDLY, HE ALLOWS HIMSELF A SELF-SATISFIED SMILE. WHATEVER THE CHOICE, **HE** SHALL WIN!

DEEP SPACE, A SHORT DISTANCE OUT FROM THE PLANET OKAARA...
"I PROMISED YOU, WONDER GIRL, THAT I WOULD AID IN RESCUING PRINCESS KORIAND'R...
"...NOW I PLEDGE THE FULL POWER OF THE OMEGA MEN TO YOUR MISSION."
"THANK YOU, PRIMUS, BUT I'M FORCED TO WONDER --"
--ARE YOU HELPING US BECAUSE YOU WANT TO...
...OR BECAUSE THE CITADEL KID-NAPPED YOUR GODDESS X'HAL AS THEY DID OUR TEAMMATE?
WHATEVER MY REASONS, THE RESULTS REMAIN THE SAME.
13

X'HAL MEANS EVERYTHING TO US. SHE MUST BE RETURNED TO OKAARA.
BUT YOU SAY YOU FEAR HER POWERS. FRANKLY, PRIMUS, I DON'T UNDERSTAND YOU.
YOU KNOW, KORY USED TO CALL UPON X'HAL EVEN AS MY SISTER CALLS UPON THE AMAZON GODS.

BUT ALWAYS IMPLICIT IN HER CALL WAS A CRY FOR VENGEANCE.
WHAT IS X'HAL? WHAT DOES SHE MEAN TO YOUR PEOPLE?
SHE WAS OUR SAVIOR. SHE IS OUR GODDESS. AND SHE IS MORE.

X'HAL IS BOTH THE EMBODIMENT OF ALL THAT CAN BE GOOD, AND ALL THAT CAN BE CORRUPTED.

SHE FLUCTUATES BETWEEN THESE TWO EXTREMES AND THERE IS NO WAY TO PREDICT HER SHIFTS...
...OR EVEN FOR HER TO CONTROL THEM.

"IT BEGAN SO LONG AGO, AND SOME OF WHAT I WILL TELL YOU HAS ALREADY BECOME THE STUFF OF LEGENDS UPON WHICH EVEN X'HAL HERSELF CANNOT SHED LIGHT.
"X'HAL WAS, PERHAPS, OUR GREATEST WARRIOR, AND SHE LED OUR FORCES INTO BATTLE AGAINST THE PSION HORDES.
14

"HER BRILLIANT MIND CREATED BATTLE PLANS WHICH REPELLED THE PSIONS, DESPITE THEIR OVERPOWERING MIGHT.

"OUR GALAXY WAS FREED AND THE ENEMY DRIVEN OFF. THE PSIONS EVENTUALLY FOUNDED A PLANET ON THE FAR SIDE OF THE UNIVERSE...

"...BUT WHAT HAPPENED TO THEM WAS BEYOND OUR CARING.
"X'HAL WAS OUR SAVIOR AND SHE WAS HAILED BY ALL 25 VEGAN WORLDS.

"UNANIMOUSLY, SHE WAS DECLARED OUR FIRST HIGH EMPRESS."

PRIMUS IS ENAMORED WITH X'HAL'S LEGEND. PERHAPS I SHOULD CONTINUE WITH A LESS GLORIFIED VERSION.
YES, X'HAL WAS OUR RULER -- AND AN EXCELLENT ONE, TOO.
SHE INSTITUTED MANY REFORMS AND BEGAN AN ERA OF PEACE THAT WAS UNBROKEN FOR MANY YEARS.
BUT EVENTUALLY IT DID COME TO AN END. IN HER QUEST FOR A FREE GALAXY SHE HAD IGNORED OUR DEFENSE. THE PSIONS RETURNED TO WAGE ANOTHER WAR.
"DURING THEIR FIRST ASSAULT THEY DESTROYED THE MOON AROUND WHAT WAS TO BECOME THE CITADEL HOMEWORLD...
"AND DURING THAT SAME ATTACK, THEY BROKE THROUGH ALL OUR MAKESHIFT BARRIERS...

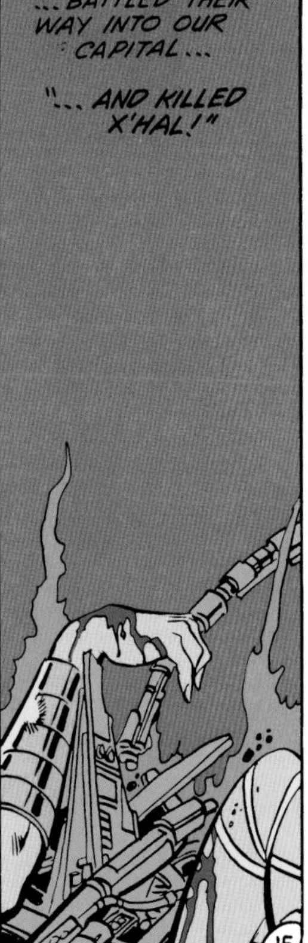
"...BATTLED THEIR WAY INTO OUR CAPITAL...
"... AND KILLED X'HAL!"
15

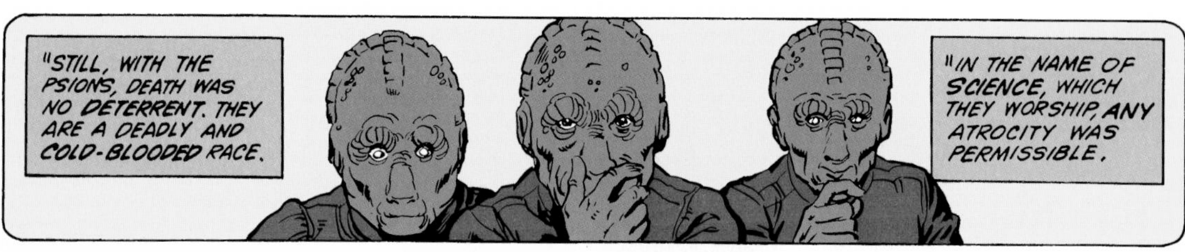

"STILL, WITH THE PSIONS, DEATH WAS NO DETERRENT. THEY ARE A DEADLY AND COLD-BLOODED RACE.
"IN THE NAME OF SCIENCE, WHICH THEY WORSHIP, ANY ATROCITY WAS PERMISSIBLE.

"AND SO THEY BEGAN TO TEST X'HAL'S LIFELESS BODY. SHE WAS BOMBARDED WITH INCALCULABLE RADIATIONS.

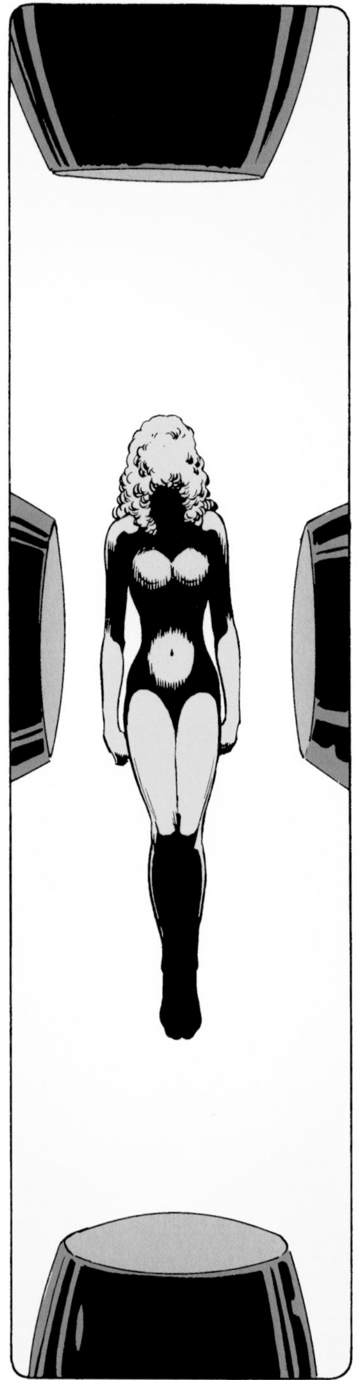

"HER BRAIN WAS REMOVED, ITS CORTEX EXAMINED.

"AND WHEN THEY WERE DONE WITH HER, SHE WAS PUT BACK TOGETHER AGAIN...

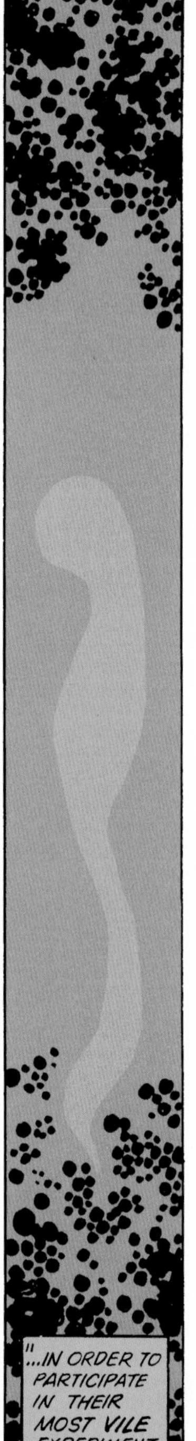

"...IN ORDER TO PARTICIPATE IN THEIR MOST VILE EXPERIMENT YET.

"WITH CALLOUS DISREGARD FOR THE SANCTITY OF HER SOUL THEY CONVERTED HER BODY-MASS INTO PURE ENERGY.

"X'HAL'S BODY FAIRLY EXPLODED WITH THE FURY OF A STAR CAUGHT IN ITS DEATH-THROES.

"IN TRYING TO DESTROY X'HAL, THEY HAD SIMPLY DESTROYED THEIR OWN LABORATORY WORLD.
"BUT X'HAL DID NOT DIE A SECOND DEATH.

"SOMEHOW SHE HAD BEEN REBORN, CONVERTED TO PURE ENERGY WHICH SHE COULD CONTROL TO AGAIN TAKE ON HUMAN SHAPE.

"BUT SHE HAD BEEN CHANGED. ONCE SHE FOUGHT FROM NECESSITY. NOW SHE BATTLED OUT OF LUST FOR DESTRUCTION!
"THE ATTACKING PSION FLEET WAS INSTANTLY OBLITERATED..."

...AND THEN SHE TURNED ON HER OWN PEOPLE.
KALISTA, PLEASE REMEMBER, SHE WAS NOT RESPONSIBLE FOR WHAT SHE DID.

"YES, PROPELLED BY HER NEW BATTLE-LUST, SHE RETURNED TO VEGA...
"AND WHERE SHE ONCE SAVED OUR PLANETARY SYSTEM, SHE PROCEEDED TO DESTROY IT. THREE WORLDS CEASED TO EXIST."

BUT SHE WOULD HAVE STOPPED HERSELF IF SHE COULD. SHE WOULD HAVE DESTROYED HERSELF BEFORE SHE SLEW HER CHILDREN. BUT THE VEGAN PLANETS COULD NOT ALLOW THEMSELVES TO BE DESTROYED, AND SO THEY BROUGHT TOGETHER THE GREATEST WARRIORS FROM ALL OUR WORLDS.

"AND THOUGH MORE THAN TWO HUNDRED OF THEM DIED IN THE ATTEMPT, THEY CAPTURED X'HAL'S LIFE-ESSENCE."

THEY TOOK X'HAL TO A WORLD WHICH HAD BEEN DEAD. THAT WAS OKAARA, AND THOSE WARRIORS BECAME THE OKAARAN WARLORDS. THEIR LIVES WERE NOW DEDICATED TO CONTROLLING X'HAL'S POWER, TO KEEPING HER CONTAINED, AND TO THE TRAINING OF ALL FUTURE VEGANS IN THE DEFENSE OF THEIR WORLDS.
17

OUR STAR-SYSTEM WAS SAFE, AND X'HAL CAME TO BE WORSHIPPED ONCE AGAIN.
BUT HER DEEDS INSPIRED BOTH AWE AND FEAR.
HAS ANYONE SEEN DEMONIA? SHE SHOULD HAVE RELIEVED ME BY NOW.
DAMN HER TRAITRESS HIDE. WHAT HAS HAPPENED TO HER?
PRIMUS, WE ARE ENTERING HOMEWARD SPACE.
WE SHOULD BE APPROACHING THEIR RINGED FORTRESS IN NINE MINUTES.
THE FORTRESS IS IMPENETRABLE. HOW WILL WE GET THROUGH?
OUR EARTH-FRIENDS ARE OUR KEY! TRUST ME, HARPIS.
GOOD. WE'RE ALMOST THERE.
I'M TIRED OF THIS DELAY.
AND I HAVE TO KNOW IF KORY'S STILL ALIVE.
BECAUSE, IF SHE ISN'T, I SWEAR THERE'S GOING TO BE HELL TO PAY!
18

TAMARAN: EIGHTH PLANET FROM THE STAR VEGA, AND HOME TO KORIAND'R, ITS CROWN PRIN-CESS. A HOME SHE HAS NOT SET FOOT UPON FOR MORE THAN SIX YEARS...

YOU HAVE ACCEPTED TRIAL BY COMBAT. NOW YOU, AND THE INHABITANTS OF VEGA'S 22 PLANETS AND OUTPOSTS, SHALL HEAR THE RULES.

THIS SHALL BE A CONTEST OF PHYSICAL PROWESS. YOU ARE NOT PERMITTED TO USE YOUR STARBOLT POWERS.

THE PSION CHUCKLES. HE KNOWS KOMAND'R CANNOT BE LONG RESTRAINED.

VICTORY IS ACHIEVED ONLY WHEN ONE IS DEAD. IS THAT UNDERSTOOD?

OF COURSE, PSION. NOW LET US GET ON WITH IT.

I'M READY.

19

EXCELLENT. VICTORY WILL BE DIFFICULT. YOU ARE EVENLY MATCHED IN STRENGTH.
SUCCESS WILL BE DETERMINED BASED ON SKILL ALONE.

OOOH, ME SURE BET KORIAND'R WIN. BET YOU THE RIGHT TO KILL ME WIFE. WHAT YOU SAY, DIMM?
KILL WIFE? SOUNDS GOOD TO ME. SURE, ME TAKE KOMAND'R.
YES, KOMAND'R MORE ROTTEN, SURE IS. SHE ENJOY TO KILL SISTER.
WELL, I FOR ONE AM UNCERTAIN AS TO THE OUTCOME. KOMAND'R DOES NOT HAVE HER SISTER'S PHYSICAL TRAINING, BUT SHE IS CRAFTY.

"KORIAND'R, HOWEVER, DOES NOT HAVE HER SISTER'S TASTE FOR MURDER.

"IT SHALL PROVE QUITE AN ...ENTERTAINING MATCH.

"THE CONTEST BEGINS--NOW!"
WELL, LITTLE SISTER, IT FINALLY COMES DOWN TO THIS, DOES IT?
BUT YOU WERE NEVER MY EQUAL, KORIAND'R. NOW, I WILL PROVE THAT!
NEVER!
20

I FIGHT FOR THE HONOR OF THE FAMILY YOU DISGRACED WITH YOUR TRAITRESS WAYS.
ONCE I SLAY YOU, OF ALL OUR FAMILY LINE, ONLY I WILL REMAIN.
OUR PARENTS ARE DEAD, KORIAND'R -- DEAD! YOU FIGHT FOR GHOSTS!
THEN YOU FIGHT FOR LOST CAUSES, LITTLE SISTER.
NO! YOU LIE, KOMAND'R.
I - I CAN'T BELIEVE YOU. IT ISN'T TRUE!
TELL ME THEY'RE STILL ALIVE! TELL ME, KOMAND'R.
TELL ME, OR--
OR WHAT, FOOLISH LITTLE SISTER?
THEY ARE DEAD, SLAIN BY OUR DEAR BROTHER THREE DAYS AFTER YOU WERE TAKEN FROM THEM.
HE WENT BERSERK, MURDERED THEM. NOW HE IS A HUNTED FUGITIVE.
WHY FIGHT, KORIAND'R? GIVE UP! JOIN YOUR PARENTS IN THAT GREAT GRAY NETHERVERSE.
YOU HAVE NOTHING LEFT TO FIGHT FOR!
NO! I...I HAVE TO FIGHT... I HAVE TO...
21

WHY, KORIAND'R? THERE IS NOTHING TO LIVE FOR.
YOU KNOW YOU'LL NEVER BE ALLOWED TO RETURN TO EARTH.
YOU HAVE NOTHING HERE!

YOU MAY AS WELL GIVE UP, LITTLE SISTER.
YOU'RE ALL ALONE.

BUT YOU DON'T HAVE TO DIE, LITTLE SISTER. BEG FOR MERCY, AND PERHAPS I SHALL GRANT IT.
ADMIT TO EVERYONE THAT I AM YOUR BETTER AND ONCE I AM LORD OVER ALL, I'LL SIMPLY SEND YOU INTO EXILE.
ADMIT YOUR WEAKNESS, KORIAND'R. YOU HAVE NOTHING TO LOSE!!

NO! I'D SOONER BE DRAGGED BY THE LIMBS OVER OKAARA'S ROCKY SURFACE THAN BOW IN SHAME TO YOU.
YOU'VE SPENT YOUR LIFE TRYING TO HURT ME.
YOU TURNED ME FROM A PERSON BRIMMING WITH LOVE INTO ONE WHO LEARNED TO HATE.

IT WAS YOUR VILE FACE WHICH KEPT ME ALIVE IN TIMES WHEN DEATH WOULD HAVE BEEN A WELCOME RELIEF.
I CANNOT DIE, SISTER-- NOT UNTIL I KNOW YOU ARE DEAD!
22

I DOUBT YOU'LL LONG THNK THAT, MY MUSCLE-MINDED LOUT.

THIS BATTLE EXISTS FOR ONE REASON ONLY. WITH ALL VEGAN EYES WATCHING THEIR FIGHTING...

...MY PSION FORCES ARE PLANTING EXPLOSIVES THROUGHOUT YOUR FABLED EMPIRE!

AT THE MOMENT THIS BATTLE IS OVER, NO MATTER WHO WINS, THOSE EXPLOSIVES WILL DESTROY EVERY CITADEL FORTRESS.

"AND THEN THE PSION EMPIRE SHALL RETURN IN TRIUMPH!"

YOU TOLD ME ABOUT OUR PARENTS TO DEMORALIZE ME, DIDN'T YOU, KOMAND'R? WELL, IT DIDN'T WORK, SISTER.
THEIR DEATHS ONLY SPUR ME ON TO GREATER GLORIES.

BUT, I'M DISAPPOINTED IN YOU, SISTER. IN MY NIGHTMARES I'VE FOUGHT THIS BATTLE A THOUSAND TIMES...

...BUT I ALWAYS SAW YOU AS SOME TERRIBLE WAR MACHINE, SO HORRIBLY POWERFUL.

BUT, IN TRUTH, YOU'RE NOT POWERFUL. YOU'RE WEAK! YOU'RE SPINELESS!
AND NOW I LAUGH AT HAVING THOUGHT THAT YOU WERE BETTER THAN I!
23

AGHHHH!
NOBODY LAUGHS AT ME!
NOBODY!!

YOU ALWAYS FOUGHT BY THE RULES, DIDN'T YOU, MY STUPID SISTER?
THAT IS WHY YOU COULD NEVER WIN AGAINST ME.

HOLD STILL, DAMN YOU. STOP SQUIRMING! LET MY STARBOLT POWERS FRY YOU FROM WITHIN!

OH, I SWEAR YOU SHALL RUE THE DAY YOU DARED LAUGH AT -- WHAT?!?
WHAT ARE YOU DOING?

STOP IT, KORIAND'R! STOP IT!
YOU KNOW I CANNOT FLY!

X'HAL'S BLOOD! SHE'LL CRUSH US INTO THE MOUNTAIN...

SHE'S CRAZED, WILLING TO KILL US BOTH, UNLESS--
24

BLACK FIRE BURNS OUTWARD FROM KOMAND'R'S FINGERTIPS, CUTTING THROUGH EARTH AND STONE...

WHILE FAR OFF IN SPACE, HIGH ABOVE THE HOMEWORLD, BRANX SECOND-LEVEL WARRIOR SEMLGH CORH-D'HN CASUALLY GLANCES AT HIS VIEWER, FULLY EXPECTING TO SEE NOTHING EVENTFUL.

NO ONE, NOT EVEN THE PSIONS, HAS SUCCESSFULLY BREACHED THE RINGED FORTRESS.
NO, THIS MONITOR JOB IS AN EASY ONE, HE THINKS.
BUT...
WHAT? ATTACK! ATTACK ON ALL FRONTS!
BATTLE STATIONS!
AS ALL HANDS RACE TO THEIR POSITIONS, SEMLGH FEELS EXTREME PRIDE EVEN AMID CONFUSION, HE REACTED AS INSTRUCTED...

...AND THIS FORTRESS, WHICH HAD BEEN BUILT UPON THE REMAINS OF THE HOMEWORLD'S SHATTERED MOON, HOLDS STRONG.

BUT, ABOARD THE OMEGA MEN'S STARSHIP...

NIMBUS, WE CANNOT BREAK THROUGH THEIR DEFENSES.
DID YOU HEAR THAT, PRIMUS? I THOUGHT YOU SAID YOU HAD A PLAN!
WHATEVER IT IS, ENACT IT NOW!

I WILL, MY FRIEND. TRUST ME.
ALL OF YOU, HEAR ME... WE ARE ABOUT TO ENGAGE IN BATTLE. IT IS POSSIBLE MANY OF US MIGHT NOT LIVE TO SEE THE END OF THIS STRUGGLE.
BUT WE HAVE NO ALTERNATIVES IF WE ARE TO BRING X'HAL BACK TO OKAARA.
THUS WE MUST FIGHT WITH OUR HEARTS AND OUR MINDS. WE MUST ENTER THIS BATTLE KNOWING OUR CAUSE IS JUST!
AS OF NOW -- THE WAR BEGINS!!
25

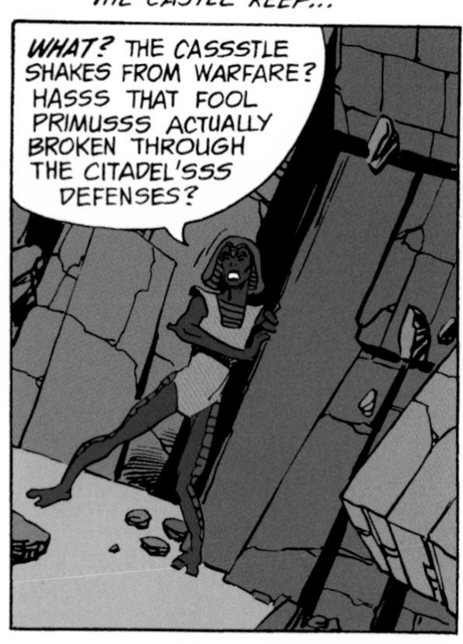
BELOW THE HOMEWORLD, WITHIN THE CASTLE KEEP...
WHAT? THE CASSSTLE SHAKES FROM WARFARE? HASSS THAT FOOL PRIMUSSS ACTUALLY BROKEN THROUGH THE CITADEL'SSS DEFENSES?

WELL, PERHAPSSS IT IS BETTER THAT HE DOES. I CAN EASILY MANIPULATE THAT TRUSSSTING DOLT...
HMMMM. PERHAPSSS, IF I CAN PLAY MY CARDSSS CORRECTLY, I CAN MANEUVER BOTH SSSIDES INTO DESTROYING EACH OTHER...
...AND THUS INSURE THAT DEMONIA COMESSS OUT ON TOP OF THIS GAME.

WHAT? WHO DARESSS--?
THE EARTHLING? I SHOULD DESTROY YOU FOR-- WAIT! YOU WERE THE ONE WHO WAS KILLED. I SSSAW IT.
YEAH, YEAH, I KNOW WHAT YOU SAW, SNAKE-LIPS, BUT GUESS WHAT?
I'M ALIVE AND WELL AND IN FULL-LIVING GREEN!
BUT HOW?
OH, IT'S NOT TOO DIFFICULT WHEN YOU CAN SHAPE-CHANGE INTO AN ITSY-BITSY SPIDER AND QUICKLY CRAWL AWAY!

SATISFIED NOW? SO HOW ABOUT TELLING ME WHERE MY FRIENDS HOPPED OFF TO.
I ASSUME YOU KNOW, DON'T YOU NOW, DEMONIA?

YES, UH, OF COURSE I DO. I SSSAW THEM BEING TAKEN OFF TO THE DOCKING AREA.
THEY'RE TO BE EXTERMINATED. I HEARD THE ORDERSSS.
THEN WE'RE GOING TO HAVE TO COUNTERMAND THOSE ORDERS, AREN'T WE?
OF COURSE, EARTHLING. I AM ON YOUR SSSIDE, AFTER ALL.
WHATEVER YOU SAY, SNAKE-LIPS.
OF COURSE, I'D PROBABLY BELIEVE WHAT YOU SAY IF YOU DIDN'T ALWAYS TALK ALOUD TO YOURSELF.
"DEMONIA COMES OUT ON TOP"? EH?
26

AT THE FAR END OF THE FORTRESS...
WHY WERE *WE* PICKED TO SHIP THOSE TWO TO EXTERMINATION CAMPS?
I WANTED TO WATCH THE *FIGHTS*.
YOU KNOW, MY MONEY-CHANGER GAVE ME 5 TO 2 ODDS THAT KORIAND'R WOULD *DIE*.
5 TO 2? I GOT BETTER ODDS THAT *THAT*, GREE.
I STAND TO CLEAR ENOUGH FOR A *VACATION* ON EUFORIX.

HMMM, MY *BROTHER-IN-LAW* WENT THERE. HE SAID HIS *ROOMS* WERE EXCELLENT BUT THE *FOOD* REPEATED ON HIM FOR WEEKS.
AND YOU CAN'T DRINK THEIR *WATER*, YOU KNOW.

WHAT ARE YOU *LOOKING* AT, GREE?
THE EARTHLING'S *WEAPONS BELT*. ONLY *ONE* WEAPON IN EACH CYLINDER. WHAT A WASTE OF *SPACE*.
OBVIOUSLY THEY KNOW NOTHING ABOUT *MINIATURIZATION*.

COME ON. THERE IS NO USE IN *COMPLAINING* ABOUT THE FIGHTS.
BESIDES, THEY WILL PROBABLY *RERUN* IT TONIGHT. LET'S GET BACK TO *WORK*.

GORDANIAN FOOLS. YOU WILL *NEVER* SSSEE THOSE FIGHTSSS.
ACCKKK
GOD, DEMONIA, YOU DIDN'T HAVE TO *KILL* HIM!
OH, YESSS I DID, EARTHLING. I *DID*.

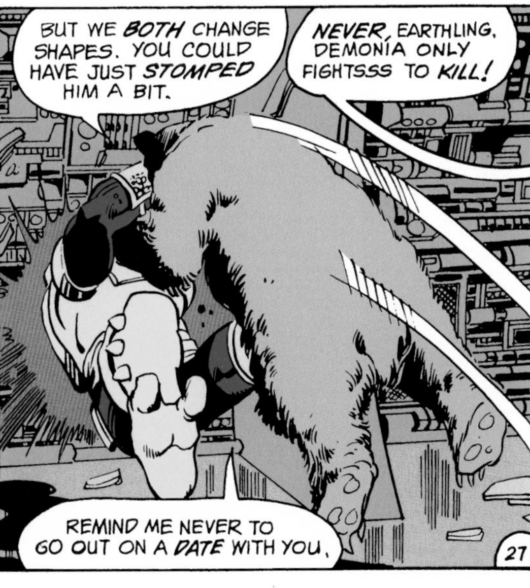

BUT WE *BOTH* CHANGE SHAPES. YOU COULD HAVE JUST *STOMPED* HIM A BIT.
NEVER, EARTHLING. DEMONIA ONLY FIGHTSSS TO *KILL*!
REMIND ME NEVER TO GO OUT ON A *DATE* WITH YOU.
27

SPACE:
YOU GOT EVERYTHING SET IN YOUR MIND, WALLY?
I'D BETTER, DONNA, IF I WANT TO COME THROUGH THIS ALIVE.
JUST HAVE TO REMEMBER TO SLOW DOWN A BIT. MY REFLEXES OPERATE FAR FASTER THAN THE SHIP'S CONTROLS.

IT'S WORKING, GUYS. MY SUPER-SPEED VISION MAKES THESE LASER-BLASTS LOOK LIKE THEY'RE STANDING STILL.
I CAN WEAVE THROUGH THEM WITHOUT BEING TOUCHED.

DON'T GET COCKY. BE CAREFUL.

YOU SEE YOUR TARGET YET?

YEAH... FIRST TARGET ON MY SCREEN. THREE... TWO ...ONE...

GIVE THE MAN A BIG CIGAR!
TELL PRIMUS HE WAS RIGHT. I AM ABOUT THE ONLY ONE WHO COULD SLIP THROUGH THIS HAIL OF FIRE.

OKAY... MAIN TARGETS AHEAD, CLOSER NOW... CLOSER... CLOSER...
DID IT! SMASHED A HOLE IN THEIR DEFENSE SHIELDS.
BAM! BLAMM!
BLAMMM!

THE WAY IS CLEAR. LET US GO!

FOR A BRIEF MOMENT, SECURITY HAS BEEN BREACHED, BUT A MOMENT IS ALL IT TAKES FOR ALMOST TWO DOZEN SKY-SKIMMERS TO SLIDE PAST A PREVIOUSLY IMPENETRABLE FORTRESS...

...AND, FOR THE FIRST TIME IN MORE THAN ONE THOUSAND YEARS, BRING WAR TO THE HOMEWORLD'S SURFACE.

EVERYTHING'S FALLING APART! VIC! GAR! C'MON, LET'S MOVE!
VIC?!?

IN A SECOND, PAL...

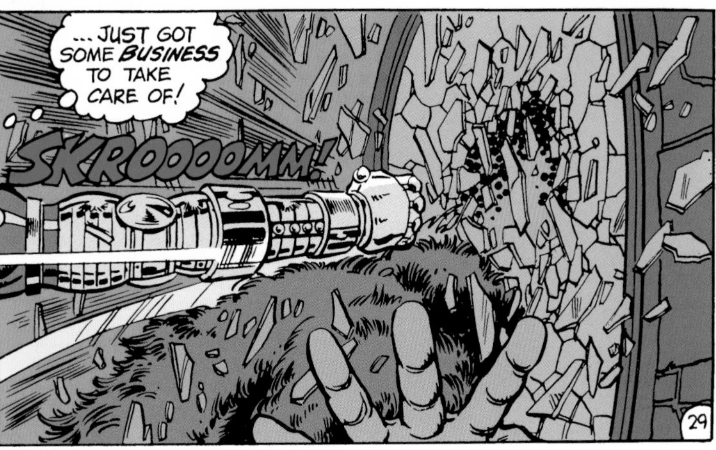

...JUST GOT SOME BUSINESS TO TAKE CARE OF!
SKROOOOOMM!
29

TAMARAN:
YOU'RE INSANE! STOP THIS MADNESS BEFORE YOU KILL US BOTH!
NO, KOMAND'R. YOU WANTED THIS FIGHT, NOW YOU'LL SUFFER FOR IT.

BUT YOU CAN SIMPLY LET GO OF ME IF YOU WANT THIS FIGHT TO END NOW.

WHY DON'T YOU LET GO, SISTER?

I-- I CAN'T FLY!

I KNOW!

X'HAL! YOU ARE INSANE!

VERY WELL, KOMAND'R... YOU WANT TO GO DOWN?

WE'LL GO DOWN!

KORIAND'R IS FURIOUS, AS A LIFETIME OF TORMENT COMES BUBBLING TO THE SURFACE. BUT...

...KORIAND'R'S RAGE HAS BLINDED HER TO KOMAND'R'S VICIOUS STRENGTH.

STEEL-JACKETED ARMS PUMMEL HER WITH REPEATED AGONIZING BLOWS,
AND SHE FLOUNDERS IN THE ONRUSHING TIDE, DESPERATELY SEEKING BALANCE...

...BUT A SOLID FOOTHOLD ELUDES HER.
KORIAND'R LASHES BACK, A POWERFUL RIGHT SMASHES INTO HER SISTER'S FACE...

...BLOOD SPURTS FREELY FROM A SHATTERED NOSE, BUT KOMAND'R'S ATTACK DOES NOT LESSEN...

WHILE ASHORE, HIDDEN IN THE SHADOWS, A TALL, LITHE FIGURE WATCHES ATTENTIVELY.

WATCHES, AND WAITS.

THIS FIGHT HAS GONE ON TOO LONG, KORIAND'R. I WANT TO BE DONE WITH YOU.
NO, KOMAND'R -- DON'T.
DON'T USE YOUR STARBOLT POWERS.

WHAT? ARE YOU FREELY ADMITTING THAT YOU ARE WEAKER THAN I AM?
SHOUT IT OUT, SISTER. LET ALL THE WORLDS HEAR THE TRUTH!

YOU FOOL, DON'T YOU KNOW WHERE WE ARE?

IF YOU USE YOUR STARBOLT HERE, NO ONE WILL--
31

IT IS ALREADY TOO LATE. FOR A MOMENT, THEY HOVER ABOVE THE RUSHING WATERS OF TAMARAN'S SEVEN FALLS.
THEN, THE WATERS BEGIN TO BOIL, BURNING AT TEMPERATURES NO HUMAN COULD POSSIBLY SURVIVE.
STONE EXPLODES WITH VOLCANIC FURY...

...AS TWO BODIES PLUNGE LIMPLY TO THEIR...

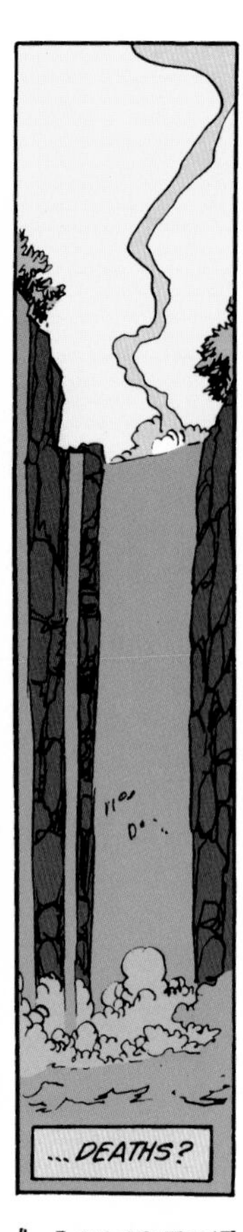
...DEATHS?

SECONDS DRAG BY LIKE ETERNITIES. THEN...

ME WIN! KORIAND'R ALIVE. EUPHORIX, HERE ME COME!
STILL, HER VICTORY ME NS NOTHING. YOU ARE ALL ABOUT TO DIE.
ASTONISHING PERSEVERANCE.
HUH?

"OH YES. IMPLANTED INTO BOTH OF THEM WAS THE TRIGGER FOR A SERIES OF QUITE POWERFUL EXPLOSIVES.

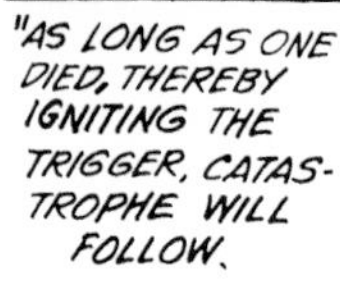
"AS LONG AS ONE DIED, THEREBY IGNITING THE TRIGGER, CATASTROPHE WILL FOLLOW.

"AND THOUGH I WILL NOT SURVIVE TO SEE YOUR DESTRUCTION...

"...I AM CONTENT IN KNOWING PSION SCIENCE WAS ONCE AGAIN VICTORIOUS."
WORLDS BEGIN TO SHAKE. A DEATH-RATTLE ECHOES THROUGHOUT VEGA...
32

BUT, SEVERAL MOMENTS BEFORE, ON THE CITADEL HOMEWORLD...
THIS IS IT. THEY HAVE TO BE HERE.
THEY ARE. I SENSE THEIR PRESENCE.
IS KORY WITH THEM, RAVEN?
SKRASH!
I--I DO NOT BELIEVE SO.
WATCH IT, DONNA-- THESE CITADEL CREEPS ARE ALL OVER THE PLACE.
GOOD! THEN THERE ARE MORE FOR BROOT TO CRUSH!
BRAK!
NO, MY BARBAROUS FRIEND, WE ARE HERE TO FIND X'HAL. ONLY SHE MATTERS TO AURON.
HER POWERS CONTROL ME. I, WHO AM HER ONLY SON--I, WHO HAVE ALWAYS STRIVEN FOR PEACE, HAVE BEEN TURNED INTO HER INSTRUMENT OF DEATH!
I MUST FIND MY MOTHER BEFORE SHE CONTROLS ME AGAIN.
BEFORE SHE MAKES ME KILL AGAIN!
ABOUT TIME YOU GUYS GOT HERE. THOUGHT WE'D HAVE TO HITCHHIKE HOME.
WHERE'S KORY?
"WHERE'S KORY?" SHEESH. NOT EVEN A HELLO TO EVERYONE'S FAVORITE GREEN PAL?
AND RODNEY DANGERFIELD SAYS HE GETS NO RESPECT! YECHH!
YOU ALL RIGHT?
WE'RE FINE, WALLY... REALLY, ALL OF US.
33

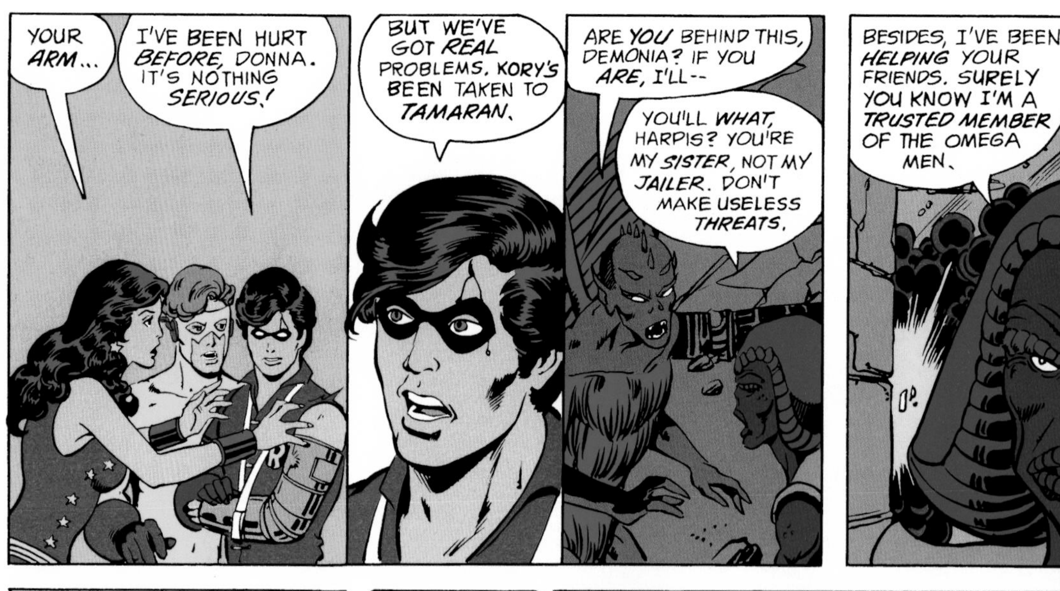
YOUR ARM...
I'VE BEEN HURT BEFORE, DONNA. IT'S NOTHING SERIOUS!
BUT WE'VE GOT REAL PROBLEMS. KORY'S BEEN TAKEN TO TAMARAN.
ARE YOU BEHIND THIS, DEMONIA? IF YOU ARE, I'LL--
YOU'LL WHAT, HARPIS? YOU'RE MY SISTER, NOT MY JAILER. DON'T MAKE USELESS THREATS.
BESIDES, I'VE BEEN HELPING YOUR FRIENDS. SURELY YOU KNOW I'M A TRUSTED MEMBER OF THE OMEGA MEN.

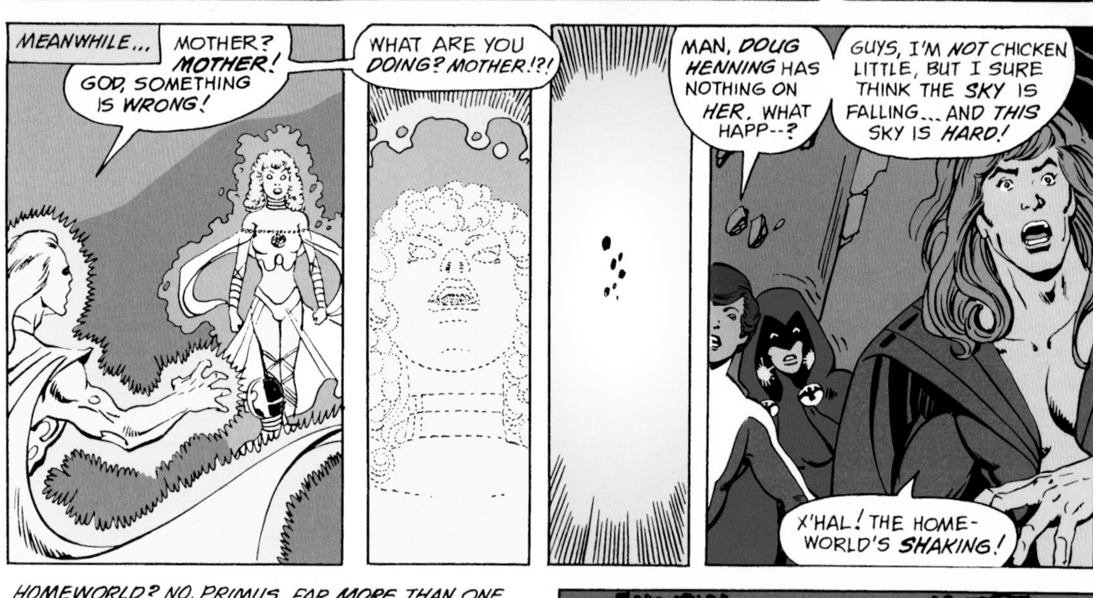
MEANWHILE...
MOTHER? MOTHER! GOD, SOMETHING IS WRONG!
WHAT ARE YOU DOING? MOTHER!?!
MAN, DOUG HENNING HAS NOTHING ON HER. WHAT HAPP--?
GUYS, I'M NOT CHICKEN LITTLE, BUT I SURE THINK THE SKY IS FALLING... AND THIS SKY IS HARD!
X'HAL! THE HOME-WORLD'S SHAKING!

HOMEWORLD? NO, PRIMUS, FAR MORE THAN ONE PLANET IS AFFECTED BY THE PSION'S QUAKE-BOMBS.
ACROSS THE BREADTH OF ALL 22 VEGAN WORLDS, A SINGLE CHAIN-REACTION BEGINS TO GROW.
MORE THAN THREE HUNDRED CITADEL WAR-STATIONS ARE MOMENTS AWAY FROM COMPLETE DEVASTATION.
BUT...
34

ONCE BEFORE SHE HAD SAVED THIS GALAXY FROM A PSION THREAT. HER REWARD WAS A FATE FAR WORSE THAN DEATH.

NOW, ALL THE PRIMAL LUSTS, ALL THE POWER, ALL THE FURY THAT IS THE GODDESS X'HAL, ALL THAT AND MORE ARE UNLEASHED.

HER POWER REACHES EVERYWHERE AT ONCE, COMBING DISTANT WORLDS, DIGGING TO THE VERY CORE OF PLANETS LONG ABANDONED--

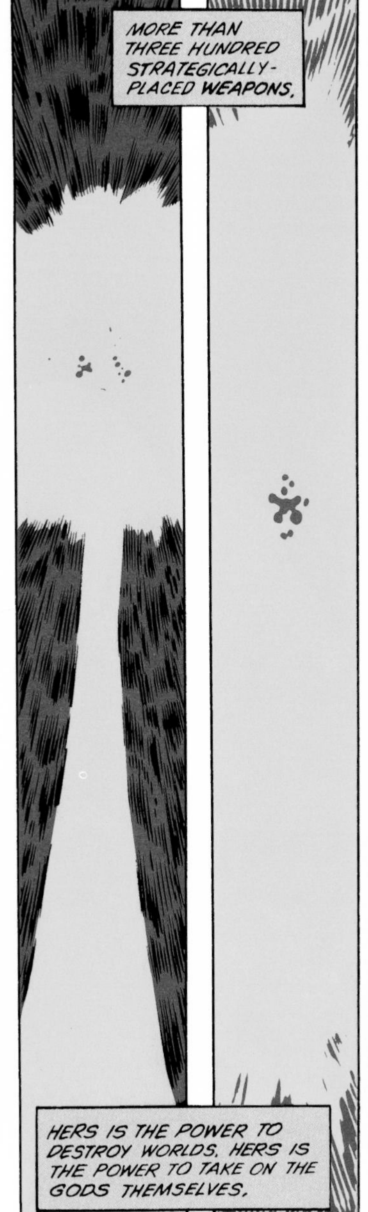

--UNTIL SHE FINDS HER TREASURE:

MORE THAN THREE HUNDRED STRATEGICALLY-PLACED WEAPONS.
HERS IS THE POWER TO DESTROY WORLDS. HERS IS THE POWER TO TAKE ON THE GODS THEMSELVES.

HERS IS ALSO THE POWER OF SACRIFICE.

HER CHILDREN WILL LIVE... NO MATTER WHAT, HER CHILDREN MUST LIVE!

35

HMMMM. SO, WORLDS WAS GOING TO DIE, HUH? SO, PSION WAS GOING TO TAKE OVER, HUH?
PSION, YOU MAY BE THE SMART ONE--

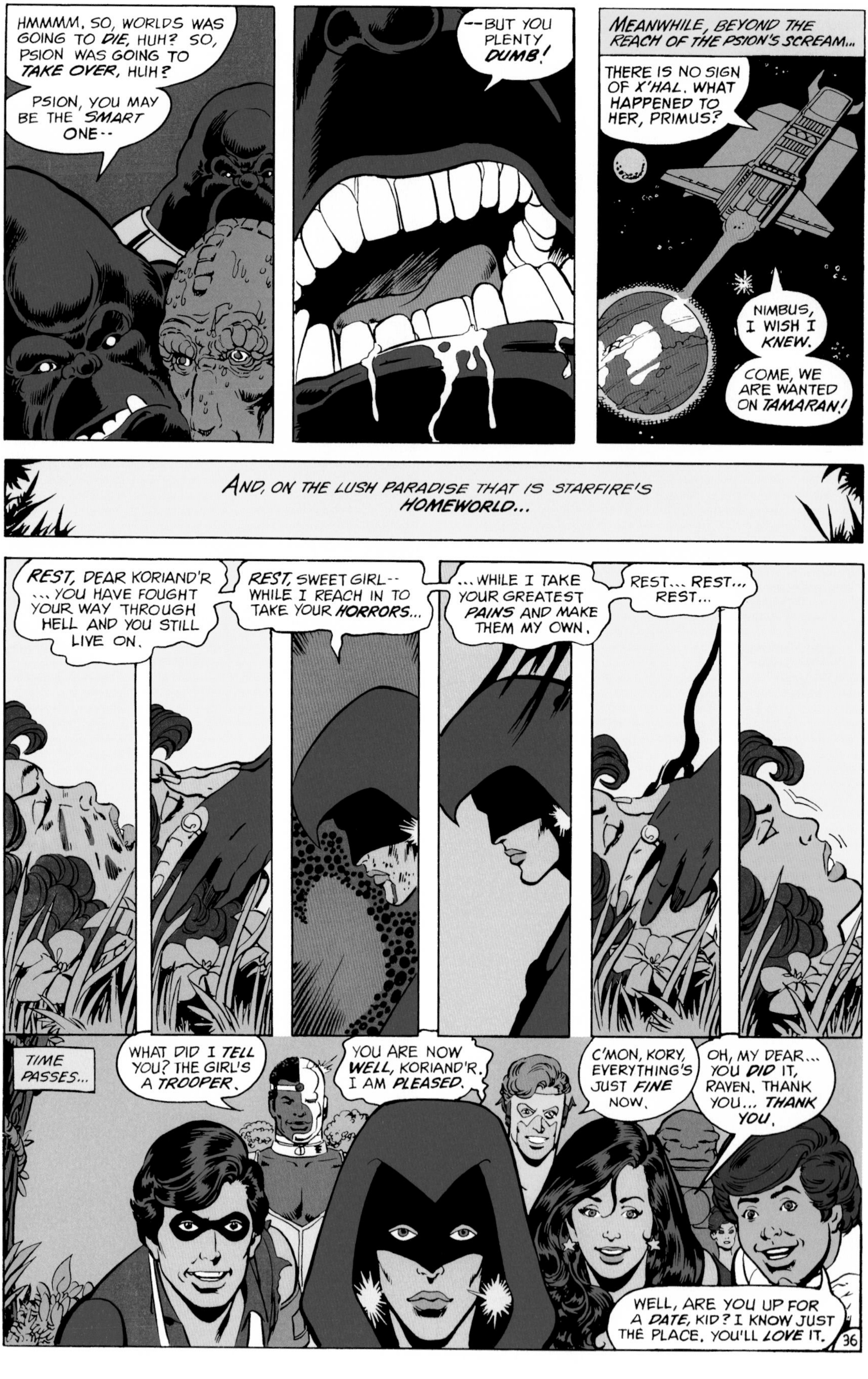

--BUT YOU PLENTY DUMB!

MEANWHILE, BEYOND THE REACH OF THE PSION'S SCREAM...
THERE IS NO SIGN OF X'HAL. WHAT HAPPENED TO HER, PRIMUS?
NIMBUS, I WISH I KNEW.
COME, WE ARE WANTED ON TAMARAN!

AND, ON THE LUSH PARADISE THAT IS STARFIRE'S HOMEWORLD...
REST, DEAR KORIAND'R ...YOU HAVE FOUGHT YOUR WAY THROUGH HELL AND YOU STILL LIVE ON.
REST, SWEET GIRL-- WHILE I REACH IN TO TAKE YOUR HORRORS...
...WHILE I TAKE YOUR GREATEST PAINS AND MAKE THEM MY OWN.
REST... REST... REST...
TIME PASSES...
WHAT DID I TELL YOU? THE GIRL'S A TROOPER.
YOU ARE NOW WELL, KORIAND'R. I AM PLEASED.
C'MON, KORY, EVERYTHING'S JUST FINE NOW.
OH, MY DEAR... YOU DID IT, RAVEN. THANK YOU... THANK YOU.
WELL, ARE YOU UP FOR A DATE, KID? I KNOW JUST THE PLACE. YOU'LL LOVE IT.
36

OH, DONNA... I FEEL SO GOOD... SO VERY GOOD.
I'M SO HAPPY TO SEE ALL OF YOU.
WE WERE WORRIED, KORY...

KORY, WE HAVE A SURPRISE FOR YOU... SOMEONE WE THOUGHT YOU'D LIKE TO SEE.
BUT ALL MY FRIENDS ARE HERE, DICK. WHO--?

HAVE YOU FORGOTTEN YOUR OWN BROTHER?
RYAND'R?
CAN YOU BELIEVE ANYTHING THAT TRAITRESS SAYS?
BUT... KOMAND'R SAID YOU KILLED OUR PARENTS...

X'HAL! X'HAL! RYAND'R... I--I LOVE YOU... I LOVE YOU!
JUST LOOK AT YOU... YOU'VE GROWN, BECOME A MAN. OH, X'HAL, YOU'RE SO WONDERFUL TO LOOK AT.
BUT... OUR PARENTS... WHY DID THEY HAVE TO DIE BEFORE I RETURNED HOME? WHY?
37

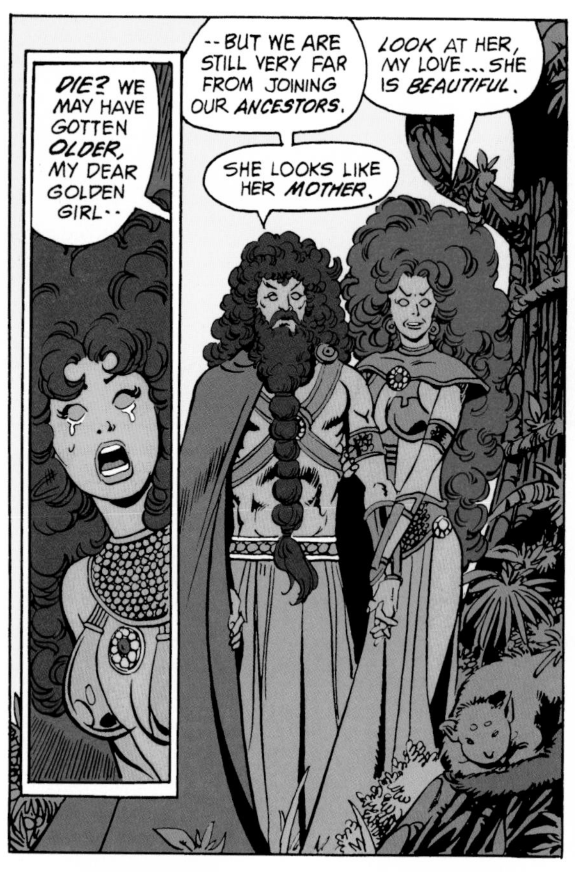
DIE? WE MAY HAVE GOTTEN OLDER, MY DEAR GOLDEN GIRL--
--BUT WE ARE STILL VERY FAR FROM JOINING OUR ANCESTORS.
SHE LOOKS LIKE HER MOTHER.
LOOK AT HER, MY LOVE... SHE IS BEAUTIFUL.

YOU'RE ALIVE? ALIVE? BUT--?
KORY, WHAT ARE YOU WAITING FOR?
YOU'RE ALIVE!
YOU'RE ALIVE!! THANK X'HAL, YOU'RE ALIVE!!

YOU'RE WONDERFUL, RAVEN-- CURING HER LIKE THAT.
NO PARENTS SHOULD EVER SEE THEIR LOVED ONE SO SCARRED.
NOW, WE SHOULD ALL LEAVE. KORIAND'R IS HOME.

I SEARCHED THE SEA-BEDS FOR KOMAND'R...
...BUT THIS IS ALL I FOUND.
SHE COULD NOT HAVE SURVIVED.
DEATH IS THE LEAST SHE DESERVED.
38

I NEVER THOUGHT I'D BE ABLE TO SAY THIS, BUT I'M HOME AGAIN... HOME TO STAY.
NO, MY GOLDEN ANGEL, NOT TO STAY -- ALTHOUGH IT TEARS MY VERY HEART TO SAY IT.
BUT, FATHER, I BELONG HERE... I LOVE --
AS WE LOVE YOU WITH ALL OUR HEARTS. BUT THE TRUTH STILL HOLDS SWAY.
SOON THE CITADEL WILL CHOOSE ITS NEW LEADERS AND THEY WILL RECALL OUR PACT.
IF YOU REMAIN ON TAMARAN, WE WILL BE DESTROYED.
YOU HAVE TO GO, KORIAND'R, BUT WE WILL BE HERE. AND I KNOW YOU WILL RETURN.
MOTHER, I DON'T WANT TO GO... PLEASE DON'T MAKE ME LEAVE YOU.

TELL THEM, DICK... TELL THEM!
YOU KNOW THEY'RE RIGHT, KORY.
BUT YOU KNOW YOU'RE NOT ALONE... WE'RE ALSO YOUR FAMILY AND WE LOVE YOU.

YOU WON'T LEAVE ME, TOO?
I WON'T LEAVE YOU.
IT IS TIME TO DEPART IF THE OMEGA MEN ARE TO ASSURE THAT ONE DAY KORIAND'R CAN RETURN.
THIS HAS BEEN A PLEASURE, ONE WHICH BROOT WILL NOT SOON FORGET.
GOOD LUCK TO YOU ALL...

BUT I THINK KORY UNDERSTANDS... IT DOESN'T MATTER WHERE SHE IS --
-- AS LONG AS SHE IS LOVED, SHE'S HOME!

END

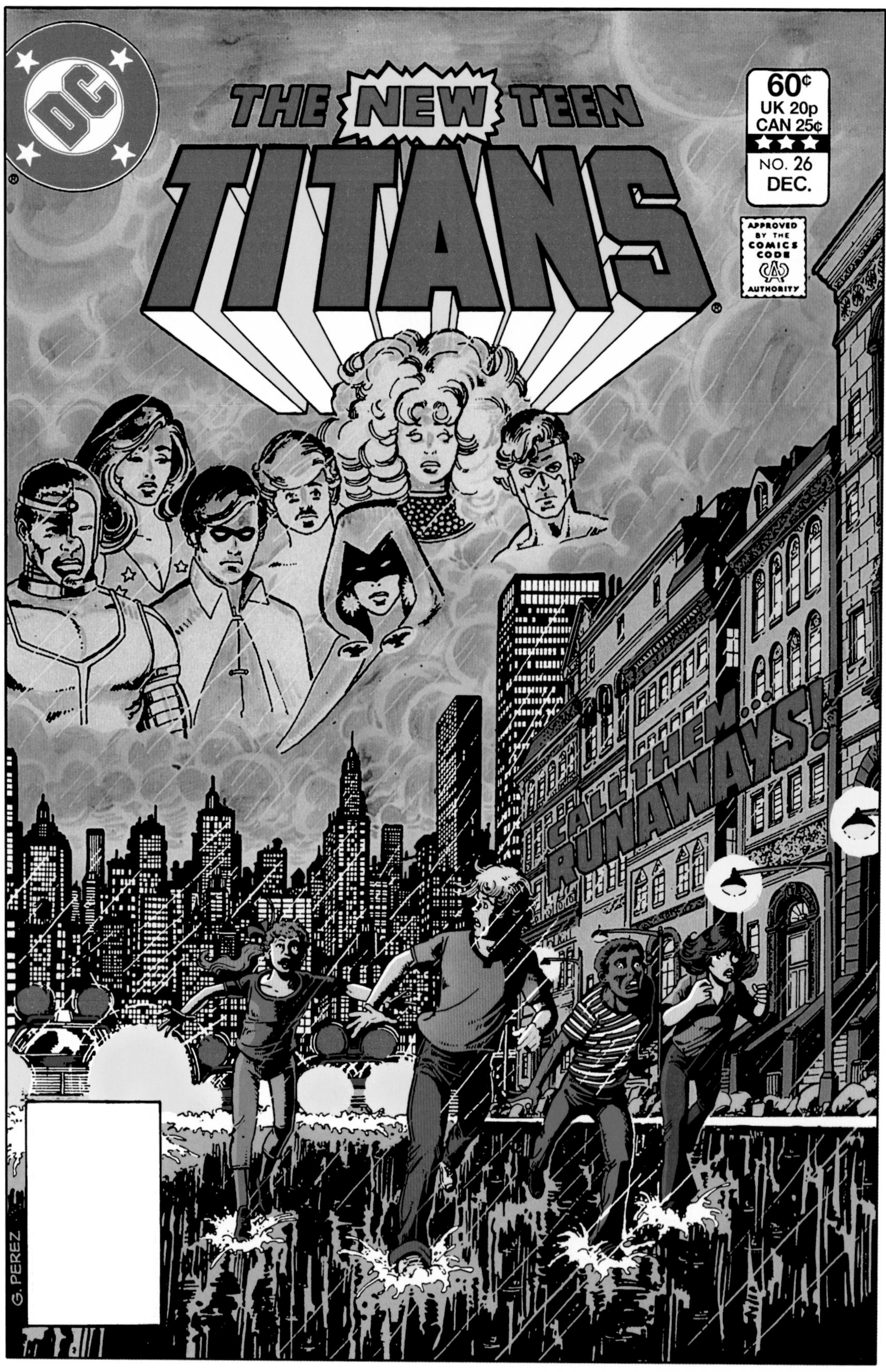
THE NEW TEEN
TITANS
60¢
UK 20p
CAN 25¢
NO. 26
DEC.
APPROVED BY THE COMICS CODE AUTHORITY
CALL THEM... RUNAWAYS!
G. PEREZ

THE NEW TEEN TITANS
MARV WOLFMAN + GEORGE PÉREZ
WRITER -- CO-CREATORS -- ARTIST
ROMEO TANGHAL
INKER
BEN ODA - LETTERER
ADRIENNE ROY - COLORIST
LEN WEIN
EDITOR
SPACE: A GREAT PLACE TO VISIT, BUT THESE TEEN TITANS WOULDN'T WANT TO LIVE THERE.
WE'RE ALMOST HOME.
YEP.
NICE DAY IF IT DOESN'T RAIN.
YEP.
YOU'RE THINKING ABOUT DICK AND KORY TOO, HUH?
UHHH, YEP.
I THINK DICK'S IN LOVE WITH HER.
I DON'T THINK DICK KNOWS WHAT HE THINKS.
I THINK HE KNOWS HE LOVES HER.
I KNOW SHE CERTAINLY LOVES HIM.
GOD, I HOPE THEY KNOW WHAT THEY'RE DOING.

WELL, LOOK AT IT THIS WAY. SHE'S GORGEOUS, BEAUTIFUL AND STACKED. HE'S GOT TO LOVE HER.
MEBBE, LOGAN.

THEN AGAIN MEBBE IT'S NONE OF OUR BUSINESS. DESPITE THE NAME OF OUR LITTLE COFFEE KLATCH HERE, THEY'RE BOTH GROWN UP.

AND WHETHER THEIR RELATIONSHIP WORKS OR NOT, IT'S REALLY UP TO THEM, ISN'T IT?

"STILL, I HOPE DICK KNOWS WHAT HE'S GETTING INTO."

KORY, CAN I SEE YOU?
OF COURSE, C'MON IN.

DOES IT STILL HURT?
IT'S FINE. KORY, CAN WE TALK?
IF YOU'RE GOING TO BE REAL SERIOUS, I DON'T KNOW.
I AM, BUT IT'S OKAY.

I JUST WANTED YOU TO KNOW WHY I'VE BEEN ACTING LIKE SUCH AN ASS LATELY.
BUT YOU'VE BEEN WONDERFUL.
NO, I HAVEN'T. PLEASE BELIEVE ME.
YOU HAVE TO UNDERSTAND SOMETHING ABOUT ME. I WAS BROUGHT UP BY THE BATMAN.
DESPITE THE TRAUMA THAT MADE HIM BECOME WHAT HE IS, HE ALWAYS TAUGHT ME TO BE GUIDED BY MY HEAD, NOT MY HEART.
BESIDES, I THINK I'VE ALWAYS BEEN TOO INTROSPECTIVE FOR MY OWN GOOD.
DICK...?
NO, PLEASE LET ME FINISH. IT'LL BE EASIER THAT WAY.
2

YOU ALSO HAVE TO UNDERSTAND THAT I JUST CAME OUT OF A ROMANCE WITH SOMEONE I THOUGHT I CARED FOR.
THAT'S WHY I'VE BEEN PUTTING YOU OFF.
YOU WERE IN LOVE WITH SOMEONE ELSE?
I DON'T KNOW WHAT I WAS.
CAN I REALLY BE HONEST WITH YOU? PART OF YOU FRIGHTENS ME. REALLY SCARES ME DOWN DEEP.
NOT THE FACT THAT YOU'RE NOT HUMAN. OR ONLY PARTIALLY HUMAN, OR WHATEVER YOU ARE... BUT SOMETHING ELSE.
IT'S HARD TO EXPLAIN. BUT, DESPITE MY REPUTATION FOR KNOWING EVERYTHING, I REALIZE I DON'T KNOW ANYTHING...
...ABOUT MYSELF.

I KNOW I LOVE YOU. ISN'T THAT ENOUGH?
I DON'T THINK SO. YOU SEE, I ONLY THINK I MAY LOVE YOU.

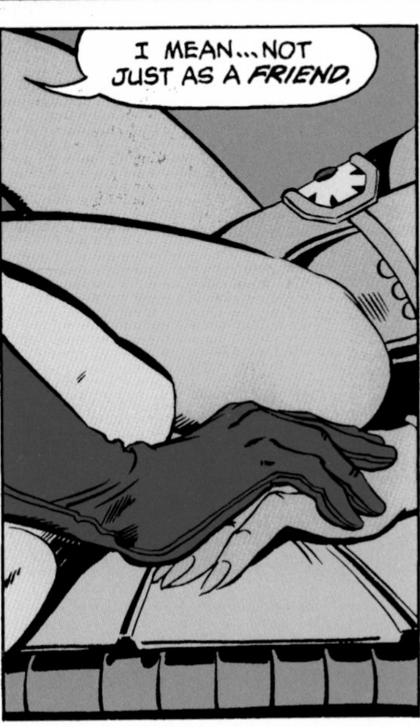

I MEAN... NOT JUST AS A FRIEND.

I MEAN... IN A ROMANTIC WAY. LORD, I DON'T KNOW WHAT I MEAN. I REALLY NEED TIME TO SORT OUT MY EMOTIONS.
I'LL GIVE YOU ALL THE TIME IN THE WORLD.

THE PLANET EARTH LOOMS AHEAD, SEEM-INGLY GROWING LARGER WITH EVERY PASSING MOMENT...

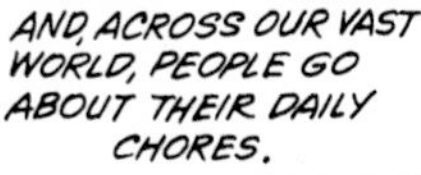

AND, ACROSS OUR VAST WORLD, PEOPLE GO ABOUT THEIR DAILY CHORES.

MOST PEOPLE WORK FOR THE GOOD.

MOST, BUT NOT ALL.
TURKEY:
HEY! CAREFUL WITH THEM BOXES. THESE "TELEVISION" THINGS MIGHT BE FRAGILE.

"TELEVISION COMPONENTS"! HAH!
3

POLICE! SURRENDER YOUR ARMS!
HELL! IT'S THE COPS! RUN!

DON'T. WE HAVE YOU SURROUNDED. LAY DOWN YOUR WEAPONS.

BUT...
...THEY DON'T. AND THEY PAY FOR THEIR STUBBORNNESS.

GRAND RAPIDS, MINNESOTA:

I DON'T WANT TO SHOW HER MY REPORT CARD.

SHE'LL BEAT ME LIKE SHE ALWAYS DOES.
YOU GOTTA UNDERSTAND ME, DON'T YOU?

C'MON, YOU KNOW SHE'D BE HAPPIER IF I LEFT.
LOOK, I GOT IT PLANNED. I ALREADY GOT THE TICKET TO NEW YORK.

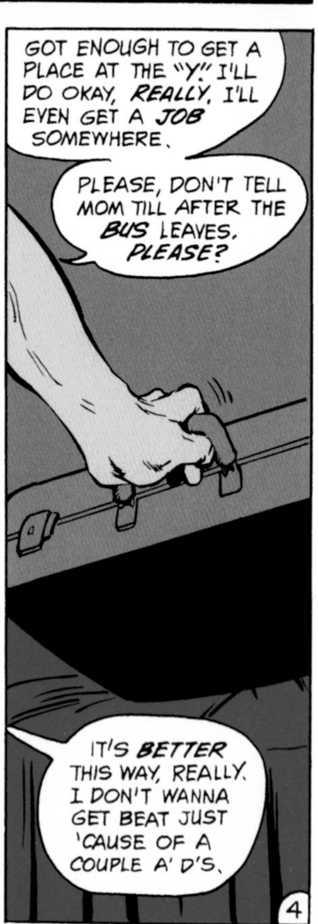
GOT ENOUGH TO GET A PLACE AT THE "Y." I'LL DO OKAY, REALLY. I'LL EVEN GET A JOB SOMEWHERE.
PLEASE, DON'T TELL MOM TILL AFTER THE BUS LEAVES. PLEASE?
IT'S BETTER THIS WAY, REALLY. I DON'T WANNA GET BEAT JUST 'CAUSE OF A COUPLE A' D'S.
4

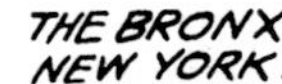
THE BRONX, NEW YORK:

PLEASE, LUIS, DON'T GO. DON'T LEAVE. WE LOVE YOU.

MAN, YOU CROWD ME, MA. BOTH OF YOU ASKIN' TOO MANY PERSONAL QUESTIONS.
HEY, I GOT RIGHTS. I DON'T HAFTA ANSWER NOTHIN'! GOT THAT, MA?
YOU WAN' ME TO STAY, IT'S UNDER MY TERMS.
I STAY OUT LONG AS I WANT. I DO WHAT I WANT. SEE WHO I WANNA SEE, AND NO QUESTIONS. COMPRENDE?

DON'T WANNA BE TOLD WHAT TO DO. DON'T WANNA BE TOLD MY FRIENDS ARE GARBAGE. DON'T WANNA BE TOLD TO GO TO NO LOUSY SCHOOL.
MAN, I WANT BREAD, AND I CAN MAKE BIG BREAD ON THE STREET. GOT THAT, MA?
DON'T NEED THIS PLACE NO MORE, MAN.

ROSA, LUIS HAS MADE UP HIS MIND. WE CANNOT STOP HIM.
GALENO, WE CAN'T LET MY LITTLE BOY GO. PLEASE, MAKE HIM STAY.
DON'T LET MY BOY LEAVE ME.

SKOKIE, ILLINOIS:
DIDN'T YOU HEAR ME, DADDY? PLEASE SAY SOMETHING.
3215
I NEED HELP. I DON'T KNOW WHAT TO DO.

YOU WANT TO KNOW WHAT TO DO, LIZZIE? I'LL TELL YOU WHAT TO DO.
YOU GO MARRY THAT SCUM.
LET HIM TAKE CARE OF YOUR BABY. I WANT NOTHIN' TO DO WITH IT.

BUT, DADDY, I DON'T WANT TO GET MARRIED. I'M NOT OLD ENOUGH. WE WERE, Y'KNOW, JUST FOOLING AROUND, THAT'S ALL.

I RAISED YOU TO BE A LADY, BUT YOU'RE NOTHING BUT A ROTTEN SLUT. GO WALK THE STREETS WITH THE REST OF YOUR KIND.
I DON'T KNOW YOU ANY-MORE.
GOD, DADDY... GOD!
5

ON AN ISLAND IN THE MIDDLE OF NEW YORK'S MURKY EAST RIVER, THERE IS A TEN-STORY T-SHAPED STRUCTURE THAT ONLY A VERY FEW NEW YORKERS KNOW AS **TITANS' TOWER**, HOME OF THE NEW TEEN TITANS...

IT IS INDEPENDENTLY FINANCED (MOST OF THE TITANS ARE WELL-TO-DO), CONTAINS ITS OWN POWER GENERATORS, AND FEATURES VIRTUALLY EVERY ACCOMMODATION NEEDED.

AND, IF YOU'VE JUST RETURNED HERE AFTER A LONG AND PAINFUL BATTLE IN SPACE, IT'S ALSO A REALLY **NEAT** PLACE TO BE.

THIS *IS* MY HOME AWAY FROM HOME. IF I CAN'T BE ON TAMARAN, THERE'S NO PLACE ELSE I'D **RATHER** BE.

I SURE COULD USE A **HOT BATH** RIGHT ABOUT NOW.

LORD, I ACHE IN PLACES I'D FORGOTTEN I **HAD**.

IT REALLY DOES FEEL GOOD BEING **BACK** HERE.

I'VE MISSED IT, TRULY **MISSED** THIS PLACE.

TOWER, I LOVE **YOU** AND YOUR WALLS AND FLOORS AND COMPUTER GIZMOS AND THINGIES AND ELEVATORS AND DOODADS AND--

DON'T YOU THINK YOU'RE GETTING **CARRIED AWAY**, GAR?

SHUT UP, RUSTHEAD. I'M A **ROMANTIC**. WE ALWAYS OVER-EMOTE.

WHERE WAS I? OH, YES, TOWER, I **LOVE** YOU. LET'S RUN AWAY TOGETHER AND MAKE LITTLE **BUNGALOWS**!

6

THIS PLACE IS MORE OF A HOME TO ME THAN PARADISE ISLAND EVER WAS.
I TRULY FEEL AS IF I BELONG HERE.
I GREW UP ON THOSE STREETS. AND I BLED ON THOSE STREETS IN MORE GANG FIGHTS THAN I WANNA REMEMBER.
YEAH, I REALLY GET OFF ON OL' WORMY, TOO.
THEY SAY THERE ARE MORE GORGEOUS GIRLS PER SQUARE INCH HERE THAN ON ANY CALIFORNIA BEACH.

I GOTTA TAKE OFF, GUYS. I HAVEN'T SEEN SARAH SIMMS OR THE KIDS IN WEEKS.
YOU KNOW, SOMETIMES I THINK THOSE KIDS HELP ME MORE'N I CAN EVER HELP THEM.

YEAH, YOU SEE SARAH. ME, I'M PRACTICIN' FOR ALL THOSE GIRLS.
I WANT TO GET MY PUCKER DOWN PAT.
SPACE: PTUI!! NEW YORK: YAY!

ARE YOU GOING TO BE ALL RIGHT, RAVEN?
I THINK SO, WALLACE. BUT I REALIZE IT IS STILL EARLY. I HAVE TO RE-REGISTER FOR MY FALL SEMESTER IN COLLEGE.
I HAVE MISSED SO MUCH ALREADY.
I'LL WALK YOU, RAVEN, IF IT'S ALL RIGHT?

THAT WOULD BE FINE, WALLACE. I THINK I WOULD ...ENJOY THE COMPANY.

DONNA, DICK'S TAKING ME TO GOTHAM CITY TONIGHT SO I WON'T BE HOME. IS THAT OKAY?
SHE'LL BE SAFE, DONNA. MY ARM'S STILL BUSTED. WE'LL PROBABLY HAVE ALFRED AS A CHAPERONE.

YOU TWO ENJOY YOURSELVES. I'VE GOT A LONG OVERDUE DATE WITH A CERTAIN HANDSOME COLLEGE HISTORY PROFESSOR.
MR. TERRY LONG AND I HAVE A LOT OF CATCHING UP TO DO...
...AND CHAPERONES ARE NOT PERMITTED.
AND SO ONE STORY ENDS, BUT ANOTHER SLOWLY UNFOLDS.
7
SEVERAL WEEKS PASS BY BEFORE WE ENCOUNTER A PROBLEM FAR WORSE THAN ANY SUPER-VILLAIN...

RUNAWAYS

NEW YORK CITY: UNDER THE GLITTERING LIGHTS OF BROADWAY...
KORY, EVERYONE SWEARS WE'LL LOVE "NINE"! IT'S THIS YEAR'S MEGA-HIT!
BEING WITH YOU IS ALL I CARE ABOUT, DICK. YOU SHOULD KNOW THAT!
TAXI
REX
CRF 49
8

AND I CAN'T BELIEVE WE'RE FINALLY ON A REAL DATE.
WHAT DO YOU MEAN? WE'VE BEEN GOING OUT FOR WEEKS NOW.

OH, I KNOW. BUT NOT LIKE THIS.
GETTING DRESSED UP AND GOING TO A BROAD-WAY SHOW IS SOMETHING SPECIAL.
DICK, LOOK OVER THERE!

ISN'T THAT THE DISTRICT ATTORNEY WE MET AFTER THE BROTHER BLOOD FIGHT?
ADRIAN CHASE. YEAH, I THOUGHT HE WAS A REAL HARD-BOILED CASE. GUESS EVEN HE TAKES TIME OFF TO RELAX.

LET'S GO OVER AND SAY "HI!"
UH-UH. YOU FORGET. HE MET STARFIRE AND ROBIN, NOT KORY ANDERS AND DICK GRAYSON.

OUR CIVILIAN ID'S AREN'T SUPPOSED TO KNOW HIM.
BESIDES, CHASE IS BUSINESS. TONIGHT WE'RE OUT FOR FUN.
THEY'LL HELP... THEY GOTTA HELP.

GOD, BUGS ALL OVER ME, ALL OVER ME. FOLLOWIN' ME.

HEY! GIMME YOUR MONEY, ALL YOUR MONEY.
YOU HEAR ME? GIMME YOUR MONEY.
WHAT'RE YOU WAITIN' FOR? THE BUGS ARE ALL OVER ME, MAN. DON'T YOU SEE 'EM? I NEED MONEY, MAN. GIMME.
ADRIAN, PLEASE DON'T FIGHT HIM.
PUT DOWN THAT BLADE, KID. YOU DON'T WANT TO HURT ANYONE.

WE'VE GOT TO HELP HIM, DICK.
WE WILL, IF CHASE CAN'T HANDLE IT.
GIVE HIM A CHANCE.

LISTEN, KID, YOU'RE NOT WELL. LET ME HELP YOU, OKAY?
HEY, I'M FINE, FLYING FINE. IT'S JUST ALL THEM DAMNED BUGS.
BUT YOUR MONEY'LL SEND THEM AWAY. THEY WON'T HURT ME.
9

Y'KNOW, THEY WERE AFTER ME. THE BUGS AND THE OTHERS. OUT TO CUT ME 'CAUSE I RAN WITH THE MONEY.
BUT I CAN PAY 'EM OFF WITH YOUR MONEY.
C'MON, MAN, WHAT YOU WAITIN' FOR? GOTTA BUY THE STUFF AND MAKE 'EM STOP!
SORRY, KID, YOU DON'T NEED MONEY. YOU NEED SOME TIME IN BELLEVUE. GIVE ME YOUR-- AGGHHH!
ADRIAN--YOUR SHOULDER!
DOESN'T HURT. C'MON, KID, LET'S GO.
SEE, KORY, CHASE HANDLED IT WITHOUT US.
SOMETIMES WE FORGET WE'RE NOT ALWAYS NEEDED.
BUT...
NO! NO! NONONONO! NOT GOIN' ANYWHERE... NO -- THEY'LL FIND ME, THEY'LL FIND ME!
LET ME GO, MAN... GOTTA GET OUTTA HERE. LET ME GO!
ADRIAN!
I'LL GIVE 'EM BACK THE CASH, THAT'S WHAT. THEY'LL TAKE THE BUGS AWAY FROM ME.
GIVE IT ALL BACK.
PLEASE, DON'T GO AFTER HIM.
THE DAMNED FOOL! HE'S NOT LOOKING WHERE HE'S GOING.
OH, GOD-- KID!!
KID!
DICK!
NO!
BEEEP
10

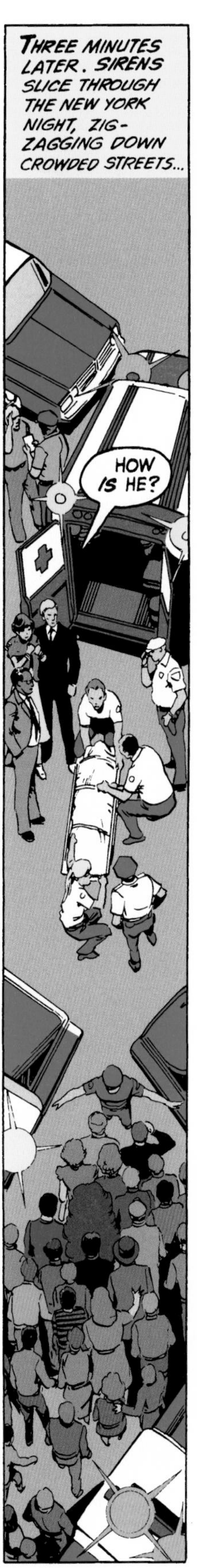
THREE MINUTES LATER. SIRENS SLICE THROUGH THE NEW YORK NIGHT, ZIG-ZAGGING DOWN CROWDED STREETS...
HOW IS HE?

DEAD.
IT MUST HAVE BEEN INSTANTANEOUS.
OH, GOD.

ADRIAN, ARE WE EVER GOING TO GET AWAY FROM THIS VIOLENCE?
I DON'T THINK I CAN TAKE IT ANY LONGER. THE CITY'S GETTING TO ME.
HONEY, IT'S THE SAME EVERYWHERE. THERE'S NO ESCAPE.
SOMETIMES I THINK THE ANIMALS HAVE TAKEN OVER.

WHAT WAS WRONG WITH THAT BOY?
MOST LIKELY DRUGS.

DAMN. IT'S A SHAME, KORY.
I REALLY FEEL SORRY FOR KIDS LIKE THAT.

TITANS' TOWER...
OH, NO -- NO! C'MON. OH, GOD -- NO!
I -- I DON'T BELIEVE IT. I CAN'T BELIEVE IT!
NONO NO!
11

LOST AGAIN! STUPID GAME! SOMETIMES I THINK ATARI HATES ME PERSONALLY.
SKRREEE
NUTS! IT FIGURES... THE EMERGENCY SIGNAL!

UH-OH, SOMETHING'S UP AT THE STATUE OF LIBERTY. WELL, GUESS I SHOULD CALL IN THE OTHERS.
THEN AGAIN, I COULD LET THE COPS HANDLE IT AND TRY ANOTHER ROUND OF SWORDQUEST.

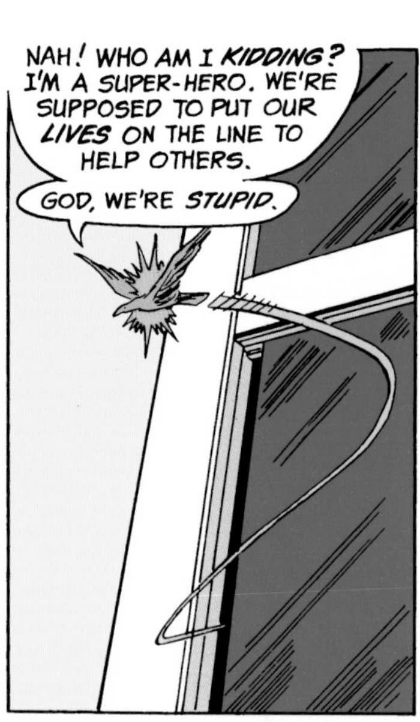
NAH! WHO AM I KIDDING? I'M A SUPER-HERO. WE'RE SUPPOSED TO PUT OUR LIVES ON THE LINE TO HELP OTHERS.
GOD, WE'RE STUPID.

KEEP AN EYE ON HER... DON'T LET HER ESCAPE.
HOW ARE WE SUPPOSED TO DO THAT?
YOU SEE HER POWERS?

MEANWHILE...
WELL, WELL, LOOK WHAT WE HAVE HERE.

HALF OF NEW YORK CITY'S FINEST HAVE GATHERED TO STOP--HER?
HI, HONEY--WHAT'S THE PROBLEM? LOSE YOUR BOYFRIEND?
COME TO UNCLE CHANGELING--I CAN HELP YOU IF SOMETHING'S WRONG.
CHANGELING? STAY AWAY FROM ME.
DON'T GET CLOSE OR I'LL HAVE TO KILL YOU.
I HAVE MY ASSIGNMENT. I HAVE TO DESTROY THIS STATUE.

YEAH, YEAH, I KNOW. IT'S A DIRTY JOB. BUT HONEY, YOU DON'T HAVE TO DO IT.
YOU LOOK LIKE YOU'RE IN TROUBLE. LET ME HELP.
NO--STAY AWAY.
YOU DON'T UNDERSTAND.

BUT YOU'RE STILL GOING TO TRY TO STOP ME, AREN'T YOU?
12

OKAY, THE STATUE STAYS IN ONE PIECE... I CAN'T LET MYSELF BE CAUGHT.
FOR NOW, CHANGELING, YOU WIN!
BUT THE NEXT TIME WE MEET, I WILL HAVE TO KILL YOU!

WHAT THE HECK IS SHE DOING?
JUMPING?
IN AN INSTANT, THE TITANS' RESIDENT METAMORPH ALTERS HIS HUMAN SHAPE...
...AND...
DON'T TRY TO CHASE ME, CHANGELING. IT CAN'T BE DONE!
I'VE GOT POWERS YOU HAVEN'T EVEN DREAMED OF!

I'M CALLED TERRA-- THAT'S AS IN EARTH POWERS!
CRUNCH!

I CAN DO MOST ANYTHING -- INCLUDING ERUPTING A SOLID COLUMN OF EARTH SKYWARD TO SLOW MY FALL--
--AND SMASH YOU INTO OBLIVION!

OKAY, KID-- DON'T MOVE. WE HAVE YOU COVERED.
I DON'T BELIEVE THIS. YOU SAW WHAT I CAN DO.
AND YOU STILL COME AFTER ME?

SHE'S GOING TO DO SOMETHING -- FIRE!
ARE YOU PEOPLE INSANE? ALL I HAVE TO DO IS RAISE AN EARTHEN SHIELD AND YOUR BULLETS ARE STOPPED IN THEIR TRACKS!
13

AND IF THE SHIELD ISN'T ENOUGH, I CAN CHANGE THAT COLUMN--
--INTO AN UNSTOPPABLE MONSTER!
SO PLEASE LET ME GO BEFORE YOU MAKE ME KILL YOU.
I DON'T WANT TO DO ANY OF THIS IN THE FIRST PLACE!
DON'T MAKE IT HARDER ON ME. PLEASE!!

SORRY, SHORT-STUFF, BUT YOU'RE NOT STOPPING ME.
LOOK, LET'S GET THIS STRAIGHT. I'M THE GOOD GUY AND YOU'RE THE BAD GUY.
IF I LET YOU GO, I'D HAVE TO TURN IN MY SUPER-HERO UNION CARD!
AND YOU KNOW HOW LONG IT TOOK FOR ME TO GET THE BLASTED THING?
SKRUNCH!
14

OH-NO--I DON'T LIKE THIS.
THEY'RE COMING FROM ALL SIDES. I'M NOT READY FOR A BIG BATTLE.
GOT TO GET OUT OF HERE.

BLAST! I THOUGHT I WAS SO MUCH BETTER. THOUGHT I HAD IT ALL WORKED OUT.
THEY'LL KILL ME FOR FOULING UP. THEY'LL JUST KILL ME.

AS IF PROPELLED FROM THE HEART OF A VOLCANO, THE GIRL NAMED TERRA SOARS OFF...

...VANISHING INTO THE FAR DISTANT MISTS...
SHE'S ESCAPING... AND I'M --I'M OUT OF POWER!
WHO IS SHE?

MEANWHILE, IN A WELL-KNOWN EATING ESTABLISHMENT IN THE MIDDLE OF NEW YORK'S TIMES SQUARE DISTRICT...
YOU'RE FULL OF SURPRISES, RAVEN. I NEVER THOUGHT YOU'D RE-REGISTER FOR PROFESSOR HOLLIS' CLASS.
NEWSTAND

AND I NEVER THOUGHT YOU'VE EVER GO OUT WITH ANY OF US.
YOU ALWAYS KEEP AWAY FROM US.
MY FRIENDS HAVE SUGGESTED I ASSOCIATE WITH OTHERS. BUT I DO FEEL AWKWARD BEING IN THIS PLACE.
THAT'S ANOTHER THING -- WHERE DO YOU COME FROM?
PLEASE, PAUL -- DO NOT ASK ME QUESTIONS.
I DO NOT LIKE TO TALK ABOUT MYSELF.

C'MON, RAVEN, WE'VE BEEN GOING TO THE SAME CLASSES FOR MONTHS. YOU CAN LIGHTEN UP WITH US.
NO! DO YOU NOT UNDERSTAND ME? I CAN NOT-- AGGHH!
THE PAIN!
WHAT IS IT? WHAT'S WRONG? WHAT'S WRONG WITH YOU?
GET AWAY FROM ME, PAUL... YOU DO NOT KNOW ME. YOU DO NOT UNDERSTAND ME.
THAT GIRL... SHE IS THE SOURCE OF MY PAIN.
I SENSE HUNGER... FEAR ...THE GIRL HAS BEEN HURT BOTH PHYSICALLY AND EMOTIONALLY.
SHE NEEDS MY HELP!

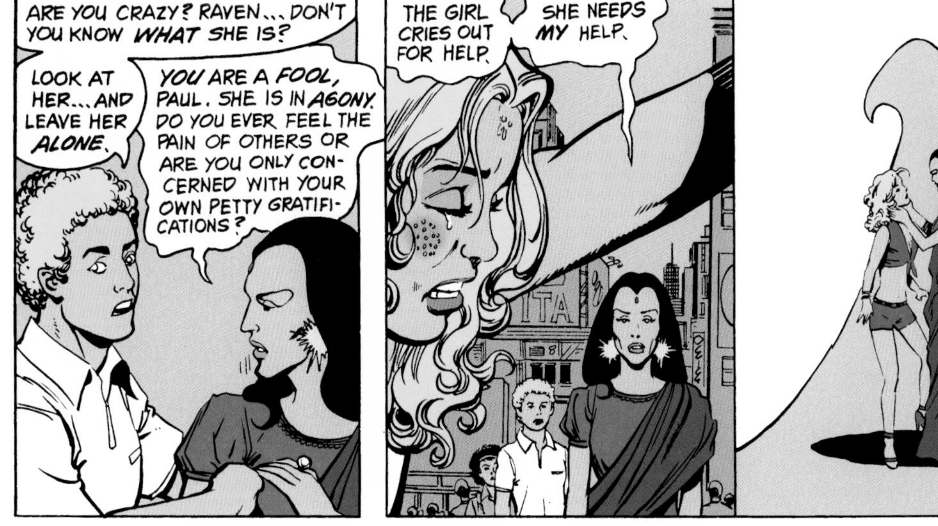
ARE YOU CRAZY? RAVEN... DON'T YOU KNOW WHAT SHE IS?
LOOK AT HER... AND LEAVE HER ALONE.
YOU ARE A FOOL, PAUL. SHE IS IN AGONY. DO YOU EVER FEEL THE PAIN OF OTHERS OR ARE YOU ONLY CONCERNED WITH YOUR OWN PETTY GRATIFICATIONS?
THE GIRL CRIES OUT FOR HELP.
SHE NEEDS MY HELP.
SHE NEEDS ME.

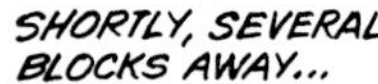
SHORTLY, SEVERAL BLOCKS AWAY...

ARE YOU ALL RIGHT NOW?
THANK HEAVEN... I NEEDED FOOD. I WAS SO HUNGRY AND IT WAS HURTING SO MUCH.
YOU HAVEN'T EATEN?

GOD, NO--NOT FOR DAYS. NOT SINCE THE COPS PICKED UP HOWARD.
HOWARD?
THE GUY I GOTTA GIVE ALL MY MONEY TO. THE COPS PICKED HIM UP AND I DIDN'T HAVE ANY MONEY.
LOOK, I WANNA THANK YOU. SAY, WHAT'S YOUR NAME?

PLEASE CALL ME RAVEN. AND YOU?
LIZZIE ANGELO.

THIS HOWARD HAS YOU WALKING THE STREETS, LIZZIE?
VICTOR, THANK YOU FOR YOUR FOOD AND APARTMENT.
'S NOTHIN', RAVEN. DID THIS HOWARD ALSO BEAT YOU, LIZZIE?

M-MY GOD! YOUR FACE!
BURT REYNOLDS HAS NOTHING TO WORRY ABOUT, DOES HE?
LIZZIE, SOMETHING TELLS ME YOU'VE BEEN TREATED REAL BADLY THESE PAST FEW WEEKS. YOU NEED HELP.
C'MON, CLEAN THAT GUNK OFF YOUR FACE. I WANT TO SHOW YOU SOMETHING.

HE WATCHES, AND HE WAITS.

THIS MIGHT BE HIS FIRST CLUE IN DAYS.
HOWEVER LONG IT WILL TAKE, HE WAITS.
AND WATCHES.
16

SEVERAL HOURS LATER...
LIZZIE, THIS IS A RUNAWAY CENTER. I THINK YOU BELONG HERE.
HUH? WHAT MAKES YOU THINK I RAN AWAY?
I DID IT WHEN I WAS A KID, TOO. SEVERAL TIMES.
AND I KEPT COMING HERE. THEY TOOK CARE OF ME AND THEY DIDN'T HASSLE ME. DIDN'T TRY'N CALL MY FOLKS, EITHER-- NOT 'TIL I WAS READY.
THEY CAN HELP YOU, LIZZIE.
AND SEVERAL MINUTES LATER...
YOU PROMISE NOT TO CALL MY DAD? HE DOESN'T EVEN WANT TO KNOW ME 'CAUSE A' THE KID.
SHE'S REALLY WORRIED, ELLIE. AND SCARED.
NO MORE SO THAN YOU WERE THE FIRST TIME, VICTOR.
MAYBE YOU WERE TOUGHER ON THE OUTSIDE, BUT JUST AS SOFT INSIDE.
DON'T WORRY LIZZIE, WE ONLY WANT TO HELP.
YOU GO WITH DR. RAYMOND. SHE'LL CHECK YOU OUT. IF YOU'RE PREGNANT, YOU HAVE TO BE ESPECIALLY CAREFUL.
SHE WAS VERY HUNGRY!
THEY MOSTLY ALL ARE WHEN THEY FIRST GET HERE. FOOD IS THE RUNAWAY'S BIGGEST PROBLEM.
YOU WOULDN'T BELIEVE SOME OF THE MALNUTRITION PROBLEMS WE'VE ENCOUNTERED.
BY THE WAY, THERE IS SOMEONE HERE WHO'D LIKE TO SEE YOU.
DO YOU KNOW ADRIAN CHASE, OUR DISTRICT ATTORNEY?
YEAH, WE'VE MET.
WELL, WELL, THE KIDDIE DO-GOODERS SQUAD IS HERE. MY DAY IS MADE.
LISTEN, LAST NIGHT A KID WAS KILLED. WE FOUND VARIOUS NARCOTICS HIDDEN ON HIS PERSON. HE WAS HUSTLING DOPE FOR A BIG SUPPLIER.
OUR SOURCES SAY WE'RE GOING TO SEE A VERY LARGE SHIP-MENT HIT THE STREETS ANY DAY NOW.
I NEED YOUR HELP.
17

HE LISTENS INTENTLY. TIME IS RUNNING SHORT-- BUT, HE THINKS, AT LEAST NOW HE KNOWS WHERE TO BEGIN.

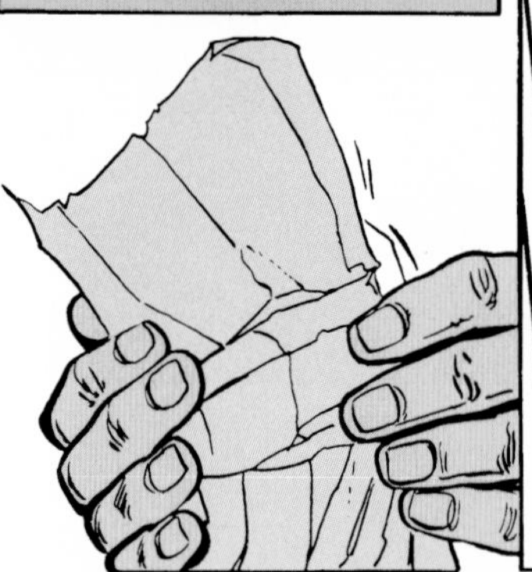
FROM HIS JACKET POCKET HE REMOVES A CRUMPLED PAPER AND GLANCES AT THE ALL-TOO-FAMILIAR HAND-WRITING...
...COMMITTING THE WRITTEN ADDRESS TO ANGRY MEMORY.

HE THEN LEAVES, KNOWING HIS REASON FOR COMING TO THIS DIRT-RIDDEN CITY IS COMING TO A HEAD AT LAST.
YOU HAVE TO REALIZE THOSE KIDS HAVE A TERRIBLY LOW OPINION OF THEM-SELVES.

SO, WHEN THE GIRLS ARE TOLD BY PIMPS HOW BEAUTIFUL THEY REALLY ARE, WHEN THEY'RE GIVEN EXPEN-SIVE CLOTHING, THEY START TO BELIEVE.

AND WITHIN A WEEK, THESE CONFUSED KIDS ARE WALKING THE STREETS, TURNING TRICKS. THAT'S GIRLS AND BOYS ALIKE.
THEY'RE ALSO RECRUITED TO SELL DRUGS--AND, MAN, IS THAT A PROBLEM FOR US.
THESE KIDS CAN MAKE A THOUSAND A WEEK. HOW THE HELL DO YOU CONVINCE THEM TO TAKE AN HONEST JOB FOR MAYBE LESS THAN A HUNDRED?

YOU JUST HAVE TO HOPE YOU CAN REACH INSIDE THEM AND MAKE THEM CARE AGAIN...
...AND THAT'S OUR HARDEST JOB. THEY HAVE TO CARE ABOUT THEMSELVES.

HOW DO YOU FIT INTO ALL THIS?
THAT KID I MENTIONED WAS A RUNAWAY. HE CAME FROM THIS PLACE.
HE WAS NOT ONLY A SUPPLIER, BUT A USER.

AND THAT, MISTER, IS WHERE YOU LONG-UNDERWEAR CHARACTERS COME IN.
18

ELSEWHERE...
THERE THEY ARE...
...THE SCUM!
ETTE

PLAYING GAMES LIKE IT NEVER HAPPENED.
MAN, ARE THEY EVER GONNA PAY--
--BIG!

...WE CALLED IN OUR SUPPLY JUST TO RESTOCK. DAMN THEM TURKS.
COST US QUARTER OF A BILLION.

BUT WE'LL MAKE IT ALL BACK, AN' THERE'LL BE NOTHIN' TO TRACE IT BACK TO US.

TWO HUNDRED STUPID KIDS ARE GONNA DO OUR DIRTY WORK FOR US!
FEW MORE DAYS AND WE'LL BE SWIMMIN' IN DOUGH!

LUIS GOMEZ PASSES ANOTHER DRINK TO ANTHONY SCARAPELLI, WHILE CASUALLY GLANCING AT THE SCANTILY-CLAD YOUNG LADIES.
THEN HE NOTICES A FAINT GLINT OF LIGHT SHINING OUT FROM A DARK CORNER OF A NEARBY DOCK.
19

MR. SCARAPELLI -- THERE'S SOMEONE OUT THERE WATCHING US.
GOOD WORK, KID.
PROBABLY A NARC. WE'LL SKRAG 'IM.

SUDDENLY, AND FOR A VERY GOOD REASON, THE YOUNG MAN IS SCARED. AND SCARED, HE RUNS...
BAM
BAM
BAM

...NOT KNOWING EXACTLY WHERE HE IS GOING OR HOW HE WILL GET THERE.
HIS CHEST NEARLY BURSTS WITH PAIN AS HIS HEART SEEMS TO EXPLODE WITH EVERY STEP.

ARE THEY STILL BEHIND HIM, HE WONDERS? HE CAN ONLY HEAR THE THUNDEROUS DRUMMING OF HIS RAPIDLY BEATING HEART.
HOPING AGAINST HOPE, HE TURNS.
"OH, GOD!"

THE CAR ROARS LIKE SOME DRAGON OF OLD...

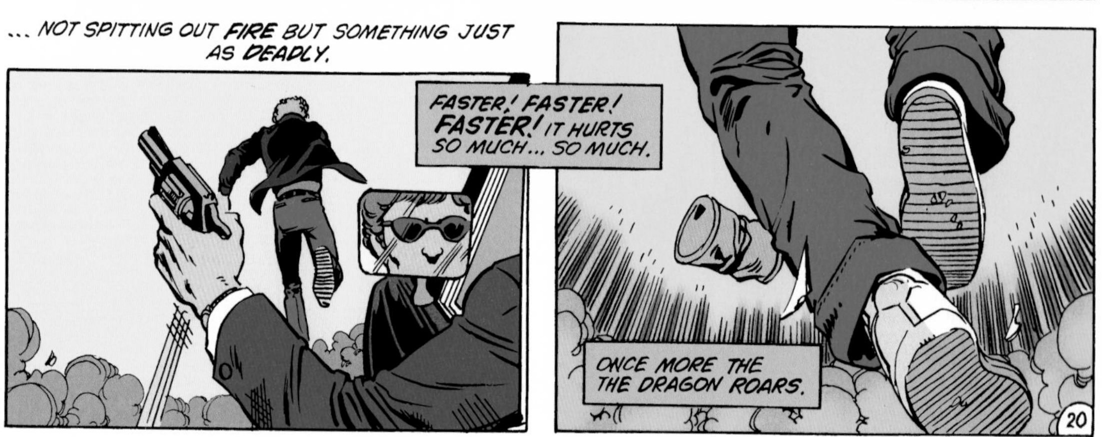
... NOT SPITTING OUT FIRE BUT SOMETHING JUST AS DEADLY.
FASTER! FASTER! FASTER! IT HURTS SO MUCH... SO MUCH.
ONCE MORE THE THE DRAGON ROARS.
20

POLICE HEADQUARTERS...
WE COULDN'T ALL MAKE IT, CHASE... BUT WE'LL DO THE BEST WE CAN.
NOW, HOW ABOUT SOME EXPLANATIONS.
SHORT AND SWEET, ROBIN. TURKISH POLICE STOPPED A BIG DRUG SHIPMENT SO SUPPLY ON THE STREETS HAS DRIED UP.

THE MOB CALLED IN ITS EUROPEAN CONNECTIONS AND A NEW SHIPMENT IS DUE HERE AT ANY TIME.
WE'VE BEEN WATCHING ALL THE KNOWN AGENTS, BUT WE'VE HEARD THE MOB IS GOING TO USE KIDS TO FERRY THE JUNK THROUGH TOWN.
SURELY THE CHILDREN UNDERSTAND THE DANGERS?
THE KIDS ARE SCARED, RAVEN. THEY'LL DO WHAT THEY'RE TOLD.
BESIDES, THESE KIDS FIGURE THEY'VE GOT NOTHING TO LOSE.
21

I CAN'T UNDERSTAND THAT. AS LONG AS THERE'S LIFE, THERE'S ALWAYS SO MUCH TO GAIN.
NOT EVERYONE'S AN OPTIMIST, STARFIRE.

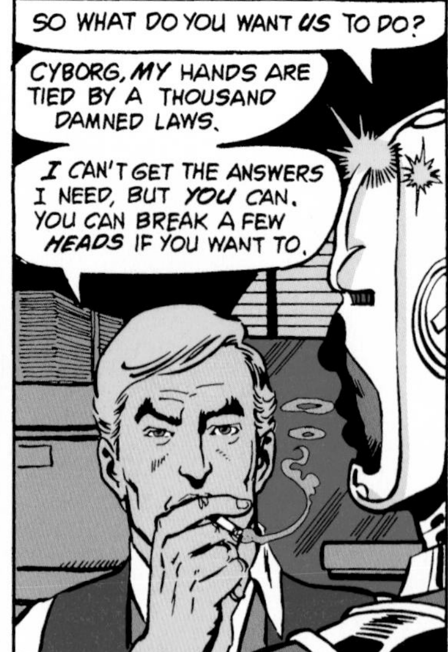
SO WHAT DO YOU WANT US TO DO?
CYBORG, MY HANDS ARE TIED BY A THOUSAND DAMNED LAWS.
I CAN'T GET THE ANSWERS I NEED, BUT YOU CAN. YOU CAN BREAK A FEW HEADS IF YOU WANT TO.

WE DON'T WORK LIKE THAT, CHASE. THERE ARE LAWS...
LAWS?

GOOD GOD, KID! THAT WORD IS STARTING TO MAKE MY SKIN CRAWL!

BUT YOU'RE A D.A.-- SWORN TO UPHOLD THE LAW.
MAYBE I NO LONGER CARE ABOUT THE LAW.

MAYBE I JUST CARE ABOUT WHAT'S RIGHT!
THOSE WORDS... ROBIN HAS HEARD THEM BEFORE, SPOKEN WITH THE SAME FANATICAL INTENSITY...

WELL, WHAT DO YOU GUYS THINK?
WE'LL GO ALONG WITH YOUR DECISION, ROBIN. THIS ISN'T OUR USUAL LINE, BUT...

ALL RIGHT, CHASE. WE'RE IN, BUT WE DO THINGS OUR WAY.
JUST GET THOSE SCUM. THAT'S ALL I CARE ABOUT.
22

RAVEN, IS HE--?

...INSIDE--?!?

DICK, HE'S NOT MOVING!

23

TO BE CONTINUED NEXT ISSUE.

DC
EXTRA! FREE 16-PAGE COMIC PREVIEW
ATARI FORCE†
THE NEW TEEN
TITANS™
60¢
UK 20p
CAN 25¢
NO. 27
JAN.
APPROVED BY THE COMICS CODE AUTHORITY
†TM Atari, Inc.

PROLOGUE
NEW YORK CITY:
OVER 30 BILLION SE
TOWN
HER NAME IS ANGELINE CAROW AND SHE IS FROM ST. LOUIS, MO....
ALONE IN NEW YORK, WITHOUT MONEY, SHE IS HUNGRY...
HEY, GIRL-- NO REASON TO STARVE, BABY.
YOU WANT FOOD, YOU CAME TO THE RIGHT PLACE. THEY CALL ME LUIS, HONEY--AND IF YOU WANT, I CAN SHOW YOU HOW TO MAKE BIG BUCKS.
Y-YOU CAN?
YEAH, HONEY, JUST COME WITH YOUR NEW BIG DADDY.
HIS NAME IS SYLVESTER JOHNSON AND HE IS FROM CLEARWATER, FLA....
NUTS. OUT OF QUARTERS.
SwordQuest
FORGET QUARTERS, MAN. I CAN GET YOU ENOUGH TO BUY THAT BIG, BAD MEAN MACHINE.
YOU INTERESTED, MAN?
YOU KNOW IT.
C'MON, HOT-SHOT, YOU JUST DONE STRUCK IT RICH!
HIS NAME IS STEVEN BROWN AND HE IS FROM SAN DIEGO, CA....
REAL BIG MONEY, BRO'-- JUST FOR CARRYIN' SOME WELL-PACKED ENVELOPES.
WHAT YOU SAY, BRO?
DON'T NEED YOUR DIRTY MONEY, MAN.
GONNA MAKE IT ON MY OWN.
SUIT YOURSELF, AMIGO, THERE ARE PLENTY OF OTHERS.
AND SO IT GOES...

THE NEW TEEN TITANS
CREATED BY WOLFMAN & PÉREZ
in
RUNAWAYS
PART 2
THE APARTMENT OF VICTOR STONE, A.K.A. CYBORG...
HE'S NOT BREATHING, IS HE, RAVEN?
WHAT HAPPENED TO HIM? WHO IS HE?
STARFIRE, I HAVEN'T THE FOGGIEST.
HE'S OBVIOUSLY BEEN SHOT, BUT WHY? WHO DID IT?
HE IS BARELY ALIVE, ROBIN.
BUT I CAN SENSE LIFE.
CAN YOU HELP HIM, WITCH?
DO I HAVE ANY CHOICE, CYBORG?
I AM AN EMPATH. I CAN NO MORE DISREGARD THIS BOY'S PAIN THAN I COULD YOURS.
WHAT I AM FORCES ME INTO ACTION.
MARV WOLFMAN, WRITER
GEORGE PÉREZ, PENCILLER
ROMEO TANGHAL, INKER
TODD KLEIN, LETTERS
ADRIENNE, COLORS
LEN WEIN, EDITOR
2

THAT DOESN'T SOUND LIKE YOU.
DON'T TELL ME YOU MISS KID FLASH?
WHERE IN BLAZES IS HE, ANYWAY?
HOME... HE HAS HIS SCHOOL WORK.
I NOTICED IT TOO, RAVEN. IS SOMETHING WRONG? CAN I HELP?
IF YOU DO NOT MIND, STARFIRE, I HAVE WORK THAT MUST BE...
...BE DONE.
THIS IS... NO EASY TASK.

HIS PAINS... SO TERRIBLE... SO VERY DEEP...
RAVEN...
THEY FLOW FROM HIM INTO ME AND THEY HURT SO VERY MUCH.
WHAT'S WRONG, RAVEN?
AZAR! THEY HURT ME... HURT ME.
RAVEN?!?

WHAT HAPPENED TO HER?
WE'VE NEVER CONSIDERED THAT ABSORBING THOSE PAINS MUST SOMEHOW AFFECT HER.
I DON'T GET IT. THIS NEVER HAPPENED BEFORE.

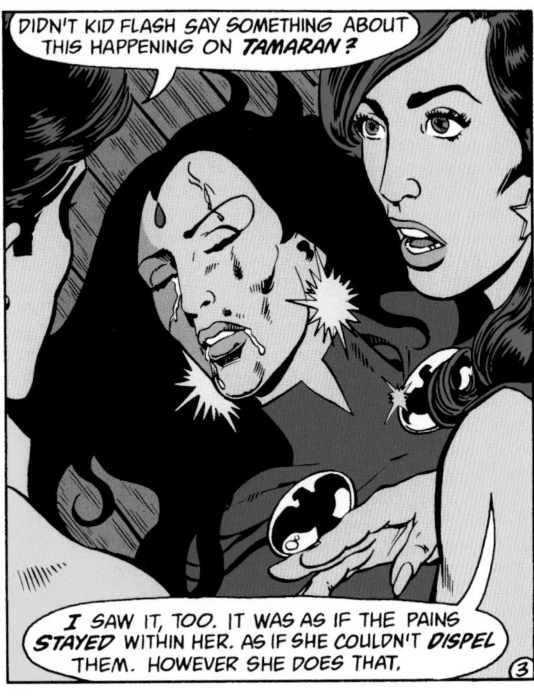
DIDN'T KID FLASH SAY SOMETHING ABOUT THIS HAPPENING ON TAMARAN?
I SAW IT, TOO. IT WAS AS IF THE PAINS STAYED WITHIN HER. AS IF SHE COULDN'T DISPEL THEM. HOWEVER SHE DOES THAT.
3

THE BOY SEEMS ALL RIGHT. THAT MEANS RAVEN SUCCEEDED.
YEAH. BUT WHAT IN HELL HAS SHE DONE TO HERSELF?
THERE WAS SOMETHING MORE. KID FLASH SAID HE HEARD THE VOICE OF HER FATHER TRIGON COMING FROM HER.
BLAST IT, WHY DOES RAVEN ALWAYS KEEP THESE THINGS TO HERSELF?

ROBIN, CAN YOU FEEL THE HEAT COMING FROM HER?
IT'S AWFUL.

NO!
I...I WON'T LET YOU TOUCH ME...

...WON'T LET YOU TAKE ME OVER.
AWAY FROM ME ...AWAY! AZAR, HELP ME, AZAR...
AWAY!

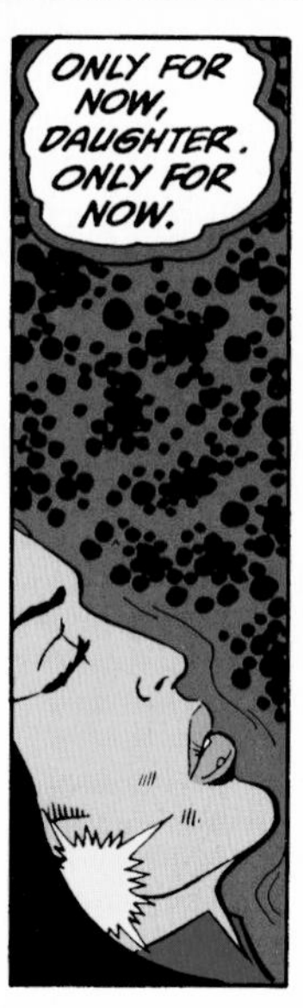
ONLY FOR NOW, DAUGHTER. ONLY FOR NOW.

RAVEN? ARE YOU--?
I AM... WELL, ROBIN.

NO, YOU'RE NOT, RAVEN.
PLEASE, TELL US WHAT'S WRONG. IT'S SO HARD TO BE YOUR FRIEND WHEN YOU WON'T TALK TO US.
THERE IS NOTHING TO TELL, ROBIN.
OUR FRIEND'S JOINED THE WORLD OF THE LIVING, TOO.

MEBBE NOW WE CAN GET SOME ANSWERS.
FIRST QUESTION, KID. HOW DID YOU GET IN HERE?
THE LANDLORD LET ME INSIDE. I TOLD HIM I WAS YOUR FRIEND.
I HAD TO COME HERE. I COULDN'T GO ANYWHERE ELSE.

OKAY, OKAY, LET'S START AT THE BEGINNING. WHO ARE YOU?
PAUL TAYLOR.
MY BROTHER DIED HERE A FEW DAYS AGO.

MIKE-- HE WAS MY BROTHER--WAS A RUNAWAY AND GOT MIXED UP IN THINGS HE SHOULDN'T HAVE.
YOUR BROTHER WAS THE ONE HIT BY THE CAR?
4

YEAH, BUT THAT WASN'T WHAT REALLY KILLED HIM. IT WAS THE DRUGS.
DID HE TAKE DRUGS BEFORE HE RAN AWAY?
NO. NOT REALLY. HE MAY HAVE TRIED A JOINT, BUT THAT'S IT. NOTHING TOO STRONG.

WHY TAKE ANY DRUGS?
HELL, HOW SHOULD I KNOW? I NEVER DID. BUT MIKE, HE SORT OF FOLLOWED WHAT HIS FRIENDS DID.
ONE OF HIS FRIENDS RAN AWAY LAST YEAR. THEN MIKE DID.
NOW HE'S DEAD.
I SPOKE WITH HIM LAST WEEK. HE SOUNDED SO SCARED... SCARED OF THE GUYS HE WORKED WITH.
HE WAS WORKING FOR A MOBSTER WHO SOLD DRUGS. MIKE WAS A STREET PUSHER.
DID HE TELL YOU WHO HIS SUPPLIER WAS?
To my brother Paul from Mike

NO. HE DIDN'T TELL ME... BUT I FOUND OUT.
...AT THE RUNAWAY CENTER AFTER I WENT THROUGH HIS CLOTHES.

SHORTLY...
YEAH, THIS IS THE PLACE. HE STAYED HERE. HE SAID THE PEOPLE HERE TOOK GOOD CARE OF HIM.
YEAH, THEY DO. THEY FEED KIDS, WATCH OUT FOR THEM, AN' EVEN TRY'N' HELP THEM FIND JOBS.
THEY GOT CENTERS LIKE THIS IN EVERY MAJOR CITY...
...THOUGH THEY DON'T HAVE ANGELS LIKE ELLIE HERE RUNNIN' 'EM.
PLEASED TO MEET YOU.
I'M SO SORRY ABOUT MIKE. WE REALLY TRIED TO HELP HIM.
BUT WE'RE NOT SURROGATE PARENTS HERE AND WE DON'T DICTATE EVERY MOVE THE KIDS MAKE. THEY'RE FREE TO COME AND GO.
AND FREE TO MAKE FRIENDS... EVEN BAD FRIENDS.
AND I'M HERE TO FIND THOSE FRIENDS OF HIS.
OH YES. TITANS, I'D LIKE YOU TO MEET...
...ROY HARPER!
5

ROY, IT'S BEEN A WHILE.
YOU KNOW EACH OTHER?
UHHH...WE WORKED TOGETHER A FEW MONTHS AGO--ON A DRUG BUST IN MIAMI.*
I'M REALLY GLAD TO SEE YOU GUYS AGAIN.

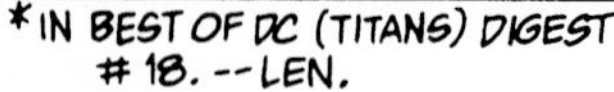
*IN BEST OF DC (TITANS) DIGEST # 18. --LEN.

C'MON, THE CREEPS WHO FED THAT CRUD TO MY BROTHER ARE PROBABLY MAKING THEIR MOVE.
CALM DOWN, PAUL. WE'LL FIND THEM WITHOUT HISTRIONICS.

SURE, SURE, BEAUTIFUL. I SEE, HARPER, THAT YOU'VE MET OUR TEENAGE VIGILANTES HERE.
BET YOU'RE REALLY CHOKED UP ABOUT WORKING WITH THEM.

ACTUALLY, MR. CHASE, THE TITANS AND I ARE OLD FRIENDS. WE GET ALONG JUST FINE, THANK YOU.
AND IF YOU'RE DONE BEING SARCASTIC, WE HAVE WORK TO DO.
YOU'RE RIGHT, HARPER, WE DO.
HARPER'S ON LOAN TO US AS A CIVILIAN EXPERT. HE'S A LIAISON BETWEEN GOVERN-MENT AGENCIES AND LOCAL AUTHORITIES.

CHASE IS COOPERATING WITH THE FEDERAL GOVERNMENT ON THIS CASE, TITANS.
A LARGE DRUG SHIPMENT HAS ENTERED THE STATES AND IS HEADING INTO THIS CITY.
WE HAVE TO FIND OUT THE POINT OF ENTRY AND HOW IT'S GETTING TO THE SUPPLIERS.

YOU ALONE ON THIS, HARPER?
AS A CIVILIAN? YEAH. BUT THE GOVERNMENT HAS DOZENS OF AGENTS ON THIS CASE.
I CAN HELP YOU. I KNOW THAT POINT OF ENTRY.
BUT I'M NOT GOING TO TELL YOU WHERE IT IS.
6

INTERLUDE
HIS NAME IS T.C. BEANE AND HE IS FROM EL PASO, TX,...
FIVE LOUSY BUCKS? THAT'S ALL YOU HAVE? SHOOT!
WASTE OF TIME, MAN. STINKIN' WASTE OF TIME.
YOU LOOKIN' FOR BIG MONEY, PAL?
HEY, WATCH WHO YOU SNEAK UP ON, BOY.
CALM DOWN, M'MAN. SYLVESTER, YOU EXPLAIN IT FOR ME.
YOU CAN MAKE BIG BUCKS, FRIEND. C'MON AND JOIN US. YOU'LL LOVE IT.
YEAH? WE'LL SEE 'BOUT THAT.
HER NAME IS JEANMARIE ROBBINS FROM SILVER SPRINGS, MD....
GOD, THAT HURT. STOMACH'S KILLIN' ME.
YOUR PIMP DO THAT TO YOU, GIRL?
HUH? WHO ARE YOU? LOOK, EVERYTHING'S ALL RIGHT, REALLY IT IS.
DON'T JIVE ME, GIRL. NOT WHEN I CAN HELP YOU.
C'MON, FOLLOW ME AND YOU WON'T REGRET IT.
UHH, OK... OKAY...
HIS NAME IS ARNIE PETOWSKI FROM PITTSBURGH, PA....
WOW, I MADE IT. NOW WHERE DO I GO?
LINES
HOW 'BOUT SOMEPLACE REAL BIG, KID...SOFT BEDS WITH NO BUGS.
HUH? WHO ARE YOU?
FRIENDS CALL ME SLY. C'MON WITH ME.
GREAT. ONLY, CAN I EAT FIRST? I'M HUNGRY. REAL HUNGRY.
AND SO IT GOES...
7

WHAT DO YOU MEAN, KID?
I'M NOT TELLING UNLESS YOU TAKE ME WITH YOU.
MY BROTHER WAS KILLED. I WANT IN ON THIS.
FORGET IT, KID. NOW, HERE'S WHAT WE DO, ROBIN...
RAVEN, DO YOU REMEMBER THAT YOUNG GIRL, LIZZIE?
OF COURSE.
SHE'D VERY MUCH LIKE TO SPEAK TO YOU.
8

ELIZABETH?
RAVEN? OH, GOD, RAVEN, I HATE IT HERE.

ARE THEY MEAN TO YOU?

OH, NO--THEY'RE GREAT, EVERYTHING'S GOOD. I MEAN I REALLY HATE NEW YORK.
I WANT TO GO HOME, BUT MY DAD...
YOU DIDN'T SEE HIM WHEN I TOLD HIM I WAS PREGNANT. HE NEARLY BIT MY HEAD OFF, RAVEN.

EVER SINCE MOM RAN OFF, HE'S BEEN SO STRANGE. I WANT TO GO BACK, ONLY I'M SCARED.
AT YOUR AGE, ELIZABETH, YOU SHOULD NOT HAVE TO WORRY ABOUT SUCH THINGS.
YOU ARE A GOOD PERSON. YOU ARE A STRONG PERSON.

FEEL YOUR STRENGTH, ELIZABETH.

DO WHAT YOU KNOW IS BEST. SPEAK STRONGLY AND YOUR WORDS CAN LEVEL THE MIGHTIEST OF MOUNTAINS.
LIZZIE RISES, FEELING AN INNER WARMTH THAT SHE HAS NOT FELT FOR MANY MONTHS...

...WHILE RAVEN ALLOWS HERSELF AN UNCHARACTERISTIC SMILE.

AT TIMES EMPATHY IS HER CURSE, BUT NOW, AT THIS MOMENT, IT IS A HEART-FULFILLING BLESSING.

THE PORT AUTHORITY BUS TERMINAL IS TWO BLOCKS AWAY. BY MORNING, SHE COULD BE **HOME**.
AS SHE WALKS, LIZZIE **SHUDDERS**. FOR THREE HORRIBLE WEEKS, SHE HAD STOOD ON CORNERS LIKE THIS ONE, CALLING TO HORRIBLE MEN SHE NORMALLY WOULD NEVER EVEN **LOOK** AT.

SHE'D **SMILE**, THEY'D SHOW HER CASH, THEN SHE WOULD GET SO COLD AND WET AND SCARED SHE'D **RUN**.
GOD, SHE WANTS TO GO **HOME**.

HEY, BABY, LIZZIE...WOW, GOOD CATCHIN' UP WITH YOU, HONEY. WHERE YOU **BEEN**, GIRL?
RONDO?
PLEASE, RONDO, DON'T **HIT** ME AGAIN.

HIT YOU, BEAUTIFUL? YOU GOT ME **WRONG**, HONEY. RONDO **LOVES** YA, BABY.
YOUR OLD MAN KICKS YOUR BUTT OUT AND IT WAS **RONDO** WHO TOOK YOU IN.
VIDEO ARCADE
9

WHO GAVE YOU **FOOD**, BEAUTIFUL? WHO GAVE YOU **CLOTHES**, BABY?
WHO SAYS YOU'S THE **MEANEST**-LOOKIN' MOMMA IN TOWN, HONEY?

I JUST WANT TO GO **HOME**, RONDO. I CAN'T DO IT WITH THOSE **GUYS** ANYMORE.
WHO'S **ASKIN'** YOU TO TURN TRICKS, HONEY?

YOU'RE **BEAUTIFUL**, BABY, JUST BEAUTIFUL.

JUST GOT ONE LITTLE **JOB**, BABY, ONE LITTLE JOB, HONEY, AND I'LL **BUY** YOU THAT TICKET HOME.
C'MON, BEAUTIFUL, RONDO LOVES YA, BABY. **RONDO LOVES YA!**

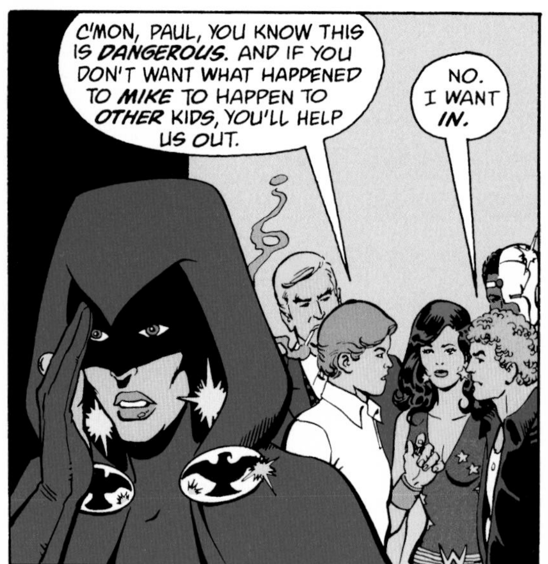
C'MON, PAUL, YOU KNOW THIS IS DANGEROUS. AND IF YOU DON'T WANT WHAT HAPPENED TO MIKE TO HAPPEN TO OTHER KIDS, YOU'LL HELP US OUT.
NO. I WANT IN.

KID, DON'T MAKE THIS HARDER THAN IT HAS TO BE. I CAN DO THINGS YOU WON'T LIKE.
I WANT THAT ADDRESS. PLAIN AND SIMPLE.

NOW, WILL YOU TELL ME, OR DO I HAVE TO--

WAIT. GIVE ME A MOMENT.

PAUL CANNOT HIDE HIS SECRETS FROM ME.
HOLD IT! WHAT ARE YOU DOING? DON'T!

AND SHORTLY...
I'LL CONTACT ALL THE AUTHORITIES. WE'LL MOVE IN AT ONCE.
GOOD. WE'LL ALL MEET THERE AT ELEVEN TONIGHT.

EXCUSE ME, ROBIN. IF YOU DON'T MIND, I'D LIKE TO GO WITH YOU.
WELL, ROY, NORMALLY WE DON'T WORK WITH CIVILIANS, BUT IN YOUR CASE, I GUESS WE CAN MAKE AN EXCEPTION. C'MON.
10

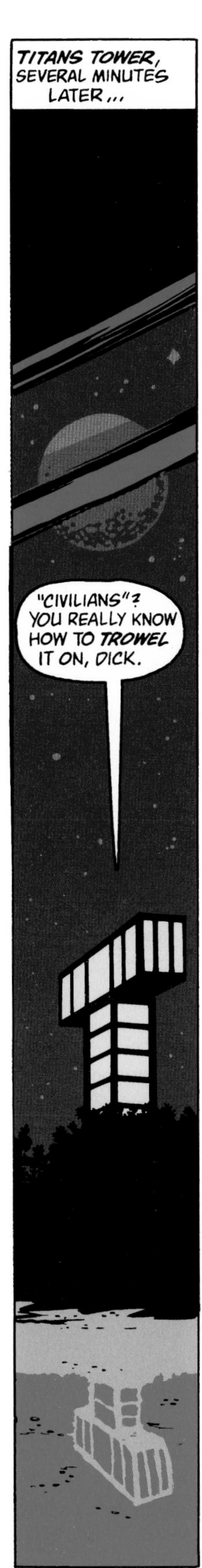
TITANS TOWER, SEVERAL MINUTES LATER...
"CIVILIANS"? YOU REALLY KNOW HOW TO TROWEL IT ON, DICK.

WELL, WHAT DID YOU WANT ME TO SAY, ROY? "YOU'RE ALWAYS WELCOME BECAUSE YOU USED TO BE ONE OF US"?
MAN, IT'S GOOD SEEING YOU AGAIN, PAL. WHAT'VE YOU BEEN UP TO?
THIS AND THAT, KEEPING BUSY. THIS TOWER IS INCREDIBLE, DICK.
WE SHOULD HAVE HAD SOMETHING LIKE THIS IN THE OLD DAYS.
YOU STILL PRACTICE PLAYING ROBIN HOOD?

NOT AS MUCH AS I'D LIKE, BUT I'M STILL AS GOOD AS I EVER WAS.
THERE! NOW TELL ME. IN THIS DAY AND AGE DO YOU THINK SPEEDY STILL HAS WHAT IT TAKES TO BE A MAJOR SUPER-HERO?

YOU CUT A MEAN COSTUME, MR. HARPER.
COMING FROM YOU, MR. GRAYSON, THAT IS A DEFINITE COMPLIMENT.
IT IS GOOD MEETING YOU AT LAST. I HAVE HEARD MUCH ABOUT YOU.

AND I'M CERTAINLY GLAD TO MEET YOU, RAVEN.
IF YOU'RE NOT DOING ANYTHING AFTER THIS BUST...
WHOA. SLOW DOWN, ROMEO. I SEE YOU'RE THE SAME AS EVER.
BELIEVE IT, PAL. REMEMBER, THEY DIDN'T CALL ME SPEEDY FOR NOTHING.
SIGH! THE MORE THINGS CHANGE, THE MORE THEY STAY THE SAME.
C'MON, LET'S GET MOVING.

THE T-JET SCREAMS INTO THE NIGHT...
11

WHILE...
YOU HEARD ME. I WANT IN ON THIS. YEAH, I KNOW, HALL--YOU'VE TOLD ME A MILLION TIMES--"D.A.S GET INVOLVED AFTER THE CRIME IS COMMITTED."
MAYBE THAT'S WHY OUR JUDICIAL SYSTEM'S GONE TO HELL LIKE--
YOU GOTTA COME. IT'S ELLIE. SHE'S BEEN HURT.
PLEASE COME WITH ME.
ELLIE? YOU MEAN MRS. CORBEN?
WHAT HAPPENED?

I DON'T KNOW. I JUST FOUND HER IN HER OFFICE, ALL CRUMPLED OVER LIKE SHE WAS SICK.

MRS. CORBEN, WHAT IS WRONG?
SHE WAS PUSHED... PAUL DID IT.
NO, NO...
HE DIDN'T MEAN TO. HE WANTED TO GO WITH YOU AND THE TITANS. I TRIED TO STOP HIM.
HE PUSHED ME ASIDE AND RAN OFF.
DAMN THAT KID. HE'LL WIND UP AS DEAD AS HIS BROTHER.
WE'VE GOT TO MOVE--FAST!

ELSEWHERE, IN THE MIDDLE OF THE NIGHT, UNDER THE WATCHFUL EYE OF A FULL MOON, A SMALL SHIP SLIPS THROUGH A SHADOW-STREWN HARBOR. ITS CARGO: TWO HUNDRED MILLION DOLLARS IN DRUGS.
12

YOU SEE IT OUT THERE?
IT'S BEAUTIFUL, MAN. I CAN ALREADY FEEL THE CASH.

JUST REMEMBER OSLO. THAT WAS A SURE BET, TOO.

YOU GOT IT, MAN. LET'S MAKE SURE THERE AIN'T ANY SCREW-UPS.
YOU TALKING LIKE THAT TO ME, BOY?

HEY! I DIDN'T MEAN ANY-THING.
PUNK! YOU'VE BEEN ACTING PRETTY HIGH ON THE HOG SINCE YOU GOT HERE. RUBBIN' ELBOWS WITH THE BIG BOYS GIVE YOU DELUSIONS, PUNK?

MR. SCARAPELLI, TELL THESE GUYS TO LET GO OF ME. I'M YOUR RIGHT-HAND MAN, AIN'T I?
HEY! HE'S STARTING TO GET ROUGH.

BOY, YOU DON'T KNOW THE MEANING OF ROUGH.

DON'T NEED NO LIP FROM NO WISE-MOUTH PUNK.
GOBEL, TEACH HIM A LESSON.

HEY, WAIT! I DIDN'T KNOW. I WON'T SAY ANYTHING AGAIN. LEMME GO, PLEASE.
WE WILL.
SOON ENOUGH.
13

C'MON, GET MOVING. JOIN THE **OTHERS.**
YOU'RE GOING TO **HURT** HIM?
YEAH.

SHORTLY...
OKAY, I WANT YOU KIDS TO UNDERSTAND ME. THIS ISN'T NO **GAME** WE'RE PLAYING HERE.
GET BACK THERE AND **SHUT UP.**

IT'S A **JOB.** YOU DO WHAT I TELL YOU AND IN THREE HOURS YOU EACH MAKE A **C-NOTE.**
ONE HUNDRED BUCKS FOR ONE NIGHT. NOT **BAD.**
YOU TRY TO **RUN,** OR YOU TRY TO **STEAL** THE PACKAGES, OR DO ANYTHING JUST A LITTLE BIT **WRONG--**

--YOU'RE **DEAD MEAT** HANGIN' ON A HOOK IN SOME GOD-FORSAKEN MORGUE.
IT'S NOT HARD, YOU'RE NOT GONNA GET CAUGHT. YOU'RE JUST DELIVERIN' A LITTLE **PRESENT.**
EACH OF YOU TO A **DIFFERENT ADDRESS.**
14

THE DRUGS BEING MOVED HERE ARE POTENTIALLY QUITE DEADLY.
USED IMPROPERLY, THEY WILL KILL.

NOT THAT IT MATTERS ONE DAMN BIT TO THESE MEN.

TO THEM, THESE YOUNG LIVES ARE AS MEANINGLESS AS THE CIGARETTE STUBS THEY GRIND INTO THE GROUND.
ALL THAT MATTERS IS THE ENORMOUS PROFIT THEY WILL MAKE.

YOU EACH GOT AN ADDRESS, RIGHT? NO ONE TALKS TO ANYONE ELSE. YOU DON'T SHOW YOUR ADDRESS TO THE KID NEXT TO YOU.

THAT WAY IF THERE'S TROUBLE YOU CAN SAY YOU DON'T KNOW NOTHIN' AND YOU'D BE TELLIN' THE TRUTH.
THEN THE COPS WON'T HOLD YOU, RIGHT? YOU'LL BE FREE, RIGHT?
EVERYONE LINE UP.
YOU GET FIFTEEN BAGS EACH.

BUT, JUST THEN...
THERE IS NO SOUND OR SMELL TO HERALD HER SUDDEN APPEARANCE, JUST SMOKE APPEARING WITH THE SUDDENNESS OF THOUGHT.
RAVEN, MISTRESS OF MYSTICISM, HAS MOVED THROUGH THE DIMENSIONAL BARRIERS, DRAWN BY THE SENSE OF SOMETHING QUITE...
...SICK. DEATH HANGS HEAVILY IN THE AIR...
...AND IT FAIRLY DRIVES THE YOUNG EMPATH MAD!
15

WHO IS SHE?
I DON'T CARE. KILL HER!
SKREEEE
NO! YOU WON'T GET A CHANCE.
I WON'T LET YOU.
I--I DON'T BELIEVE IT.
I THOUGHT THEY ONLY FOUGHT THINGS FROM OUTER SPACE!

WRONG, CREEP. WE'RE AFTER TRASH LIKE YOU-- WHO WOULD POISON THE WHOLE WORLD IF YOU COULD MAKE A BUCK.
FORGET THE CHATTER, ARCHER. TRASH 'EM!
I KNEW CRUD LIKE THESE WHEN I WAS GROWING UP.
THEY'RE THE LOWEST FORM OF SCUM TO EVER WALK THE EARTH.
PAL, NORMALLY I'D SUGGEST YOU'D SURRENDER JUST TO SAVE YOURSELVES THE BEATING...
16

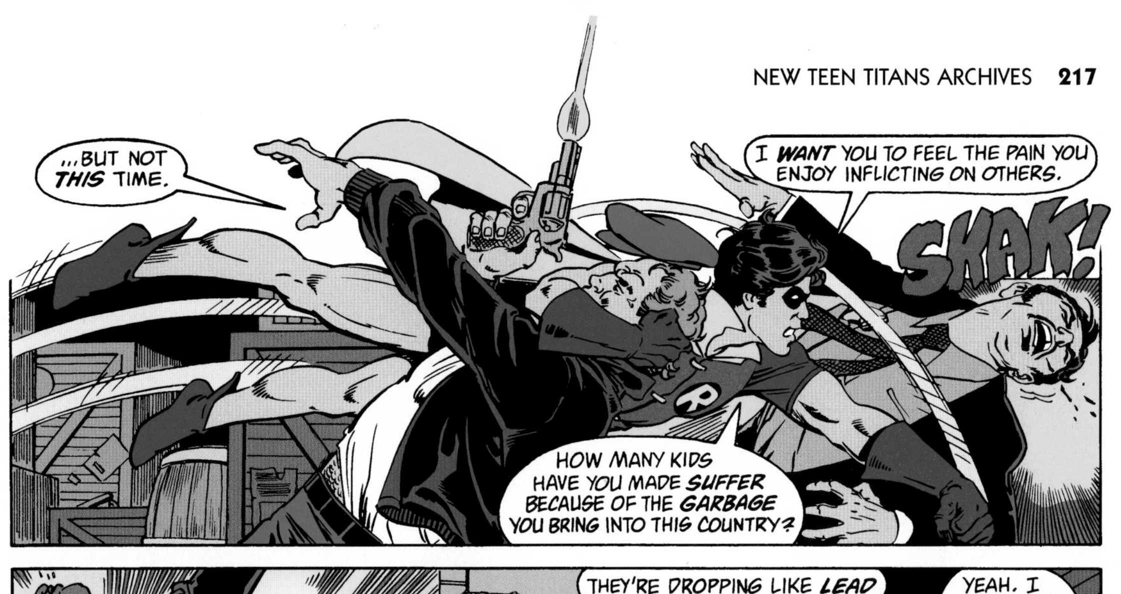
...BUT NOT THIS TIME.
I WANT YOU TO FEEL THE PAIN YOU ENJOY INFLICTING ON OTHERS.
SKAK!
HOW MANY KIDS HAVE YOU MADE SUFFER BECAUSE OF THE GARBAGE YOU BRING INTO THIS COUNTRY?

THEY'RE DROPPING LIKE LEAD FLIES, ROBBIE.
YEAH. I NOTICE, PAL. GOOD SHOOTING.
POOM!
SHUCKS, 'TIS NOTHIN' ANYONE ELSE EQUIPPED WITH A BOXING GLOVE ARROW AND YEARS OF PRACTICE COULDN'T DO.

WH-WHAT'S THAT SHADOW COMIN' AT US?
NOTHIN' YOU'RE GONNA LIKE, SLIME-BREATH!
CYBORG, LET ME DEAL WITH THESE MEN MY WAY.

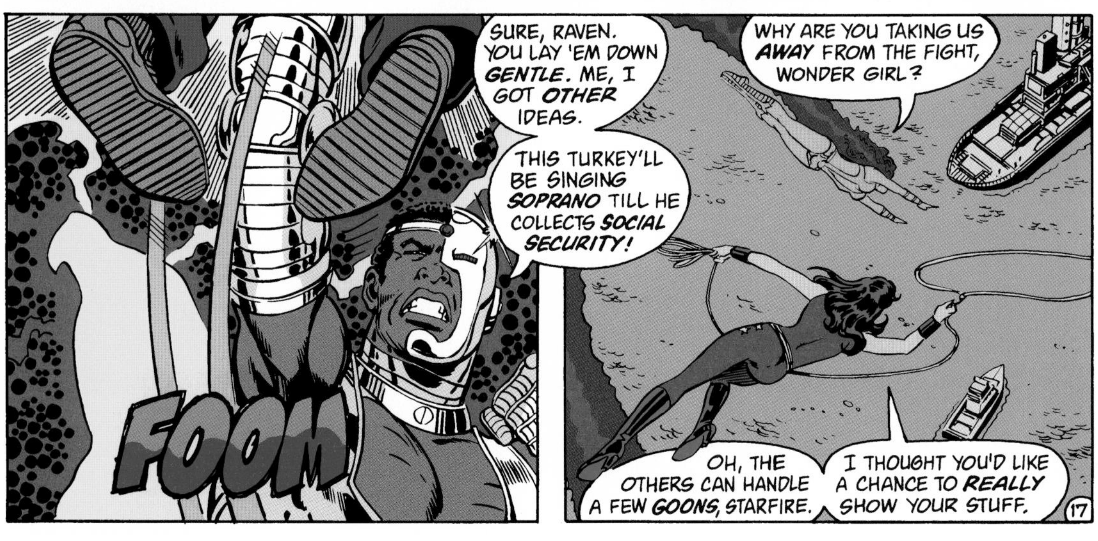
SURE, RAVEN. YOU LAY 'EM DOWN GENTLE. ME, I GOT OTHER IDEAS.
THIS TURKEY'LL BE SINGING SOPRANO TILL HE COLLECTS SOCIAL SECURITY!
FOOM
WHY ARE YOU TAKING US AWAY FROM THE FIGHT, WONDER GIRL?
OH, THE OTHERS CAN HANDLE A FEW GOONS, STARFIRE.
I THOUGHT YOU'D LIKE A CHANCE TO REALLY SHOW YOUR STUFF.
17

I'LL HANDLE THE SUPPLY BOAT.
WHY DON'T YOU TAKE CARE OF THEIR EUROPEAN FRIENDS?
BAM
BAM
BAM
OUR BULLETS ARE BOUNCING OFF HER BRACELETS!

YOU GOT IT, PAL.
SPING
SPING

YOUR TOY GUNS ARE AS USELESS AS YOU ARE!
GO AHEAD, STARFIRE-- DO IT!
SPAMM!

I'VE NEVER TRIED USING MY STARBOLT POWERS LIKE THIS BEFORE, BUT I THINK I CAN DO IT.

FOCUSING A CONSTANT WEDGE OF ENERGY BEFORE ME, I CAN SMASH THROUGH THIS SHIP LIKE A DRILL THROUGH PAPER!
WHOOM!
18

T.C., WHAT DO WE DO NOW?
DO, MAN? WHO GIVES A BLOODY DAMN 'BOUT ANYTHIN' NOW?

YOU SEE WHAT'S OUT THERE, MAN?

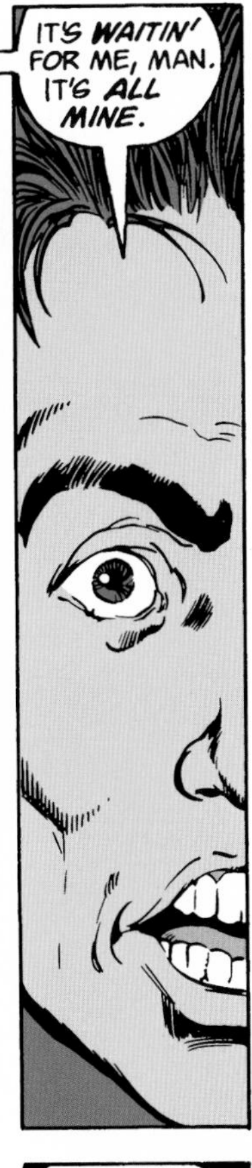
THE STUFF, KID ...FOOD, MAN. ENOUGH FOR A WHOLE DAMN LIFE!

IT'S WAITIN' FOR ME, MAN. IT'S ALL MINE.

JEEZ! THAT KID'S GOING AFTER THE COKE.
NO WAY... NO WAY!
BAM!

HIS NAME WAS T.C. BEANE FROM EL PASO, TEXAS. HE WAS FIFTEEN.

YOU SCUM! YOU LIKE PLAYIN' WITH YOUR TOYS, HUH, MAN?

YOU LIKE BEATIN' UP ON GUYS, DON'T YOU?
NO MORE, MAN... NO MORE! IT'S ALL OVER NOW.

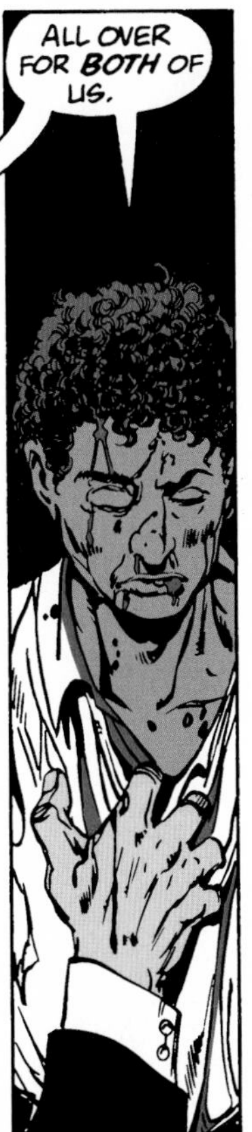
ALL OVER FOR BOTH OF US.

COULD RUN. PROB'LY GET AWAY, TOO. RIGHT, CHIEF?
YEAH, COULD RUN.
NAH.

I THINK I'LL SIT HERE AND WAIT.
IT'S A BEAUTIFUL DAY IN THE NEIGHBOR-HOOD!
19

HURRY, CHILDREN... MOVE QUICKLY OUT OF HARM'S WAY.
THERE IS STILL DANGER HERE.
RAVEN. HOLD IT-- INTERNAL AMPLIFIER'S PICKIN' UP SOMETHIN' --BEHIND US!

WATCH OU--
ARGGHH!
BAM!
BAM!

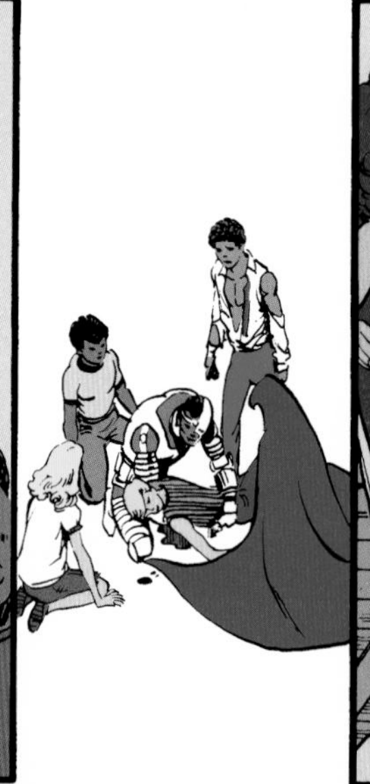

SLY! MAN, C'MON, DON'T YOU DIE ON ME, TOO.
DO SOMETHIN' TO HIM. DO SOMETHING!
I... CANNOT.
I AM NOT ...GOD!

MANY YEARS AGO, VICTOR STONE, KNOWN NOW AS CYBORG, ALSO RAN AWAY.
HE UNDERSTANDS THE PAIN, THE HELPLESSNESS AND THE HOPELESSNESS.

AND HE CRIES.
HIS NAME WAS SYLVESTER JOHNSON. FROM CLEARWATER, FLORIDA. HE WAS THIRTEEN.
20

OH, GOD... NO PLACE TO RUN.
COPS ARE EVERYWHERE.
LOOK! THERE'S ONE OF THEM NOW.
WATCH IT. HE HAS A RIFLE.

SHOOT!
WE CAN'T, SIR. WE HAVE RULES!
N-NO... I'M NOT GOING. YOU HEAR ME. I'M NOT--
13TH PCT
LAY DOWN YOUR WEAPON. WE HAVE YOU SURROUNDED!

YOU'RE NOT DOIN' NOTHIN', CREEP.
SPAMF!

I'M HOLDING EVERYTHING IN, MAN, BUT I AM VERY ANGRY.
AND, VERY QUIETLY, VERY EFFICIENTLY, I AM GOING TO TAKE MY ANGER OUT ON YOU!

UNDERSTAND?
SPOOOOOOOOOM!

IS HE DEAD?
NO.
SHAME, CYBORG. HE DESERVED TO DIE.
I'M NOT GONNA ARGUE, CHASE. THE WAY I FEEL, I MIGHT FIND MYSELF AGREEING WITH YOU.
AND MISTER, THAT SCARES ME SPITLESS!
21

CAPTAIN HALL, I FOUND THIS ONE TRYING TO DRIVE AWAY.
NEEDLESS TO SAY, A $90,000 ROLLS ROYCE IS NOW FIT FOR THE JUNK PILE!
WELL, WELL, ANTHONY SCARAPELLI. I HAVE A FILE ON YOU SO THICK IT COULD CHOKE A DINOSAUR.
MR. SCARAPELLI, LET ME DRIVE YOU... DOWNTOWN.
YOU GOT NOTHIN' ON ME.
I'LL BE FREE IN AN HOUR.

SPEEDY, IS HE...?
I'M AFRAID SO, STARFIRE.
LOTSA FUN, WASN'T IT?
DAMN!

COME ON.
YEAH, I'M GOIN'.
DON'T WORRY.
OH, GOD, RAVEN... I'M SO SORRY. I DIDN'T KNOW WHAT TO DO.
EVERYTHING WILL BE FINE, DARLING... DO NOT WORRY. ALL WILL BE...?
PARDON ME, ELIZABETH. I SENSE...

...SOMETHING FAMILIAR.

PAUL.
I GOT HERE WHEN ALL THE FIGHTING BEGAN.
I... WAS SO SCARED. I COULDN'T DO ANYTHING.

Y'KNOW, I CAME HERE TO FIND OUT WHY MIKE DIED. I THOUGHT IT WOULD MAKE ME FEEL BETTER.
GOD, I FEEL SO SICK INSIDE.

THEN YOU MUST WORK TO MAKE CERTAIN SUCH THINGS DO NOT HAPPEN AGAIN.
COME. TAKE MY HAND. WE MUST GO.

YOUR BROTHER AND OTHERS LIKE HIM FACE PRIVATE DEVILS EACH DAY OF THEIR LIVES. WE ALL DO.
THE DIFFERENCES BETWEEN US ARE IN HOW WE FIGHT WHAT WE MOST FEAR.
22

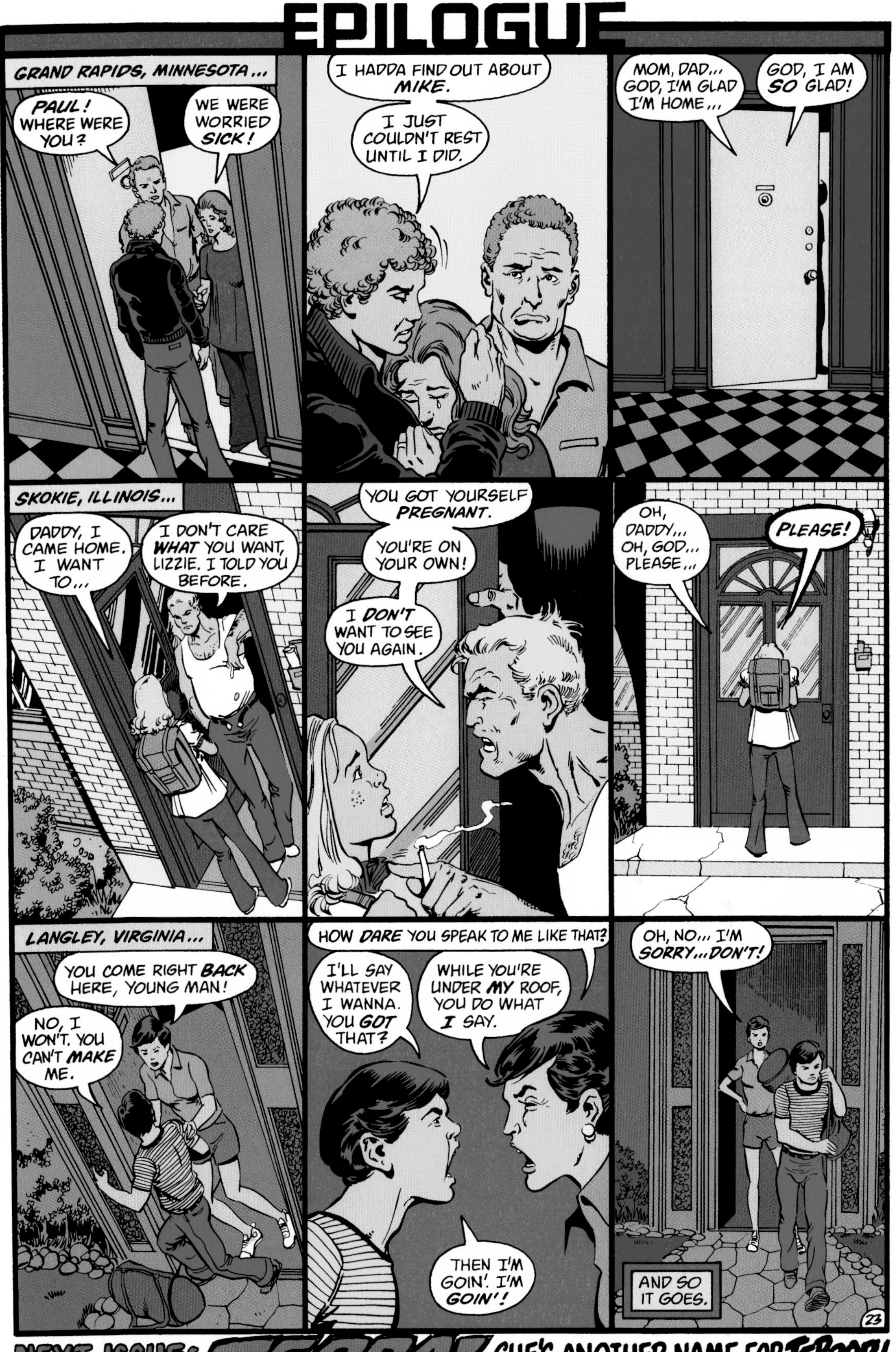
EPILOGUE
GRAND RAPIDS, MINNESOTA...
PAUL! WHERE WERE YOU?
WE WERE WORRIED SICK!
I HADDA FIND OUT ABOUT MIKE.
I JUST COULDN'T REST UNTIL I DID.
MOM, DAD... GOD, I'M GLAD I'M HOME...
GOD, I AM SO GLAD!
SKOKIE, ILLINOIS...
DADDY, I CAME HOME. I WANT TO...
I DON'T CARE WHAT YOU WANT, LIZZIE. I TOLD YOU BEFORE.
YOU GOT YOURSELF PREGNANT.
YOU'RE ON YOUR OWN!
I DON'T WANT TO SEE YOU AGAIN.
OH, DADDY... OH, GOD... PLEASE...
PLEASE!
LANGLEY, VIRGINIA...
YOU COME RIGHT BACK HERE, YOUNG MAN!
NO, I WON'T. YOU CAN'T MAKE ME.
HOW DARE YOU SPEAK TO ME LIKE THAT?
I'LL SAY WHATEVER I WANNA. YOU GOT THAT?
WHILE YOU'RE UNDER MY ROOF, YOU DO WHAT I SAY.
THEN I'M GOIN'. I'M GOIN'!
OH, NO... I'M SORRY... DON'T!
AND SO IT GOES.
23
NEXT ISSUE: TERRA! SHE'S ANOTHER NAME FOR TERROR!

MARV WOLFMAN

One of the most prolific and influential writers in modern comics, Marv Wolfman began his career as an artist. Realizing that his talents lay more in writing the stories than in drawing them, Wolfman soon became known for his carefully crafted, character-driven tales.

In a career that has spanned nearly 30 years, Wolfman has helped shape the heroic careers of DC Comics' Green Lantern, Blackhawk and the original Teen Titans. In addition to cocreating THE NEW TEEN TITANS and the universe-shattering CRISIS ON INFINITE EARTHS with George Pérez, Wolfman was instrumental in the revamp of Superman after CRISIS, the development of THE NEW TEEN TITANS spinoff series VIGILANTE, DEATHSTROKE THE TERMINATOR and TEAM TITANS, and created such characters as Blade for Marvel, along with NIGHT FORCE and the retooled DIAL "H" FOR HERO for DC.

In addition to his numerous comic book credits, Wolfman has also written several novels and worked in series television and animation, including the Superman cartoon of the late 1980s and the hit Teen Titans show on Cartoon Network.

GEORGE PÉREZ

George Pérez started drawing at the age of five and hasn't stopped since. Born on June 9, 1954, Pérez started his professional comics career as an assistant to Rich Buckler in 1973. After establishing himself as a penciller on Marvel Comics' Man-Wolf and Sons of the Tiger, he moved on to such Marvel titles as ***The Inhumans***, ***Fantastic Four***, ***Marvel Two-in-One*** and ***The Avengers***. Pérez first came to DC in 1980, where his highly detailed art style was seen in such titles as JUSTICE LEAGUE OF AMERICA and FIRESTORM THE NUCLEAR MAN.

After co-creating NEW TEEN TITANS with Marv Wolfman in 1980, Pérez and Wolfman collaborated again on the landmark maxiseries CRISIS ON INFINITE EARTHS.

In the midst of the revamps of BATMAN and SUPERMAN that came in the wake of CRISIS, Pérez took on the difficult task of revitalizing WONDER WOMAN. As the series' writer and artist, he not only reestablished Wonder Woman as one of DC's preeminent characters, but also brought in some of the best sales the title has ever experienced.

TODD KLEIN

One of the industry's most versatile and accomplished letterers, Todd has been lettering comics since 1977 and has won numerous Eisner and Harvey Awards for his work. One highlight of his career is his work with Neil Gaiman on nearly all the original issues of THE SANDMAN, as well as BLACK ORCHID, DEATH: THE HIGH COST OF LIVING, DEATH: THE TIME OF YOUR LIFE and THE BOOKS OF MAGIC.

BEN ODA

Ben was one of the most prolific letterers in the world of comic books and comic strips. His work has graced literally thousands of pages for every major and minor publisher, dating back to comics' Golden Age. Ben died in 1984.

ROMEO TANGHAL

A veteran comic-book inker, Romeo's work has been seen in such books as JUSTICE LEAGUE OF AMERICA, WONDER WOMAN, GREEN LANTERN and, of course, NEW TEEN TITANS.

LEN WEIN

A mainstay of the comics field, Len Wein has created dozens of characters and held numerous editorial positions at both DC and Marvel Comics. Perhaps best known as the cocreator of DC's SWAMP THING (with artist Bernie Wrightson), Wein was the editorial guiding light for the early years of THE NEW TEEN TITANS. He was also instrumental in the genesis of CRISIS ON INFINITE EARTHS (working again with Wolfman and Pérez) and the original edition of WHO'S WHO.